THE PASSING OF THE BLACK KINGS

KHAMA AND HIS WIFE MA-BESSU 382

(Frontispiece)

THE PASSING OF
THE BLACK KINGS

BY

HUGH MARSHALL HOLE, C.M.G.

FORMERLY CIVIL COMMISSIONER OF BULAWAYO

Author of 'The Making of Rhodesia', 'The Jameson Raid', Etc.

NEGRO UNIVERSITIES PRESS
NEW YORK

Originally published in 1932
by Philip Allan, London

Reprinted 1969 by
Negro Universities Press
A DIVISION OF GREENWOOD PUBLISHING CORP.
NEW YORK

SBN 8371-2421-2

PRINTED IN UNITED STATES OF AMERICA

TO MY OLD FRIEND

THE HON. HOWARD UNWIN MOFFAT, C.M.G.

PRIME MINISTER OF SOUTHERN RHODESIA,

*The third in descent of a line of
distinguished pioneers who have
devoted themselves to the cause
of civilisation in South Africa.*

'The important thing is not the native's inferiority, or his equality, or his superiority; what is important is just the fact that he is different from the white man. The recognition of this difference should be the starting-point in South Africa's native policy.'

South Africa, by JAN H. HOFMEYR.

INTRODUCTION

FOR over a hundred years British colonists, inspired in a few cases by religious or philanthropic motives, but mainly for commercial aims, have been endeavouring to impose their own institutions and ideals upon primitive South African tribes.

The story of the advance of civilisation from the Cape into the interior has generally been told from the point of view of the white pioneers. If, however, their set-backs and successes are to be placed in proper perspective it is necessary to look on the other side of the picture—to study the character of the blacks whom they encountered in their progress, and especially of those outstanding chiefs who in some cases met them half way, in others vainly strove to keep them back. This aspect has not hitherto been sufficiently considered, and it is with this that the following pages are principally concerned.

The story has also been overlaid and obscured by the loose and inaccurate writings of casual or biased observers, and I have used my own experience (dating back more than forty years) to separate the grain from the chaff. To avoid burdening the text with footnotes, references to authorities have been made sparingly, and only to support statements which might otherwise be regarded as personal or prejudiced.

My warm thanks are due to Dr. Robert Unwin Moffat and to Mrs. Henson (grandson and granddaughter of the celebrated pioneer missionary) for several of the portraits ; to Miss Alice Werner (late of the School of Oriental Studies) for assistance with native names, and to Mr. H. H. Kitchen, of the British South Africa Company, for kindly preparing the maps.

H. M. H.

May, 1932.

CONTENTS

ILLUSTRATIONS

MAPS

CHAPTER I

THE BANTU

I. WHO THEY ARE

THE peoples whose rulers, wavering fortunes, struggles and settlement are dealt with in this volume were fragments of that great division of the human race known, of recent years, as the ' Bantu '. Their savagery kept civilisation at arm's length for the best part of a century. The problem of their control still overshadows those parts of Africa south of the equator where Europeans are busy digging themselves in.

The word ' Bantu ' is not, as a good many seem to think, the designation of an African tribe, nor is it used by any section of the black folk to describe themselves. A native might tell you ' I am a Zulu ', or ' I am a Basuto ', but he would not say ' I am a Bantu ', for he does not know that he is one. Like ' Aryan ' or ' Mongol ', it is a convenient term adopted by modern ethnologists to embrace a large group of negroid races whose members, while speaking a variety of tongues—over two hundred in all, according to the late Sir Harry Johnston [1]—and possessing many diversities of habit and custom, have certain definite affinities and resemblances pointing to descent from a common stock. One of the most noteworthy is that the inflexions of their speech are based on a system of prefixes repeated through each sentence, and not, as with many other

[1] *A Comparative Study of the Bantu Languages*, p. 2.

1

nations of the world, on changes in the form of individual words.[1]

Where the Bantu peoples had their origin is a matter of doubt and controversy. Up to nearly the end of the eighteenth century the old Cape colonists knew little or nothing about them. They were till then chiefly concerned with the tawny-skinned races who inhabited the extreme south of the continent—the intractable little Bushmen, whom they regarded more or less as wild beasts, and the Hottentots, rather higher in the scale of humanity, with whom they established a rough kind of alliance, broken now and then by local squabbles about cattle thefts. Between 1780 and 1800, however, they came in contact with the ' Caffres ', as they called them, on their eastern borders. White settlement had then been pushed as far as the Fish river, which enters the sea a few miles east of the modern town of Grahamstown. On the other side of this were the ama-Xosa, a troublesome tribe, whose chiefs, besides being constantly at loggerheads among themselves, developed a habit of making frequent darts across the boundary to raid the cattle of the farmers on the west bank. Reprisals were undertaken from time to time, and a state of something like war was maintained for nearly forty years. Finally in 1819 a serious attack on Grahamstown—then an outpost—led to more practical measures. The Colonial Government defined a buffer area east of the Fish river and erected forts to keep the marauders at a respectful distance. This as I say was, up to about 1820, the only point at which the Dutch and British settlers of Cape Colony had come into

---

[1] The word *ba-ntu* (more correctly *aba-ntu*, though the initial *a* is nearly mute) means ' men ', and is the plural form of *mu-ntu*, or *umu-ntu*, ' a man ', made by changing the prefix of the root-word *-ntu*, which, with slight modifications, is found, with the same meaning, in a large number of the languages of this group. In its generic sense the term was first employed in 1856, by Wilhelm Bleek, a German philologist, who was placed by Sir George Grey in charge of the Capetown Public Library about that time.

direct contact with any Bantu tribe. As regards the
immense hordes who roamed freely over the unexplored
interior there was absolute ignorance and profound indifference. There were of course many blacks employed in
Capetown and its surroundings, but these were, with few
exceptions, slaves imported from West Africa—not Bantu,
but Negroes.

Nowadays it is fairly established that the Bantu have for
long ages been a migratory sort of race, with a general
tendency to drift from north to south. It is also clear that
some of them, in the course of their wanderings and temporary settlements, became associated with widely distinct
branches of mankind and acquired, in various degrees, an
admixture of alien blood. In the north and east there were
infusions from Hamitic and Arab stocks ; in the south,
where they approached the coast, from Bushmen and
Hottentots. The results of this interbreeding may be seen
to-day. In many of the villages of Nyasaland and Rhodesia you will find, side by side with the black skins and
typical negroid countenances, individuals who have aquiline
features and lighter complexions, pointing unmistakably to
an Arab strain ; while in the south there are whole tribes
with an apparent infusion of Bushman blood.

The units of the Bantu family were constantly multi-
plying, like bacteria, by division. Offshoots were thrown
out which strayed far afield; formed new colonies and new
alliances ; conquered and preyed on other tribes ; rose to
power, and then declined, as they in turn were conquered,
enslaved or absorbed by later arrivals. But they carried
with them their languages, totems, superstitions and customs, some of which survived and are, in most cases, the
only clues we possess to tribal origins. Points of resemblance in speech and tradition are found between tribes
now separated by hundreds of miles—as for instance,
between the Angoni of Nyasaland and the Zulus of Natal,

from whom they broke away a century ago. Some tribes have disappeared, but left their language behind them. This is what happened with the Makololo, of whose extraordinary career an account will be given later. In Livingstone's time they dominated a large part of the upper Zambesi valley; they were afterwards slaughtered to a man by the people they had conquered, but their language survived, and is spoken to this day by many of the river tribes in that locality.

These migratory and predatory processes have been at work in Africa for long ages, and were still going on when the first tentative explorations into the interior were attempted by Europeans, and the first recorded observations made of the habits and characteristics of the inhabitants. The whole native population south of the equator, beyond the narrow limits of the Cape Colony, was, up to recent times, in a state of flux, and the task of elucidating the history of its various elements is more difficult than that of reading the records of the earth from the fossils found buried in the rocks. For anything further back than the last hundred years or so we have largely to depend on native traditions, which, though carefully handed down from father to son, must of necessity have become blurred with the passage of time. Outside the established colonies official data, meagre and superficial at first, only became available forty or fifty years ago, when European powers began their greedy scramble for territory, and the interior was mapped out in 'protectorates' and 'spheres of influence'.

II. MISSIONARY RECORDS

Between the traditional period and the 'Blue Book' period there is a big gap to be bridged—a gap of fifty years, from about 1820 to 1870. The dark age with its legendary kings, its fables of the Mountains of the Moon and of

Solomon's Mines, was slipping away, and the dawn of a new era was approaching. The diamonds and the gold were as yet unsuspected, but explorers were already trying to pierce the gloom which hung over the interior. The land was pregnant with great events and the figures of outstanding native rulers were beginning to emerge and attract attention. For this transition period we have some account of what was happening in the written journals and published books of the pioneer missionaries and occasional hunters and travellers, but they are disconnected, and it is not by any means easy to piece them together into a consecutive story. As regards the missionaries, while nothing can detract from the honour due to these intrepid and single-hearted men, who endured every kind of peril, personal sacrifice and, in many cases, family bereavement, in their endeavours to carry out their self-appointed and often thankless task, it has to be admitted that, as chroniclers of historical incidents, they were not always satisfactory. In saying this I do not forget the immense debt which the colonising powers of Europe, and especially Great Britain, owe to their splendid efforts, and I also recognise that history writing was no part of their business. They were there first to spread the Gospel, and their books were primarily intended for the edification of those in the old country who were interested in evangelistic work among heathen races. Still they enjoyed a unique opportunity of relating in a matter of fact and impartial manner episodes which were likely to become of historical value, and of which they were the only eye-witnesses, and one cannot help regretting that they failed in many cases—Robert Moffat and John Mackenzie are outstanding exceptions—to regard what they saw going on round them with a proper sense of proportion, and were inclined to view the time-honoured customs of the native tribes through the lenses of their own religious convictions. Such institutions as polygamy, the initiation

ceremonies of boys and girls at puberty, and witchcraft
were repulsive to their ideas of propriety, and while they
spent a good deal of their time, and incurred considerable
odium, in a vain effort to suppress them, they shut their
eyes to their sociological interest and simply treated them
as manifestations of the power of Satan. Prominent native
chiefs were condemned or applauded by them according to
the way in which they responded to Christian teaching.
They seemed too often to be incapable of realising that the
savage who openly denounced such teaching as revolutionary, and therefore detestable, was true to his tribal traditions, and possibly more to be trusted than the one who
cunningly professed Christianity in order to gain some
material advantage. Examples of both types were frequent,
and even so acute a judge as Livingstone allowed himself on
several occasions to be taken in by the latter.

In almost every case the early missionaries were enthusiastic students of native languages. One of their chief
objects was of course to preach to congregations in their
own tongue, and another to translate the Gospels into it.
Their contributions to Bantu etymology are of great value,
but are very often impaired by strained efforts to transcribe
the sounds of Bantu words into equivalents of their own
choice. In this they followed no settled rule. Each created
a system for himself, and the identification of people and
places mentioned by different writers is consequently
difficult. When a man is generally known as ' Lobengula '
it is confusing to find his name spelt ' Ulopengule ', and it is
doubtful if many would recognise the Matopo hills when
disguised as ' Amadobo '. Some of the missionaries seem
never happy unless they can torture a native name into an
unusual shape.[1]

---

[1] There are so many instances of these mannerisms that I have
thought it useful to add an appendix giving a list of the variants used
by missionaries and others of familiar native names.

My last complaint is that the missionary chroniclers display, as a rule, a cheerful disregard for dates. They seem to think it sufficient to use such phrases as ' in the following June ', or ' two years later ', unconscious of the trouble this gives to one who tries to fit events into their proper place. Their stories wander on from month to month, and year to year without punctuation, and it is impossible, except by tiresome examination and constant reference to back pages, to follow the sequence. Livingstone is a bad offender. His observations on native customs, the botany and natural history, the meteorology and physical features of the countries he passed through were minute and exact, and his avoidance of exaggeration amounted almost to an obsession. But he had a tendency to ramble inconsecutively, and only to give dates at irregular intervals. It requires no little research, for example, to find out from his own account the year in which he discovered the Victoria Falls ! Livingstone's books too, like most of the others, are marred by the absence of an index.

From hunters and casual travellers one does not expect so much. They did not stay for any length of time in one spot, and such cursory remarks as they made on the wars, habits and characteristics of the tribes they came across were too disjointed to have great importance. Nevertheless the books of Gordon Cumming, Cornwallis Harris, and later on of Selous have a distinct value in enabling us to check the statements of more permanent (and therefore less impartial) observers. Selous, in particular, was a most accurate recorder of what he saw around him, and anything related by him may be treated as absolutely free from bias or exaggeration.

III. WHERE THE BANTU LIVED

It is outside the purpose of this volume to attempt to follow the ceaseless and intricate movements of the various tentacles springing from the main Bantu stock. Yet it is essential that the relative positions of the main tribes of southern Africa in the early years of the last century should be made clear. Without a preliminary knowledge of these it would be impossible to understand the conduct and motives of those three notable kings whose careers it is my object to sketch, and who stood out like islands when the tide of civilisation swept round their countries.

The accompanying map shows roughly what is known of the distribution of the natives living and moving between the Zambesi-Congo watershed and Cape Colony about 1820.

That year was an important landmark for several reasons. It was the year when the first attempt at an organised South African emigration scheme was undertaken by the Home Government. During March and April upwards of 3000 British settlers arrived in Table Bay and were provided with land—chiefly in the eastern part of the Colony. Before their coming the British residents, outside officials and soldiers, were a mere handful.[1]

In 1820 also Robert Moffat, the pioneer of the London Missionary Society, and afterwards father-in-law of Livingstone, opened an advanced mission station outside Cape Colony among the Bechuana natives. In itself this may seem a small thing. In reality it was a milestone on the road to civilisation—the first step of a forward movement which grew and gathered impetus until it culminated in the occupation and settlement of the twin colonies of Rhodesia. Not long after he established his station Moffat was a spectator of some of the terrible episodes of the last two Bantu migrations—the avalanche of looters and desper-

---

[1] According to a census taken in 1819 the population of the Colony consisted of 42,217 white people, mainly Dutch; 31,696 slaves; 24,433 Hottentots ; 1,883 free blacks and 1,428 negroes taken out of captured slaveships. (Theal, *History of South Africa*, vol. iii, p. 224.)

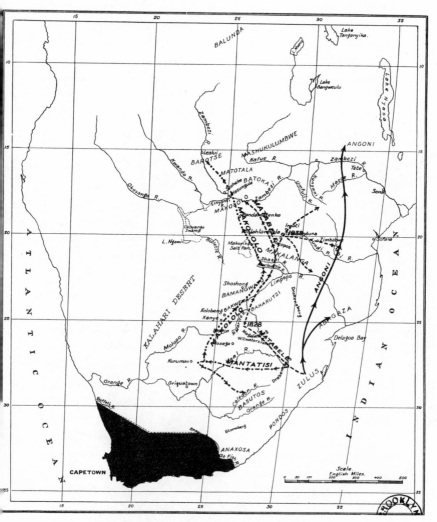

SOUTH AFRICA IN EARLY PART OF 19th CENTURY.

Area of European Settlement in 1820 Coloured Red.

The Red Lines show Migrations of Matabele and Other Tribes, 1820-1840.

adoes led by the Amazon Ma-Ntatisi, and the series of murderous swoops made by the Matabele, after their break-away from Zululand.

It will be seen from the map that European settlement had not, in 1820, been pushed beyond the ranges of mountainous country known as Sneeuwberg and Stormberg. The depth of the strip between these ranges and the 34th degree of latitude (on which lie Capetown and Port Elizabeth) is barely two hundred miles, and at that time it was this strip that constituted Cape Colony. The most advanced towns were Beaufort West and Graaf Reinet on the north and Grahamstown on the east, but they were little more than outposts.

To the north of the Colony, beyond the Orange river, stretched the vast and arid plains of the Kalahari desert and the scantily watered bush country of Bechuanaland. On the north-east was an elevated, fertile region, better provided with streams, whose centre was the watershed of the Orange, Vaal and Limpopo rivers. It was occupied, more or less densely, by various weak tribes whose manhood was later to be regularly mowed down by the scythe of invaders from the east.

The Colony of Natal had not then been thought of. The Drakensberg mountains, which afterwards formed its western boundary and run roughly parallel with the sea-coast at a distance of about 150 miles, split the Bantu tribes into two groups, with marked physical and temperamental distinctions. Each of these had many subdivisions, but to avoid wearying my readers with a string of crabbed names I will term them, for brevity, the Zulu group, occupying the eastern, or sea side, and the ba-Suto group, on the western. Between the component units of both there were incessant feuds, bursting out from time to time into open warfare, with its invariable accompaniments of massacre, the seizing of women and the looting of cattle.

Out of this welter of strife there had emerged, early in the century, Tshaka, the Zulu, an upstart but a genius. By the strength of his personality, the adoption of new methods of attack, and the invention of improved weapons he converted a petty tribe into a fighting machine of extraordinary efficiency. All the neighbouring tribes were in turn reduced to submission or exterminated by his ruthless army. Their ferocity has no parallel in history except perhaps in the marauding bands of Vandals, Goths and Mongols who overran western Europe in the fifth century.

By 1820 Tshaka and his Zulus had laid waste the whole of the coast area from Delagoa Bay to Pondoland. Those tribes that resisted were wiped off the face of the earth ; young females only were spared for breeding purposes, and such boys as were considered fit for absorption in the Zulu army. Numbers fled in panic across the Drakensberg, and drove before them others, until a general movement set in towards the Kalahari in the west. Tshaka's persecutions were the motive force that started a series of restless waves of migration, involving in the long run all the Bantu population between the Orange river and the Zambesi. Their repercussions convulsed the sub-continent, and for many years held back the advance of civilisation. It is hardly too much to say that they constitute the main story of South Africa from 1820 to 1880—from Tshaka to Rhodes.

Up to 1820, however, the tribes on the inland side of the Drakensberg had not felt the full force of the westward rush. In the country between the Orange and Vaal rivers, with branches extending along the edges of the Kalahari, there was a large collection of inter-related tribes with ba-Suto affinities, who, for convenience sake, may be described as the ' Bechuana '. Though frequently rent by the rivalries of chiefs and the incurable craving for each others' cattle they were less fierce on the whole, and more inclined to tribal fraternisation than the turbulent members of the Zulu group. They were cattle breeders and hunters. Some of them did a fair amount of trade in ivory, and all were skilled in wood-carving and in the manufacture of *karosses*, or rugs made of the pelts of wild animals sewn together by means of sinews. Among them were the ba-Mangwato, who will figure prominently in the following pages, and the ba-Kwena and others who will come into the story incidentally.[1]

Of the tribes still further north practically nothing was then known. Later discoveries revealed that the wide uplands between the Limpopo and Zambesi rivers were occupied by a number of comparatively peaceful clans of some antiquity and a fair degree of intelligence. There are vague accounts of inroads by invaders known as Varoswi and Banyai (whose descendants still retain these names), one or other of which gained temporary ascendancy over the older occupants, loosely allied under the name Makalanga. They eventually settled down amicably, and busied themselves with cattle-raising and agriculture. At the time we are speaking of some of them were doing a steady trade with their neighbours in iron implements of their own smelting, and a small and diminishing one with east coast merchants in gold dust washed out of the river beds. Collectively these are the people now called Mashona. They had been approached from Sofala three hundred years before by the Portuguese colonists, who left detailed accounts of their industries and customs, and of the Zimbabwe and other stone buildings scattered in a semi-ruinous condition

---

[1] The coast peoples—Zulu, Pondo, Xosa, Tembu and others were all distinguished by the prefix *ama-* (ama-Xosa, etc.) ; the ba-Suto and Bechuana tribes by the prefix *ba-* (ba-Mangwato, ba-Kwena, and so on). There were broad differences between the two types, both in language and custom. One of the distinguishing marks of the Zulus and their offshoots was the *dhlodhlo*, or headring, worn in different shapes by the male elders of all.

over their country. Without doubt the Makalanga, whose identity is now hardly distinguishable from the general body of Mashona clans, are the disintegrated remnants of the tribes formerly united in the romantic kingdom of Mono-motapa. For our first acquaintance with this name, which was sprawled over most of the maps of Africa between the sixteenth and eighteenth centuries, we are indebted to the Portuguese. In process of time it became encrusted with legends of ancient gold-miners and strange cults. The land of Monomotapa was long regarded—and even to-day the claim cannot lightly be dismissed—as the Ophir of the Old Testament—the source from which King Solomon obtained the gold and ivory brought by Phenician sailors for the building of his temple. Interest in this theory was rekindled in the 'eighties by one of Rider Haggard's novels, and the opening up of Mashonaland a few years later revealed that a vast gold-mining industry had indeed been carried on there in ancient times.

The map also shows a portion of the country between the Zambesi and the great lake system of Central Africa. All that was known of this spacious region in the early nine-teenth century was derived from the reports of a few Por-tuguese explorers and half-caste traders. The most notable was a learned professor named Lacerda, who, in 1797, made a bold attempt—which cost him his life—to conduct an expedition across the continent from Mozambique to Angola on the west coast. Strangely enough none of them succeeded in discovering the chain of lakes which Living-stone revealed to the world sixty or seventy years later. But the Portuguese explorations did disclose the existence of the ancient Lunda kingdom, a confederation of Bantu tribes under a king bearing the hereditary name Mwata Yanvo,[1] whose rule extended from the watershed of the

[1] Livingstone calls him Matiamvo, and places his main town in about latitude 7·20 south and longitude 23·20 east.

Zambesi to the eastern tributaries of the Congo. The Lunda kingdom was divided into a number of provinces under local governors, who, at the time we are dealing with, were already beginning to break away from the central authority. Among them were certain tribes on the south which eventually fell wholly or partially under the influence of the King of Barotseland, as will be related in due course.

One of the effects of Tshaka's cruelties was to create disaffection among his own adherents, and several large bodies made their escape at different times. One section worked its way northwards and finally settled in Nyasaland, where it became known as the Angoni tribe. Another—the aba-Gaza or ama-Shangana—took refuge in the coast lands north of the Limpopo river. Some thousands of warriors, led by Mziligazi, one of Tshaka's principal commanders, crossed the Drakensberg range and betook themselves to the fertile district of Marico, in what is now the western Transvaal. There they soon became notorious as the Matabele—' the people of the long shields '. A fourth offshoot—the ama-Hlubi—pursued a more southerly course, and found a sanctuary on the head-waters of the Caledon river, near the modern town of Harrismith. In each case the fugitives carried on among their new neighbours the system of rapine and slaughter which they had practised under their former king.

Such was the position in 1820. The whole of South Africa, from the Orange river to the sources of the Zambesi, and from the Kalahari desert to the eastern seaboard, was seething with violence and bloodshed. It was hardly a favourable opportunity for any white man—still less a white woman—to venture beyond the range of the forts which dotted the frontiers of Cape Colony. Yet this was the moment chosen by Robert Moffat, of the London Missionary Society, who had already spent a year or two in less disturbed districts, to fare forth, accompanied by his young

Scottish wife, and take up his residence among the Bechuana. It is true that these were of milder disposition than
the Zulus ; but they were rent by incessant tribal feuds,
and were now, in addition, exposed to assaults from the
human beasts of prey let loose by Tshaka's tyrannies.

CHAPTER II

BANTU LIFE

CONSIDERATIONS of space preclude a detailed description of the many interesting customs of the Zulus and Bechuanas, but such of their characteristic institutions and beliefs as affected their relations with white men and reacted on the advance of civilisation must be briefly touched on. Different tribes had of course their own special observances, but there were certain general principles common to all.

Among Bantu peoples every action of life and train of thought sprung from one or other of a few fundamental and absorbing interests. Some of these were instinctive and individual, as for instance their sexual and family relations, and the urge for hunting, at the back of which was the necessity of obtaining meat. Others were more concerned with communal needs, and paramount among these were the success of the crops, depending on the rainfall, and the possession of cattle. The diversions of kraal life were restricted to feasting, beer-drinking and dancing, all of which had a social importance and, to some extent, a ritual of their own. But permeating the whole of their private and public conduct, and linking up all their interests by subtle and infinite connections, was the belief in magic. This term is here used in its widest sense, to cover the superstitious practices arising out of ancestor worship, the recognised and legitimate use of occult means to ensure an early and abundant rainfall or success in war, and the

15

illicit and reprehensible employment of spells and charms to bring death or misfortune upon a private enemy.

The above general statement applies to all the various branches of the Zulu and Bechuana stocks.

Under the word ' sex ' may be grouped a host of special customs connected with the attainment of puberty by boys and girls, the system of marriage, the position of the wife or wives, and the resultant status of the children. Among many tribes there was an elaborate preparation of young people for their future career as adult members of the community. With the Bechuana this took the form of a series of rites (known as *Boguera* in the case of boys, and *Boyali* for girls) held every two or three years when sufficient candidates of the right age were forthcoming. *Boguera* included circumcision, and initiatory ceremonies lasting over some weeks, under the supervision of special instructors, with the object of educating the youths in sexual matters, training them in the use of arms and instilling into them their duties to the tribe and its chief. The most severe discipline was enforced. The initiates were constantly subjected to cruel floggings, and were expected to endure the pain stoically. Those who went through the ceremonies at the same time remained bound together by a sort of brotherhood, and, in theory, were companions for life. The sons of chiefs were not exempt, and in after years would normally become the leaders of their ' school ' mates in hunting and warfare. Similar usages were observed among the Zulu group, though Tshaka is said to have vetoed circumcision.

The girls' initiation was on corresponding lines. They were instructed in the physical side of wifehood and motherhood, in the cultivation of the land, and in the domestic tasks which would fall to them on marriage.

During these proceedings both boys and girls wore a distinctive dress, and were jealously secluded so that no profane eye might pierce the mysteries. It is doubtful whether they were ever seen by white men, though Livingstone describes [1] a portion of the rite of circumcision, of which he was, apparently by accident, a spectator. From details extracted from older natives it is clear that a great part of both ceremonies was of a kind repugnant to European ideas of decency. Consequently they were regarded with strong aversion by the early missionaries, who used all their efforts to get them suppressed. Their well-meant interference provoked, in some cases, resentment among the chiefs, who felt responsible for the proper maintenance of the traditions of their tribes. They regarded it as a shameful thing for any male or female to grow up without this necessary instruction—something which would create wrath among their ancestral spirits—and much of the trouble encountered by Christian workers in Bechuanaland and elsewhere arose from the conflict of ideas on this point. It is possible that the antipathy of the missionaries was based too much on externals. The primary object of the rites was to inculcate courage and self-control in the boys, and domestic virtues in the girls, and even though accompanied by obscene details they did not appear to unprejudiced persons to exercise a demoralising effect in after life.

Another institution which the missionaries worked indefatigably to repress was polygamy. In theory the men of all Bantu tribes were polygamous. Actually, however, the number of wives a man might acquire depended on his capacity to pay for them by the arrangement known as *bogadi* among the Bechuana, and *lobola* with the Zulu. The richer a man in cattle the higher his social standing, and so it came about that the chief, who was frequently the owner of the bulk of the cattle of the tribe, had most wives, and that men of humbler rank had to content themselves with one, or even—though this was rare—remain unmarried.

[1] *Missionary Travels*, etc., p. 146.

The wife was not, as is sometimes thought, a chattel, but had definite rights, an important share in the kraal life, and special duties to see to. Women were, however, of secondary consequence in matters relating to war, hunting and cattle.

A chief's marriages were frequently contracted for political purposes—to establish or cement friendly relations with the ruler of another tribe, or to honour a favourite or influential subject.[1] The relative status of the wives of a chief did not depend on the order in which they were taken. There was always one who, either on account of her superior birth or through special nomination by the chief, enjoyed the rank of ' Great Wife '. Her sons were entitled to succeed their father in preference to any others—even though born earlier—whose mothers were not so designated. This rule had far-reaching results, and a good many tribal disturbances and disruptions arose out of attempts to contest the right of succession of the ' great wife's ' family. Another curious development may be mentioned. The great wife retained her privileges even after the death of her spouse. In many tribes it was customary that she, together with the other ' widows ', should be taken over by a brother or other near relative (sometimes a son) of the deceased chief, and her subsequent offspring would remain in the line of succession.[2]

[1] Thus Livingstone relates in his second Cambridge lecture that Sechele, Chief of the ba-Kwena, had five wives. His father had been murdered, and four of his principal men had assisted in restoring the son (Sechele) to the chieftainship. To show his gratitude he had married a daughter of each of his benefactors. Livingstone interfered in this domestic arrangement, and admits that in consequence these women and their friends became bitter opponents of Christianity.

[2] The Rev. John Campbell, an early colleague of Moffat, in a curious little book entitled *A Journey to Lattakoo* (1835) gives an instance of this among the Bechuana. ' The Chief of the Marootzee [ba-Hurutsi] died, leaving no children by his great wife. After his death this woman became the wife of one of his brothers, who, according to the Jewish custom, raised up seed to the deceased. By

There were other interesting features of the marriage customs, such as child betrothal, and the strange etiquette of *hlonipa*, which made it a shameful thing for a woman to use words resembling the names of her husband or his male relatives, and necessitated the adoption of a special vocabulary for use in each domestic circle. But these and many others had no direct bearing on politics or the relations between natives and white men, and need not here be dealt with.

A fruitful source of tribal dissension was the jealousy and suspicion with which a chief often regarded his sons in the direct line of succession. If such a one became too popular his father was prone to assume that he was conspiring to kill him and step into his shoes. This led to feuds which had a far-reaching effect on the tribes in which they occurred.

From time immemorial all Bantu natives have had a passionate and insatiable craving to accumulate cattle, which were the equivalent of wealth, and, in the case of chiefs, implied political power. Cattle-lifting was the invariable accompaniment, and, in most cases, the primary motive, of wars. The ownership of the cattle of a tribe was usually vested in its chief, but he was in the habit of assigning the custody of herds to local sub-chiefs, who were allowed to make use of the milk, but accounted to their master for natural increases and losses, and could not kill them for food without permission. In other cases the chief would bestow cattle as a gift on a deserving subject in reward for meritorious service, so that private proprietorship was recognised within limits. Cattle were also the ordinary medium for the purchase of wives ; but the

him she had a son whose dignity is the same as though he had actually been the son of the king ; by law he is the king's son, and will be acknowledged as the rightful successor when he comes of age.'

Theal (*History of S. Africa since 1795*, vol. i, p. 401) quotes a case occurring in the pedigree of Moshesh, the famous Basuto Chief ; and Stow (*Native Races of S. Africa*) gives further examples.

acceptance by the father implied a guarantee of his daughter's good behaviour, and a refund was demanded if she was guilty of infidelity—among the Matabele also if she failed to produce children.[1] This principle led to constant disputes and litigation, prolonged sometimes to the second and third generation.

At Bulawayo cattle were slaughtered freely for the king's consumption, and for distribution to the soldiers and other favoured subjects. On ceremonial occasions, such as the annual celebrations of the harvest, or to provide a feast in honour of some signal victory, large numbers were killed, moderate portions of the flesh being formally reserved for sacrificial purposes. The natives were inordinately fond of beef, though there should have been no lack of fresh meat at any time, for a hundred years ago elephant, rhinoceros, giraffe and many species of antelope ranged in inconceivable numbers throughout Bechuanaland and Matabeleland. Such large game could, however, only be successfully attacked by organised hunting parties, and by the construction of *mahopo*, or pits, into which herds were driven to death. In ordinary times the Bechuana were not squeamish about feeding on a lion's leavings, and were always eager to attach themselves to white hunters for the sake of a share in the meat. Among the Makalanga, beasts that died a natural death were never wasted but eaten without hesitation. Before leaving the subject of cattle it may be added that their care was exclusively the province of the men. It was unseemly for a woman even to approach the kraals where they were enclosed.

The next big interest in the native mind was the rainfall. In South Africa generally the year is divided sharply into dry and wet seasons. To people who had no knowledge of the conservation of water the success of the crops—in other words the year's supply of meal and beer—depended upon

[1] P. Nielsen, *The Matabele at Home*, p. 16.

an early and copious rainfall, and any delay in its arrival at the usual period, which was in November, might spell great privation—if not actual famine. Very seldom was any provision made in time of plenty against a possible dearth. If in any season there was an abundant harvest it meant that more beer was brewed, and only so much grain saved as would suffice for seed. It is easy to understand the vital importance attached to the first rains, which softened the soil and rendered it fit for hoeing.

The absence of rain was invariably attributed to supernatural causes—the displeasure of the vague beings in the unknown realms outside mortal vision, whose good-will must be won back by those who understood how to do it. This brings us to the subject of magic, which was extensively employed by all Bantu peoples when assailed by troubles outside their ordinary comprehension. In every tribe were skilled professional rain-makers, whose services were in great request as the time for the ' ploughing rains ' drew near. They were generally a close corporation, and went through an elaborate training to qualify for their calling. They guarded their secrets jealously and took drastic measures against outsiders who tried to encroach upon their practice. At their head was the chief himself whose reputation and popularity largely depended on his capacity for influencing the weather, or at least offering a plausible explanation of any unusual drought. He presided over the hocus-pocus employed to propitiate the ancestral spirits and, as the great *Ngake*, *i.e.* ' doctor ' or high priest, was expected to have an intimate knowledge of the correct methods of approaching them. His mysterious intercessory rites were, advisedly, always held in private, with only the initiated in attendance. The materials used in rain-making consisted of ' medicines ' and charms of a most nondescript and varied nature. Some were obtained from herbs whose virtues were kept secret ; others from the bladders, bones and intestines of selected birds and beasts. A goat would be cut open and its steaming entrails studied by the diviners, who would then repair to the hills, light sacrificial fires, blow horns, whistle and shout, and go through a variety of antics recalling the efforts of the prophets of Baal when they strove to break the drought which afflicted Samaria. If, in spite of these cantrips, the rain held off for a prolonged period, it was not unusual for the blame to be laid on a scapegoat. Cases of ritual murder were at one time fairly common, and may even now take place where detection is unlikely. Only a few years ago the chief of a district not far from Salisbury had his own son burnt to death to appease the spirits and induce them to send rain.

The hastening of the rains was one of the principal functions of the hierarchy of necromancers, but their powers were invoked to placate the spirits on other occasions of national emergency, as during an invasion of locusts, or before a war. Coillard describes the elaborate steps taken by Lewanika, King of Barotse, before sending an expedition against a neighbouring tribe. ' The war drums were beaten all night. The King went through various rites, and sent offerings of calico, beadwork, milk and honey to each of the royal tombs, and a sheaf of spears, which remained lying there for 48 hours to give the dignitaries of the other world time to bless them '.[1] At one time the wizards may have actually accompanied the armies into battle. Dos Santos, quoted by Theal, mentions that when Barreto attacked the Makalanga chief Mongazi near the Mazoe river, in 1572, the natives were led by an old female witch-finder with a calabash full of charms, which she threw into the air in the belief that they would cause the Portuguese to become blind and palsied.[2] In later days the wizards were careful to keep in the background during actual fighting,

[1] On the Threshold of Central Africa, p. 303.
[2] Theal, The Beginning of South African History, p. 245.

and save their own skins. It is interesting to find this early record of witchcraft among the Makalanga, for down to quite modern times they had a specially high reputation for knowledge of magic. Their *ziwosana*, or diviners, were consulted and treated with respect by Mziligazi, the Matabele king, even after he had conquered them, and reduced them to slavery. They professed to have the power of holding direct intercourse with a supernatural being whom they called *Mwari*,[1] and who could only be propitiated by valuable gifts, and was in the habit of speaking with an oracular voice from caves in the hills—a phenomenon easily attained by ventriloquism, in which the Makalanga wizards were proficient. Mwari was, at the outset, essentially the regulator of the rainfall, though in 1896 his aid was invoked under his Matabele name Mlimo, to engineer the native rebellion against the Chartered Company.

There were other ghostly beings termed *ma-dzimo* (*ama-dhlozi* among the Matabele), who were supposed to be the spirits of departed chiefs. They were regarded as continuing to take an interest in tribal affairs, and as responsible also for occurrences of a more personal kind, such as disease and death—neither of which was ever attributed to natural causes. As a consequence of this superstition it was customary at the obsequies of a chief to give him a good ' send-off '. Care was taken to bury with his body the things which he used in his lifetime—the weapons, utensils, garments and furniture which he might require in the next existence—and to sacrifice cattle whose spirits would accompany and comfort him. In some cases it was the custom to kill some of his slaves so that he should not enter the spirit kingdom unattended.[2] Afterwards further offer-

---

[1] Known to the Bechuana as *Morimo* (Moffat, *Missionary Labours*, etc., chap. xix), and adopted by the Matabele under the name of *Mlimo*.

[2] This, according to Livingstone, was the practice among the ba-Rotse. (*Missionary Travels*, etc., p. 318.)

ings in the shape of beer and beef would from time to time be placed in the neighbourhood of the grave.

None of these usages can be taken to imply belief in a soul or in immortality. The Bantu are not concerned with such abstractions. All that can be said is that they express the vague subjective idea of a continuing influence which has to be respected and humoured. The homage to ancestral spirits seldom extended beyond three generations—the father, grandfather and great-grandfather.

Misfortunes to individual members of a tribe were commonly attributed to the machinations of evilly disposed persons (*ba-loi*), who resorted to magic to induce the spirits to help them to gratify private animosities. This was the explanation offered for illness, death, epidemics among men or cattle and other natural events of a similar kind. Illicit sorcery, especially when aimed against the chief, was the most heinous crime known to the Bantu imagination, and was always punished by death. It was the business of the official witch-doctors to counteract these malign influences by stronger ' medicine ', and if possible to track down the offender and expose him. In some cases this was effected through a trial by ordeal, in others by the simple means of public denunciation. It will readily be understood what a fearful instrument was thus placed in the hands of the chief, whose creatures the witch-doctors were, and it was freely used by Mziligazi, Lobengula and others to get rid of subjects who had incurred their enmity or aroused their jealousy.

There are a number of other native superstitions which might be touched on if space permitted. We may smile at some of them, but almost all can be matched among modern nations who boast a high degree of civilisation. Totems, for example—a far too complicated subject to be condensed into a single chapter—have certain analogies with coats of arms and crests, while the odds and ends worn on the person by African natives to bring good luck, or avert misfortune, have their counterpart in the mascots, swastikas and sacred emblems carried by thousands of educated people in London to-day. The belief in witchcraft formerly prevalent throughout Europe has only been scotched in recent times and still lurks in unsuspected places. Even those who are sceptical about spiritualism or crystal-gazing generally cherish some little superstitions of their own, and, though they may be surprised, should not affect to be shocked at the Bantu with their fetiches, the shades of their ancestors and their magic-mongers.

CHAPTER III

THE CLASH OF THE BANTU

I. THE BA-MANGWATO

AUTHENTIC records of Bechuanaland commence with the arrival of Robert Moffat, who, in May, 1820, started work for the London Missionary Society near Lattakoo (or Letakong) and shortly afterwards founded a permanent station a few miles away on the Kuruman river, from which it took its name. That was his headquarters for close on fifty years, and from there he made frequent journeys to visit neighbouring chiefs. Over several of them he succeeded in gaining an extraordinary influence, equalled perhaps by none of his colleagues with the exception of David Livingstone. He was a scrupulously accurate observer, and his writings form our main authority for the conditions of native life and politics at a time when these savage parts were still unlapped by the first ripples of civilisation.

The traditions of the Bechuana themselves carry us a good deal further back than Moffat's days. They had, it is true, no means of reckoning time except by vague reference to so many moons or harvests. Nor is it possible, except in rare cases, to link up their stories with contemporary events outside. But it would be unwise altogether to reject them on that account. Inside the ring of huts which formed each family tenement was a small courtyard (*kothla*) and here, in times of peace, when the day's work in the fields or among the cattle was over, and it was too dark to stitch the skin rugs, the older men were wont to gather round a fire of logs and cowdung, to smoke, exchange snuff, scratch themselves and drink their millet beer (*boyalwa*), while the youngsters squatted outside the circle, edging forward now and then to drain the dregs from the calabashes, and picking up scraps of the talk of their elders. On moonless nights, when there was no dancing, there was nothing to do but talk, and, apart from the trivial occurrences of the day, nothing to talk about except the deeds of bygone heroes of the tribe— those who had left them, but were still, in some mysterious fashion, watching over their interests. In this way names and pedigrees, long recitals of raids and hunting exploits, became stamped, by constant repetition, in the memories of successive generations. Any deviation from an accepted version would be challenged and corrected, as by children to whom one relates a fairy tale. In course of time the fabric of a narrative might become embroidered, but it cannot for that reason be wholly discarded nor relegated to the category of folklore. Old Testament chronicles of Pharaohs and Israelites, Homeric ballads of the wars of Greeks and Trojans, even our own legends of King Arthur and Robin Hood, must have been handed down in the same way, and, though coloured strongly by romance, are based on a background of real places and actual men and women. It is fair to assume that people who had no other means of preserving records would have taken care to stick as closely as possible to what they had heard from their fathers, and to pass it on in the same form to their sons.

The kraal-fire stories are a thing of the past. The young Zulu or Bechuana no longer passes his life with his tribe. He goes off to work at the mines or in the white man's towns, and apes the white man's ways. Tradition has been lost in the general disintegration of tribal ties. The talk to-day is of the compounds of Kimberley and Johannes-burg ; of train journeys, secret drinking-dens and brothels.

Some of the moderns have been to school, and have oil
lamps to read by ; others can play mouth organs and con-
certinas, and there are even cheap gramophones. But not so
long ago there were those who kept the tribal spirit, and
missionaries who interrogated them and took down their
words. By this means a good deal of traditional history has
been recorded. It may not always be consecutive, and it
may be exaggerated, but without doubt it has a sub-
stratum of fact, and with that assurance we must rest
content.

The old men of the Bechuana when questioned as to the
past were ready to recite the names and deeds of a long
succession of mighty ancestors, many of whom were
probably mythical. The earliest of whom they could give a
clear account was one Masilo, the paramount chief of a tribe
whose offshoots were destined to play leading parts in the
affairs of the Transvaal and adjacent territories. They
called themselves ba-Kwena, after their *siboko*, or tribal
emblem, which was the crocodile (*kwena*). Deductions
based on the number of generations between this Masilo and
his successors of Moffat's time indicate that he must have
flourished about the middle of the seventeenth century.

As seems to have been almost a universal rule among the
families of Bantu chiefs a dissension occurred between two
of Masilo's sons—Malopi, the elder, breaking away and
taking with him a portion of the tribe, while the other,
Kwena, who though younger by birth was the old man's
son by the ' great wife ', and therefore his legitimate heir,
remained with his father, and eventually succeeded him.
The adherents of Kwena continued to be regarded, even by
the seceders, as the mother stock. They retained the
crocodile totem, and the chiefs that followed were accorded
a certain precedence over those of the other branches.
They enjoyed priority in partaking of the first fruits of each
new harvest. For any of the other chiefs to disregard this

prerogative would have been a gross breach of etiquette, and would probably have led, in the old days, to war. The ba-Kwena retained this dignity down to the time of a much later chief, Sechele, who was an astute man with a good deal of diplomatic skill, and played his cards well with Livingstone, by whom he was held, undeservedly it would seem, in high estimation. He figured prominently in the intrigues of the various Bechuanaland tribes in the mid-nineteenth century. He posed as their guardian. On several occasions he harboured—for a consideration—chiefs who were obliged to fly for political reasons, and was always ready to interfere in tribal disputes. After his death the ba-Kwena declined. His successor, Sebele, who visited England in 1895, was of a different calibre, hopelessly addicted to drink. Though tolerant and friendly to the missionaries he was for many years a thorn in their side owing to his reluctance to abandon witchcraft and other practices which were to them anathema.

Masilo's elder son, Malopi, the seceder, had many sons of his own, and three of them, Hurutsi, Ngwaketsi and Ngwato,[1] following the family tradition, became leaders of disruption. This portion of the crocodile people—the junior branch—was in consequence split into three factions, which went their several ways, and settled at a distance from each other. The people of the first called themselves, after their chief, ba-Hurutsi—a subtribe which retained the crocodile, but adopted the baboon as an additional totem. In later years it fell into misfortune. In 1823 it was sorely harassed by the terrible Mantatees, whose story follows, and the tribe was finally broken up by the Matabele under Mzili-gazi. The few survivors fled into the Kalahari desert, and in the long run relapsed into a condition almost of serfdom.

[1] The sound expressed by *ngw* in these names, and in the language of the Bechuana and allied tribes generally, is the same as in the English word ' ringworm ', and not hard as in ' anguish '.

The second subtribe retained their independence, and continued to call themselves ba-Ngwaketsi, after their founder, down to our own times. They migrated in a southerly direction, and endeavoured to settle in the Marico district of what is now the Transvaal, but it was a vulnerable position in a fertile and attractive country. They were driven back by the successive raids of Zulu and other marauders, at whose hands they suffered cruel persecutions. One of their chiefs, Makabi, lost his life in an affray with the Matabele in 1835, and another, Gaseitsive,[1] fell foul of the Transvaal Boers, who made him a prisoner. The tribe took refuge at last in the country round Kanye, about a hundred miles north-west of Mafeking, where their descendants are found to-day. Their chiefs were undistinguished, and have mostly been forgotten, but in 1895 Bathoen, who then ruled them, was dragged into prominence for political reasons, and was permitted to pay an official visit to England, where he, together with Khama, the ardent temperance advocate, and Sebele, the equally ardent tippler, were received by Queen Victoria.

It is with the fortunes of those that followed the third of Malopi's sons, Ngwato, and their posterity, who called themselves ba-ma-Ngwato,[2] that we are chiefly concerned.

---

[1] Mackenzie, in *Ten Years North of the Orange River*, calls him Hasiitsiwe.

[2] In this and similar cases it is probable that tribes, when first separating from the parent stock, adopted the name of their leader, though some hold that the converse rule was followed, *i.e.* that the founder of a new section took the name of the tribal *siboko* (totem), to show that he was its representative. The word *ngwato* has no connection with the emblems of the ba-Mangwato, which were the crocodile and the duiker-buck. Mr. J. C. Harris (in his life of Khama, p. 11) says that the word means ' a poor piece of beef ', and that it was a ' sinister gift made to Ngwato's mother by her ironical husband when she was childless. When later she bore him a son she named him Ngwato as a subtle reprisal.' This implies that, according to a common Bechuana usage, she herself would be known as ma-Ngwato, but it seems rather a far-fetched explanation.

From this stock sprung the famous Khama, who, from amid the most adverse surroundings, rose to become the greatest reformer that any Bantu race has yet produced.

Ngwato and his following formed, probably about the year 1700, a colony among the hills in the vicinity of Shoshong. Reduced and reinforced from time to time by defections and additions, they remained in this part of the country through many vicissitudes, and, after two hundred years, they are there still. During the lifetime of their founder the tribe seems to have remained intact, but in the reign of his successor, Matipi, the usual family split occurred. This man had two sons—Khama (hartebeeste), the first of that name, and Tauwana (young lion), who was his favourite. The brothers quarrelled, and Tauwana, with a portion of the tribe, either of his own accord or under compulsion, forsook his ancestral home and formed a new settlement near Lake Ngami. Strangely enough the chief, Matipi, accompanied him, leaving Khama to rule the main body of the tribe. Tauwana afterwards turned against his father,who thereupon sought reconciliation with the elder son. His overtures were rejected, however, and finding that he had fallen between two stools he hanged himself in despair.

The ba-Mangwato retained their veneration for the crocodile, but in the course of time adopted an additional totem— the small antelope familiar throughout South Africa as the *duiker*, and called by them *phuti* (the *ph* being pronounced as in the English word *haphazard*), in consequence of which they were sometimes known as ba-Phuti—the 'duiker people'. The fortunes of the tribe fluctuated, but a period of prosperity set in with the accession of Khama's son Khari (grandfather of the famous Khama of the nineteenth century). He was a chief of strong capacity, and it was to him that the ba-Mangwato owed their first emergence as a self-contained unit of the Bechuana family. Under him they acquired an ascendancy over many of the Makalanga dwelling on their northern borders, and, according to the missionary Mackenzie,[1] even over some outlying groups of the Mashona, who were scattered over the wide region beyond the Shashi and Limpopo rivers. It seems to have been Khari's practice to make occasional raids into these parts for the purpose of exacting tribute—in other words of seizing cattle. But he did this once too often. The people in these parts had not then sunk into the abject condition to which they were afterwards reduced by Matabele depredations, and one of the tribes against which he led a pillaging expedition lured his force into a trap and utterly defeated it, killing the chief himself, and some of his principal commanders. This took place in the rocky fastnesses of the Matopo Hills.[2]

Thus far we have been relying on native tradition. With Khari we have approached surer ground, for he overlapped the historical period, and was, in fact, ruling the tribe at the time of Moffat's arrival in Bechuanaland in 1820. For some time after his death, however, the ba-Mangwato were demoralised, and little was heard of them as a tribe until they came once more into the limelight through their relations with Mziligazi and other alien invaders. Before dealing with these it may be useful to recapitulate, in the form of a genealogical table, the line of descent of all the offshoots of the ' crocodile people ', from the time of the legendary Masilo to the middle of the nineteenth century, when Moffat, Livingstone and others were working and travelling among them.   (See opposite page).

II. THE MATABELE

Of the early days of Mziligazi, the founder of the Matabele nation, no very precise details have come down to us.

[1] *Ten Years North of the Orange River*, p. 358.

[2] Evidence of Khama at Grobler inquiry ; *Blue Book*, C. 5918, p. 72.

THE BA-KWENA (CROCODILE PEOPLE)

PEDIGREE OF CHIEFS

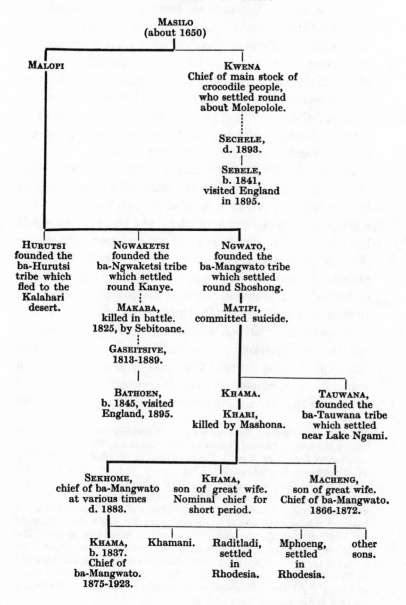

MASILO
(about 1650)

MALOPI

KWENA
Chief of main stock of
crocodile people,
who settled round
about Molepolole.

SECHELE,
d. 1893.

SEBELE,
b. 1841,
visited England
in 1895.

HURUTSI
founded the
ba-Hurutsi
tribe which
fled to the
Kalahari
desert.

NGWAKETSI
founded the
ba-Ngwaketsi tribe
which settled
round Kanye.

NGWATO,
founded the
ba-Mangwato tribe
which settled
round Shoshong.

MAKABA,
killed in battle,
1825, by Sebitoane.

MATIPI,
committed suicide.

GASEITSIVE,
1813-1889.

BATHOEN,
b. 1845, visited
England, 1895.

KHAMA.

KHARI,
killed by Mashona.

TAUWANA,
founded the
ba-Tauwana tribe
which settled
near Lake Ngami.

SEKHOME,
chief of ba-Mangwato
at various times
d. 1883.

KHAMA,
son of great wife.
Nominal chief for
short period.

MACHENG,
son of great wife.
Chief of ba-Mangwato.
1866-1872.

KHAMA,
b. 1837.
Chief of
ba-Mangwato.
1875-1923.

Khamani.

Raditladi,
settled
in
Rhodesia.

Mphoeng,
settled
in
Rhodesia.

other
sons.

It is generally accepted, however, that he was born about 1790, the son of Matshobane, petty chief of a small clan known as the Kumalo, which was absorbed into the Zulu hegemony by Tshaka. His father having met the not uncommon fate of assassination in some tribal quarrel, Mziligazi was chosen to lead the clan. His personal bravery and success as a raider rapidly brought him into favour with his king, who before long placed him in charge of one of his military kraals—Gibixegu, or Bulawayo [1]—and gave him the command of some 20,000 fighting men.

In the year 1817, after a successful foray, he was guilty of keeping back a number of cattle which, according to custom should have been handed over to Tshaka. It was a grave act of treason, for which he and his headmen would have been put to death without compunction. To escape this fate Mziligazi and his army fled over the Drakensberg mountains and having thus made themselves outlaws, embarked on a course of organised brigandage against the Bechuana tribes then settled in the Transvaal.

At this time Mziligazi was about twenty-seven years of age, and was possessed of extraordinary vigour and athletic strength. During the next few years he gradually assumed autocratic powers over his following, extended his raids and increased the distance between himself and his former

[1] I am informed by Miss A. Werner, the well-known authority on Bantu languages, that *Gibixegu* means 'Drive out the old man', in allusion to Zwide, or Mzwiti, the murderer of Matshobane. Captain W. Cornwallis Harris, in his *Wild Sports of South Africa* (p. 98) explains that *Gibbeklaik*—as he spells it—denoted 'pick out the old ones', and was humorously bestowed on the kraal in commemoration of a barbarous massacre ordered by Tshaka of all those veterans of his army who were no longer fit for active service, and were consuming his beef without making any return for it. *Bulawayo* means 'The place of slaughter'. Both names were many years afterwards adopted for the new town which Mziligazi's son, Lobengula, founded in Matabeleland on his accession. The word *Mziligazi* means 'track of blood'. All these expressions are grimly significant of the ruling passion of the Zulu nation and its offshoots.

master. By 1830 he had laid waste the whole area between the Drakensberg range and Witwatersrand, and had robbed the wretched inhabitants of the greater part of their cattle and small stock. He and his army followed the routine they had learnt from Tshaka. Whenever they swept down upon a village they mercilessly butchered the older men and women, and the helpless infants—often with indescribable tortures and mutilations. Only the marriageable girls were spared, and such of the boys as were likely to be useful for training as soldiers. These latter were fed on a meat diet and put through a course of the harshest discipline, which resulted in the elimination of all weaklings, while the survivors acquired the ferocity and blood-lust of their captors.

Mziligazi copied Tshaka's methods also to strengthen his personal authority. His word was the only law. The penalty for the slightest insubordination or failure was death. The cattle captured in war were his, and could only be slaughtered for food by his orders. The young men could not marry until he had given his sanction, which was occasionally granted to a whole regiment at the same time as a reward for some exceptional feat of arms. For his own delectation a large number of women were distributed among the various kraals who kept him informed as to what was going on, and, when he got tired of them, were sometimes allotted to favourite headmen. In his youth he had contracted orthodox marriages with two of the daughters of Mzwiti, the man who afterwards murdered his father, and one of these, Umoaka, he recognised as the ' great wife '.

III. THE MANTATEES

We must leave Mziligazi and his tribe for a moment in order to describe the progress of the further waves of westward invasion which began to develop before the Matabele had settled down in their new country. The initial impetus came, as before stated, from Zululand, and each mob as it broke away set in motion those in front of it, until the whole population was moving in successive jerks and bumps after the manner of a string of railway trucks in shunting operations.

About 1821 came the ama-Hlubi (Fingos) who took a more southerly route than the Matabele, and followed the course of the Caledon river, along the borders of Basutoland, until they came perilously near to Cape Colony. They were checked, however, by the Orange river, which was in flood, and turning back spread through the districts now comprising the Orange Free State. The disturbed tribes in these parts fled to the north and west. Out of the general tumult a number of clans of different origins, living on the high *veld* between the Caledon and Vaal rivers, made common cause. Dispossessed of their homes and robbed of their cattle they became desperate, and rapidly there grew up an immense rabble—part fugitives and part banditti—which swept over the Vaal river and fell upon the peaceful Bechuana tribes on its northern side. A fierce woman leader now appeared —one Ma-Ntatisi, who, aided by her son Sikonyela, infused some sort of discipline and organisation into the heterogeneous mass. The most hideous outrages were perpetrated by this couple and their furious following. Of the virago Ma-Ntatisi herself (from whom the horde of brigands took its name Mantatees or Makatees) the wildest rumours gained currency among the surrounding peoples. She was said to be of enormous stature, with a single eye in the middle of her forehead, and to feed her army with her own milk when they were short of beef or human flesh—for some of them were reputed to be cannibals.[1] The Bechuana believed these fantastic tales, and were so paralysed with

---

[1] Theal, *Hist. of S. Africa since 1795*, vol. v, p. 383. Moffat, *Missionary Labours*, etc., chap. xxi. J. S. Moffat, *Lives of R. and M. Moffat*, letter quoted from Mary Moffat, p. 112.

fear that they could form no plan to save their lives other
than flight to hiding places among the nearest mountains.
A state of panic pervaded the whole of the country in the
line of the Mantatees' advance.

One after another the Bechuana tribes were attacked and
routed, often with terrible slaughter. On the northern
slopes of the Magaliesberg range, near the headwaters of the
Limpopo river, and somewhere between the modern sites of
Rustenberg and Pretoria—one of the most fertile and well-
watered spots in the Transvaal—the ba-Hurutsi, of the ba-
Kwena group, who had not so far been molested by
Mziligazi, were leading a tranquil life and tending large
herds of cattle. Suddenly down came the Mantatees and
drove them in scattered remnants towards the desert.
They then turned south-west, and in June, 1823, advanced
in the direction of Kuruman. Fortunately the terrified
natives sought the advice of Moffat, who in this crisis behaved with great coolness and decision. About a hundred
miles to the south of his station was a settlement of Griqua
half-breeds. Many of them had horses and were armed
with flint-locks and other muzzle-loading guns. Moffat
resolved to call in their aid, and travelled with all speed to
Griquatown. He explained the situation to Mr. Melvill, the
Government agent, and with his co-operation induced the
Griqua chiefs Andries Waterboer, Adam Kok and others to
march to the support of the Kuruman natives with a
' commando ' of a hundred mounted men. A few days later
they came in contact with advanced parties of the Mantatees
horde at Takoon near Lattakoo. The main body was
estimated by Moffat at upwards of 40,000, but there was
little cohesion among them ; they were undisciplined, and
exhausted by the privations and hardships of their long
campaign. They could make no stand against the tactics
of the Griquas, who never allowed them to come to close
quarters. Galloping within range they discharged their

old-fashioned muskets and then returned to reload. They were skilled shots and did great execution among the Mantatees, who were unaccustomed to gunfire, and could not get near enough to use their assegais. After several hours of this one-sided fighting they began to give way and finally took to flight, leaving a large number of wounded on the field, and many women and children too weak to escape. The Griquas pursued them for about eight miles, and as soon as they saw their dreaded enemy in retreat the Bechuana, who had so far been watching the struggle from a safe distance, rushed forward like voracious wolves, and fell upon the wounded and helpless women and children with their spears and battle-axes. A grisly scene of butchery ensued. Moffat, who had not fired a single shot, rode in and strove to stop the carnage, but the Bechuana were maddened with blood, and he could do little to check them. He reckoned the number of Mantatees killed at between 400 and 500.

It seems incredible that a party of only a hundred should have been able to turn and rout a force so greatly outnumbering them, but it is clear that the Mantatees were reduced to the last extremity by hunger, and in fact both men and women were found afterwards devouring the bodies of their own killed. The part played by Moffat was worthy of the highest credit, but he writes of the affair with great modesty, only expressing the shame and disgust which he felt at the revolting cruelty displayed by the local natives, among whom he had been carrying on his mission work. No man hated bloodshed more, and the atrocities he was forced to witness made him sick with horror. But his courage and determination had saved the situation. Had the murderous rabble not been checked they would in all probability have crossed the Orange river and descended upon the defenceless border farmers of Cape Colony, where they might have played still more serious havoc.

After this reverse the Mantatees began to break up. Some turned back towards the Caledon river, and with these we are not here concerned ; some hundreds of them under a remarkable leader, Sebitoane, who lived to make a good deal of history, struck northwards, and it was not long before they came into collision with the Matabele, whose acquaintance they had not till then made. But no trustworthy information can be obtained as to their movements or those of the tribes they encountered during the next few years. Owing to its disturbed state the country north of the Orange river remained a sealed book to white men. There are vague and scrappy references in the literature of the day to attacks from Zululand beaten off by Mziligazi, and to conflicts between his *impis* and the Makololo, as Sebitoane's followers were now called, while the latter were working their way towards the Zambesi. From time to time we hear also of the wretched plight of the ba-Hurutsi and other Bechuana tribes who were alternately harried by one or the other and were driven from pillar to post, but it is impossible to piece together a clear story from such disconnected items, and we must pass over a period of seven or eight years in silence.

IV. MZILIGAZI

The curtain is lifted for a space in 1831 by Moffat. His work had begun to provoke the curiosity of Mziligazi, who thought it would be rather a fine thing to have a missionary of his own, and sent messengers to Kuruman to investigate. By this time he had finally dispossessed the ba-Hurutsi from their rich Marico valley and had taken up his own quarters at Kapain (or Gabeni) near Zeerust, where there was abundant grazing for the enormous herds of cattle he had collected in his raids. The tyrant Tshaka, his former master, had been murdered in 1828 by his brother Dingaan (who then assumed the chieftaincy of the Zulus) and with that threat removed Mziligazi had ceased to lead his soldiers personally into battle, and was living a life of pleasant ease, relieved by visits to his numerous military kraals to review his troops, to feast his eyes on his stock, and to enjoy the society of his concubines. These had no official standing, though, as the king's favourites, they could claim a good many privileges. In later years, with an eye to political advantages, Mziligazi made several marriages ; but in 1831 he would appear to have had only the two orthodox wives before mentioned, and against these, as daughters of his father's assassin, he cherished a secret grudge. The elder, Umoaka, was however the 'great wife', and no private feelings on the king's part could destroy her status, or deprive her offspring of their inherited rights. About the year 1828 she bore a son, whose original name I have been unable to discover, though he afterwards figured prominently under another—Nkulumane. Her sister also had a son called Ubuhlelo, who, being of pure Zulu stock, would in the normal course have been the next heir after Umoaka's family.

Mziligazi's messengers, one of whom was Umnombate, his chief councillor, were really spies, but they brought with them a pressing invitation to the missionary to visit their king, and after some hesitation Moffat accepted it and returned in their company. His account of the ten days he spent in the Matabele country is valuable as supplying one of the few pictures we possess of the king himself as he was in the days of his prime. 'In person', he says, 'Mziligazi was below the middle stature, rather corpulent, with a short neck, and in his manner could be exceedingly affable and cheerful. His voice, soft and effeminate, did not indicate that his disposition was passionate'. Moffat goes on to say that from the period of his revolt from Tshaka until the time of this visit 'his career formed an interminable catalogue of crimes. Scarcely a mountain, over extensive regions, but bore the marks of his deadly ire. His experience and native cunning enabled him to triumph over the minds of his men, and made his trembling captives soon adore him as an invincible sovereign. Those who resisted, and would not stoop to be his dogs, he butchered'. [1]

. In spite of these unpleasant traits Moffat seems during his short visit to have found some element of human kindness in his composition, and to have regarded him as a possible convert. This demonstrates Moffat's freedom from prejudice and at the same time suggests that behind Mziligazi's ruthless policy there may have been some other motive than a mere lust for murder. The king, for his part, appears to have been captivated by the missionary's personality, and to have conceived a strong affection for him. On subsequent occasions he certainly sought his advice, and followed it—even against his own interests. He paid him the compliment of naming his eldest son Nkulumane (the Matabele pronunciation of Kuruman) in memory of the visit. But one cannot exclude the idea that his crafty mind had some ulterior purpose in these outward demonstrations. In any case it is an exaggeration to speak, as many writers have, of the existence of a ' strong friendship ' between natures so diametrically opposed as those of Moffat and the barbarous and ensanguined chief.

It is interesting to compare Moffat's description of the man with that of Captain W. Cornwallis Harris, who visited him five or six years later. According to the latter Mziligazi's figure was ' rather tall, well-turned and active, but through neglect of exercise, leaning to corpulency. . . . The expression of the despot's features, though singularly cunning, wily, and suspicious, is not altogether disagreeable. He appeared about forty years of age, but being totally beardless it was difficult to form a correct estimate'. [2]

[1] Moffat, *Missionary Labours*, etc., chap. xxx.
[2] Harris, *Wild Sports in S. Africa*, p. 123.

Both writers agree that he kept up an appearance of great state. Whenever he moved he was preceded by heralds, who capered and pranced about, flourishing short wands, and shouting out his titles in a string of unbroken sentences, and behind him came a procession of women carrying calabashes of beer and bowls of steaming beef. Whenever he rose or sat down all within sight hailed him with the royal salute 'BAYETE!' and vied in screaming out effusive compliments such as 'Great King!', 'King of Heaven!', 'Elephant!', and the like.

Mziligazi's dress was hardly in keeping with this regal display. Here is Harris's description : 'The elliptical ring on his closely shorn scalp was decorated with three green feathers from the tail of the paroquet, placed horizontally, two behind and one in front. A single string of small blue beads encircled his neck ; a bunch of twisted sinews encompassed his left ankle, and the usual girdle dangling before and behind with leopards' tails completed his costume'. [1]

The full dress of the soldiers was far more elaborate, and was designed no doubt to add to the terror which the *impis* inspired in the minds of the local tribes who were continually harried by their raids. It consisted of a thick fur kilt composed of triple rows of cats' or monkeys' tails, descending nearly to the knee. A tippet, formed of white cows' tails, covered the shoulders, the knees, wrists, elbows and ankles being ornamented with a single ox-tail fastened above the joint. In later days the white tippet was replaced by a thick cap and cape of black ostrich feathers, which gave them a still more savage and martial appearance. They were armed with the broad-bladed assegais which Tshaka had introduced to supersede the throwing javelins carried by other Bantu tribes, and carried a long shield of ox hide, oval in shape but pointed at each end and stiffened by

[1] Harris, *Wild Sports*, etc., p. 123.

strips of hide plaited vertically.[1] Many also wielded knobkerries made of rhinoceros horn. They had learnt to throw
these with such precision that they were able to bring down
a bird on the wing or a running antelope. The effect of a
regiment in mass thus equipped was splendid and awe-
inspiring. Their method of attack was to manoeuvre their
enemy into open ground where they could rush upon them in
crescent formation, striking their shields by way of intimida-
tion. The horns of the crescent would be rapidly closed and
their victims surrounded and finished off by stabbing.

The paramount interest of the Matabele—occupying their
minds to the exclusion even of sexual matters, which bulk
so largely among other African tribes—was warfare and the
shedding of blood. Their devotion to their chief, whom they
regarded as a god ; whose creatures they were—slaves of
his caprice and instruments for his aggrandisement, can
only be accounted for by admitting that he possessed a
subtle and magnetic personality. Added to this he was
undoubtedly endowed with exceptional powers of statecraft—possibly surpassing even Tshaka in his capacity for
governing a nation of cut-throats. If other proof were
absent one need only point to the fact that, surrounded at
all times by sinister influences of his own creation, he yet
managed to live to a ripe old age and to achieve the distinction—rare indeed among Zulu tyrants—of dying a
natural death.

[1] The generally accepted explanation of the name ' Matabele ' is
that it means ' the people of the long shields ', but Mr. F. J. T.
Posselt, a recognised authority, in a paper on Mziligazi, read before
the Rhodesia Scientific Association in 1919, states that it was a term
applied to them by the ba-Suto tribes, and denotes ' aliens ', or
people who could not speak the Suto language.

The Rev. A. T. Bryant (*Zululand and Natal*, p. 425) says that the
ba-Suto styled them ma-Tebele as signifying ' those who disappear
or sink down out of sight (Suto *teba*) behind their immense war-
shields '.

If spelt as pronounced by themselves the name would be *ama-
Ntebele*.

CHAPTER IV

THE MATABELE IN THE TRANSVAAL

I. FIRST CONTACT WITH WHITE MEN

OF what was happening in the storm area on the borders of the Transvaal and Bechuanaland during the four years following Moffat's visit to Mziligazi in 1831 we have very meagre knowledge. At Kuruman Moffat was in a back-water ; at any rate he has left no detailed account of events beyond those that took place in his own immediate surroundings. Our only information is gleaned from the reports brought back by two or three white traders who were courageous enough to travel in their ox-waggons into these turbulent parts in the early 'thirties, and they are vague and not altogether trustworthy.

For some years there had been a deadly competition in pillage between Sebitoane's brigands and Mziligazi's butchers. From time to time there were fierce clashes between them. The country could not long contain two such destructive forces. The Matabele had the advantage of a settled base and better organisation. Being of Zulu origin they were of more highly tempered metal than their rivals, who were mainly Basutos. Gradually the latter began to yield to pressure and to retire. Having eaten the country bare they passed like a swarm of locusts and disappeared towards the north.[1]

[1] Theal (*History of S. Africa since 1795*, p. 396) estimates the number of individuals that perished in the ravaged country between 1820 and 1830 as nearer two millions than one.

All this time the unhappy Bechuana tribes had been ground between the upper and the nether millstone, and even now there was no respite for them. With the departure of the Makololo the Matabele incursions became more savage and more continuous. By 1831 most of the older communities of the raided zone were either broken up and scattered or had secured a precarious immunity by accepting a state of serfdom and paying tribute to Mziligazi. Among the worst sufferers were the ba-Kwena (the elder branch of the 'crocodile people'), who lived near the headwaters of the Limpopo river, and were thus close neighbours of the Matabele, and peculiarly exposed to attack. They survived the depredations of Sebitoane, who had, in fact, taken them under his wing, and had installed as their chief Sechele, a young member of the reigning family, with a great capacity as it turned out, for governing. The ba-Mangwato, being more remote, suffered less severely, but after the defeat and death at the hands of the Mashona of their powerful chief Khari they had become disintegrated, and remained in obscurity until they too were pulled together by one of his sons, Sekhome. Both Sechele and Sekhome played a prominent part in the recovery of their respective tribes during the next few years.

The only serious resistance encountered by Mziligazi came, not from the local tribes, but from the settlements of half-breeds on the south side of the Vaal river, most of whom were as inveterate cattle thieves as the Matabele themselves. In 1831 an expedition composed of Griquas and Korannas, many of them mounted and armed with guns, crossed the river and made a sudden descent on some kraals near the present site of Pretoria. The Matabele could make no stand against firearms, and were at first compelled to beat a retreat, leaving some thousands of cattle in the hands of the invaders. A few days later they rallied and made a counter-attack in great strength. The Griquas were taken by surprise, and were cumbered by the looted cattle. A bloody engagement followed in which the Matabele managed to get home with their short stabbing assegais, and did fearful execution. The Griqua force was nearly annihilated, their leader, Barend, and a handful of his men escaping with difficulty. The Matabele returned triumphant, having recovered the whole of their stock, and captured alive the daughter and nephew of Davids, one of Barend's lieutenants. After this affray Mziligazi issued orders that no one should cross the Vaal river from the south, and kept up a system of continuous patrols to ensure obedience. Even traders, hunters and missionaries were prohibited from entering his country by any road but that which passed through Kuruman.

Not until 1835 was the veil which covered these dark and troubled days once more drawn aside. The reports of traders of the fertility of the region beyond the Vaal river, and of the abundance of big game to be found there, had excited the cupidity of enterprising spirits at the Cape. A subscription was raised, and a strong expedition equipped with the support of the government to explore and gain more accurate information. It was placed under Dr. (afterwards Sir Andrew) Smith, a retired army surgeon with a taste for zoology, who left Graaf Reinet with twenty waggons and fifty persons, including some volunteer troops, in August, 1834. The expedition first visited Basutoland, and, in spite of the warnings of Moshesh, the ruler of that country, Smith resolved to push his investigations into the districts ravaged by the Matabele. First he went to Kuruman, where he found Moffat in poor health, but eager to help him. Messengers were sent to Mziligazi to ask permission for the entry of the exploring party; and, on a favourable reply being received, the missionary volunteered to accompany it. At the Molopo river the expedition was

JOHN SMITH MOFFAT
IN 1858

(At the time of his departure for Matabeleland.
See page 97)

(face p. 46)

ROBERT MOFFAT
IN 1816

(The year in which he began his labours in South Africa.
See page 13)

met by Kalipi, the Matabele commander-in-chief, who personally escorted it over the border.

In June, 1835, Smith and Moffat found the king at Tolane, one of his military kraals, to which he had betaken himself owing to an outbreak of disease at his capital town of Mosega. There Moffat remained for two months while Smith pursued his investigations in the surrounding country. He travelled as far north as latitude 24°.30′, where he found a Bechuana village under a Matabele *induna*, and was informed that this was the last of Mziligazi's posts in that direction. Dr. Smith's report, which was afterwards printed in an abridged form in the *Journal of the Geographical Society*,[1] is a dull, uninspiring document, mainly occupied with notes on the natural history of the countries he passed through, and unrelieved by any description of its inhabitants or their chiefs. He tells us nothing about Mziligazi, by whom he appears to have been well received—probably as a result of Moffat's good offices. The visit had, however, one interesting and surprising sequel. Mziligazi, for the second time, betrayed his curiosity about the British by deciding to send a mission of his own to Capetown. Smith on his return journey was accompanied by a deputation of Matabele headed by Umnombate, the chief councillor, who was charged with the duty of ' greeting the white man's Chief ', *i.e.* the Governor.

The visit was an eye-opener to the Matabele delegates. It was, of course, the first time they had seen anything more imposing than an up-country mission station, and they were deeply impressed by the evidence of the military strength and commercial activity of the capital, the shipping, the houses and public buildings. It would have been a good opportunity for the Governor, Sir Benjamin D'Urban, to warn them that their king must put a stop to

[1] Vol. vi, 1836.

his bloodthirsty methods or take the consequences. But nothing of the kind was done. A 'treaty' was drawn up pledging the Matabele king to act as a faithful friend and ally of the Colony, to maintain peace with the British Government, to give his protection to white people visiting his country, to encourage missionaries, and generally to promote civilisation, and to this precious document the Governor affixed his signature, and Umnombate his mark. It cannot be supposed that Umnombate grasped the full import of such an agreement or realised the sanctity attached to written contracts by the British. He probably never suspected that he was giving any guarantee on behalf of his chief, still less that he was restricting his freedom of action. The 'treaty' was, except for that part which related to missionaries, a dead letter. Precisely six months after its execution the Matabele crowned their atrocities by the cold-blooded massacre of a party of Boer emigrants from the Cape Colony.

II. ENTER THE BOERS

As this was the first time that Mziligazi's soldiers had dipped their assegais in the blood of white men the reasons which led the Boers to put themselves within his reach must be shortly explained.

For twenty years or more the Cape colonists had been subjected to growing injustice at the hands of ignorant or misguided politicians in Great Britain. The outburst of emotional philanthropy which seized Englishmen in the early part of the century found its first outlet in the emancipation movement. This culminated, so far as South Africa was concerned, in 1834, when 40,000 slaves, the legal property of the white settlers, were declared free by an Act of the Imperial Parliament. Public opinion in Cape Colony had been prepared for this step, and would not have resented it had the provisions for compensation been honourably carried out. But the assessed value of the slaves had been cut down to less than one half, and it was further decreed that payment (which was to be partly in cash and partly in Government stock) could only be made in London —6,000 miles away. The slave-owners were in consequence unable to get the amounts awarded to them except by the employment of agents, to whom they were obliged to sell their claims at a ruinous loss. The aggregate amount which actually reached the owners was about £600,000, or one-fifth of the total assessed value, and many colonists, whose slaves represented their invested capital, and who depended on them for their labour supply, were reduced to bankruptcy.

The history of all social reform movements—temperance, puritanism, pacifism, and a dozen others—shows that they tend to branch out into freakish growths. Owing to confusion of ideas, and in their righteous zeal to put a sudden end to an institution which was as old as human society, the champions of negro emancipation allowed their vision to become distorted. It came to be thought that white men could not live side by side with blacks without oppressing them. There was in Cape Colony a small but active clique, headed by Dr. Philip, a missionary of extreme pro-native views, which spared no effort to besmirch the character of the colonists by allegations of cruelty towards the black population. The effect of their persistent campaign was to create in England, both in official and private circles, a conviction that the white settlers in South Africa could not be trusted to deal fairly with the indigenous inhabitants. This belief grew into a dogma which coloured the relations between the Imperial Government and the Colony for many years. It was productive of incessant misunderstandings and seriously handicapped the efforts of colonial statesmen whose aim was to develop the dark places of the continent by the gradual introduction of British officials, and by the firm and sane treatment of the aboriginal natives. The mistrust of their own countrymen was extended to British settlements in other parts of Africa. That it is not yet dead is proved by the restrictions which recent governments have sought to impose on our East African colonies in regard to their native policy.

Incidentally also the agitation started by Dr. Philip did irreparable mischief to the missionary cause which he claimed to represent. It created an impression, which to this day has not entirely evaporated among South Africans, that missionaries must of necessity be allied with the blacks against the whites. The work of evangelising and uplifting the natives began to be surrounded with a suspicion which has never been completely shaken off.

In 1835 the Imperial authorities—admittedly with a large section of the public behind them—refused to pay attention to the sober reports of unprejudiced officials on the spot. They preferred to rely on the wild denunciations of Dr. Philip and the small party of fanatical extremists who sided with him. They were induced to believe that the constant depredations of the ama-Xosa and other cattle-raiding tribes on the eastern borders of the Colony, which had desolated the frontier districts and ruined many of the settlers besides creating a condition of semi-warfare, were justified as retaliation for systematic persecution. The colonial troops employed to keep the marauding natives within bounds were branded as robbers and murderers. The marking out of a buffer area between the colonial and native territory was denounced as an act of spoliation. Lord Glenelg, the Secretary of State for the Colonies, ignoring the arguments of his responsible officials at the Cape, ordered the evacuation of this area and the removal of the troops. He gave other directions which showed that he had utterly failed to grasp the real situation, and accompanied them with insulting and odious insinuations as to the conduct of the white colonists. As a result of his instructions the border relapsed into a condition of chaos and anarchy, and many farmers in the eastern districts found it impossible to make a livelihood, and unsafe even to remain.

The outcome of these acts was that a number of respectable and substantial citizens of Boer descent decided to cut adrift from the country of their birth, where they despaired of getting fair treatment, and to work out their salvation elsewhere.

III. THE GREAT TREK

The thoughts of those who had made up their minds to break away from the Cape Colony naturally turned to the open country beyond the Orange river of which they had heard such favourable reports. In these wide spaces, which seemed to belong to no one, they hoped to find room to make new homes, with freedom to lead their own lives unhampered by the interference of distant authorities. During the winter of 1836 several large parties, comprising some hundreds of farmers, began to move northwards in detachments from the border districts of the Colony— those exposed to the Kaffir marauders. They took with them their wives and families, and their household effects, together with their cattle and small stock ; in fact they made a deliberate root and branch abandonment of their former habitations. After crossing the Orange river the various groups took different courses. One band succeeded in reaching without molestation the Zoutpansberg district in the north of the Transvaal, but here they were cut off by a force of natives—possibly one of Dingaan's *impis* from Zululand,[1] though no actual details came to light—and massacred. Others settled on the south banks of the Vaal,

---

[1] Dingaan was Tshaka's brother, who murdered and then succeeded him.

while a number, with an idea of working towards the sea-coast, followed the north bank and spent some weeks in hunting elephants and exploring. Hardly any natives were at first encountered in this part of the country, and the emigrants were so unsuspicious of danger that they broke up into small parties of a few families, each with its private waggons.

On the 2nd of September two such parties were surprised simultaneously by Matabele patrols. Men, women, children and coloured servants were hacked to death, the cattle seized and the waggons carried off. Stephanus Erasmus and another Boer, who had been after elephants, on returning to their camp and finding it in the hands of the natives, rode at once to give the alarm to a larger group which was thirty or forty miles in rear. These had barely time to draw up their waggons into a rough *laager* when they too were attacked by a regiment of Mziligazi's warriors. They defended themselves with their muzzle-loaders for the best part of a day and eventually managed to drive off their assailants with considerable loss. The whole body of emigrants in that neighbourhood then hastened back across the river and formed a strong *laager* of fifty waggons on the south side. It was afterwards found that from the first camp attacked—that of Erasmus—the Matabele had seized three little children—a boy and two girls—whom they took away with them alive to Mosega as a present to their king.

On the 29th of October a force of 5000 Matabele under Kalipi, the commander-in-chief, advanced against the party on the south side of the Vaal, which had placed itself under the command of Hendrik Potgieter. Though only forty in number the white men rode out to give battle, and by alternately firing volleys and retiring held the enemy in check while the *laager* was strengthened and made secure ; then taking up their position on the waggons they kept up a deadly fire of slugs and buckshot at short range, the women

doing their share by reloading the guns as they were discharged and passing up spare ones to their men-folk.

Again and again the Matabele made fierce rushes, rattling
spears and knobkerries against their shields, hissing and
screaming their war-cries, after their manner when attacking a Bechuana village, but each time they were driven back
by the steady volleys of the defenders. Kalipi himself was
wounded in the knee, and at last gave the order to retreat,
leaving 150 of his *ma-tjaha* dead round the waggons. In
their baffled fury the Matabele hurled hundreds of their
assegais into the *laager*, wounding twelve of the Boers and
killing two. But they never succeeded in breaking through
the cordon, or in coming to close quarters with their deadly
blades. The emigrants had saved their lives and their
waggons, but nothing more. When the Matabele retired
they drove in front of them nearly 5,000 head of cattle,
100 horses and 50,000 sheep and goats. With the remaining
horses—those they had been riding when they fell back on
the *laager*—Potgieter and his men pursued them, but
although they managed to shoot down a few stragglers they
were unable to retrieve the captured animals. The party
were ship-wrecked on the veld, incapable of moving until
the arrival of other bodies of their fellow-emigrants a few
days later enabled them to withdraw to a safe distance.

They were not the sort of men to sit down tamely under
these reverses, but it took them some months to organise a
counter-attack, and they made their preparations with great
care. It was decided to advance on Mziligazi's main kraal
with a mounted column unencumbered by waggons, and
early in January a determined commando crossed the Vaal
river under Potgieter and Gert Maritz, a wealthy farmer
who had recently arrived from Graaf Reinet. It was composed of over a hundred white men, together with about
fifty half-breeds under Pieter Davids, the Griqua captain,
who was eager to avenge his defeat by the Matabele five

years before and to rescue his captured daughter Gertrude. A few Bechuana natives on foot accompanied the commando. The force approached Mosega by the Kuruman road from which side no attack was likely to be expected, and succeeded in reaching their objective unobserved. On Jan. 17, 1837, at the first streak of dawn, they suddenly emerged from a pass in the hills and opened fire on the kraal. The Matabele were completely taken by surprise. The dreaded Kalipi was fortunately absent at the time, and the fighting men were somewhat demoralised in consequence. The attack was an absolute success. The Matabele fled pursued by the Boers, who shot down at least 400 before returning to set fire to the huts and granaries. They recovered most of Erasmus's waggons and seized over 6,000 head of cattle with which they marched back to the Vaal river. Three American missionaries whom Mziligazi had allowed, at Moffat's request, to open work at Mosega, realised the danger of remaining, and joined the victorious commando.

This was the first real reverse Mziligazi had experienced since leaving Zululand seventeen years before. But there were further blows to fall. The news of Potgieter's victory at Mosega reached the ears of Dingaan, the Zulu king, who thought the opportunity of paying off old scores too good to be wasted, and at once despatched an army to strike down the Matabele before they could recover. A hand to hand battle was fought near the Vaal river and large numbers were slaughtered on both sides. In the end the Zulus were beaten off, but managed to drive away most of Mziligazi's remaining cattle.

Finally, towards the end of the year, a still more effective chastisement was administered by the Boers. A new expedition was formed under the joint command of Potgieter and Pieter Uys, and marched boldly into the heart of the Marico district. After the previous disaster at Mosega the King had shifted his head-quarters to Kapain, about fifty miles further north, and here he was mercilessly hunted down by the Boers, who taught him the lesson he so richly deserved. For nine days they chased him from one position to another, inflicting such heavy losses on his regiments that they were utterly broken up. His cattle were seized, and his kraals fired. The morale of the Matabele was, for the time being at all events, destroyed, and Mziligazi realised that the country which had been his happy hunting-ground for so many years had now become too hot for him. He ruefully collected his shattered regiments and turned his face northwards.

Early in 1838 the whole nation was on the move towards the Limpopo river, preying, whenever they got the chance, on the weaker tribes on the road—Bechuana and Makalanga, to whom the name of Mziligazi still spelt terror. The women and children shared the hardships of the long march, and among them the king's great wife and his two sons Nkulumane and Ubuhlelo. There was also a son by an inferior wife—a little lad scarce old enough to toddle—whose name was Lobengula.

IV. DIFFERENT VIEWS OF THE TREK

The above outline of the encounters between the Matabele and the emigrant Boers has been drawn mainly from the much more detailed narrative given by the historian Theal. Theal never quotes authorities, but he had access to the early official records of the Cape and Transvaal, and was in touch with many of the relatives of those who took part in the Boer trek. His account is corroborated in essentials by the Hon. Henry Cloete, High Commissioner for Natal, who possessed an intimate knowledge of the events, gathered directly from participants, and described them in a series of lectures some years later. Theal's account may therefore be accepted as substantially correct.

Beyond the Boers engaged there were no white eye-witnesses except the three American missionaries—Messrs. Lindley, Venables and Wilson—who were present at Mosega during the attack in January, 1837, and none of these has left records. There were, however, two British army officers in Mziligazi's country engaged on independent hunting trips—Captain Sutton and Captain Cornwallis Harris—and the latter wrote a book of reminiscences which throws some interesting sidelights on these stirring events.[1] Harris first heard of the trouble from Sutton and Moffat at Kuruman, when he passed through in September, 1836, but it did not deter him from proceeding with his visit to Mosega for which he had secured the King's permission. On arrival there he saw Erasmus's waggons standing in the King's kraal, and heard from the missionaries that Kalipi had already started with a very large force for the Vaal river ' to complete the destruction of the emigrant farmers '. He also learnt that on the day before his arrival two Dutch girls had been sent away in a waggon by Mziligazi, who was anxious that their presence should not be made known to him. These of course were two of the three children carried off in the assault on Erasmus's camp in the previous month. Harris was present at the kraal when the news arrived of Kalipi's ' successful ' engagement with the emigrants at the Vaal river, and describes the King's delight at receiving it ; but he thought it prudent to affect ignorance of the hostilities, and to ask no questions about Erasmus's waggons. On his way down country he actually met the Matabele army returning with their spoil of cattle, and had some difficulty in satisfying their commander Kalipi, that he was there with the King's consent. Harris also has a good deal to say about Gertrude or ' Truey ', the daughter of the Griqua chief Davids, who, with her cousin, had been kidnapped in the fight with the half-breeds in 1831, and at the

[1] *The Wild Sports of Southern Africa*, published in 1839.

time of his visit was one of the King's concubines. Some idea of the carnage during that fight may be gathered from Harris's description of the battlefield, which was pointed out to him. ' It was a perfect Golgotha, thickly strewed with the whitened bones of men and horses, broken guns and tattered furniture '.[1]

As regards the Boer emigrants the tenor of Harris's comments indicates that he had little sympathy with them, and thought their misfortunes had been brought on by themselves. It is strange to find that so far-sighted a man as Dr. Moffat, who had every reason for wishing the country freed from the tyranny of the Matabele, held the same view, though to him the principal offence of the Boers was that they had interfered with the progress of the Christian missions. ' The prospects of our American brethren ', he says, ' were unexpectedly blasted by an inroad of some disaffected farmers, who had located themselves on the Yellow [Vaal] river. It appears that the farmers had hunted on what Moselikatse [Mziligazi] considered his dominions, and had used some people who acknowledged his authority rather roughly. This the haughty monarch would not brook, and sent his men more than once to attack them ; and on one occasion a desperate conflict ensued, when the farmers repulsed their assailants, who, seizing the cattle, retired with them, leaving many of their number dead on the spot where they had intended to mas-sacre the farmers. Exasperated at this, the latter came down in a large body on the mission premises, in rather savage style ; and there being only a handful of Matabele in the Mosega basin, these were cut off ; and the farmers, with the cattle they had seized, made a precipitate retreat to the Orange river, taking with them the American missionaries, who were so dispirited by the effects of disease, as to be scarcely able to judge how they should act. The

[1] This was borne out by Dr. Smith, who also visited the spot.

latter were prevailed on to leave their property behind, except that which the farmers took for their own use. Thus was the Mission to Mosega again broken up. Into the merits of the case we do not pretend to enter. It was altogether a melancholy affair, like many others which have resulted from the unrestrained power of the farmers who emigrated from the Colony ; and it is deeply to be regretted that there should have been causes, either real or alleged, for such a procedure '.[1]

Disapproval of the *trek* movement would appear indeed to have been the common attitude of Englishmen then in South Africa. They resented the independent spirit of the *trekkers* and were slightly shocked at the idea of people seeking to escape from the blessings of British rule—even people who had not asked for those blessings. In this frame of mind they lost sight of the signal service which Potgieter and his commandos had rendered to the whole community, irrespective of race or colour. The Boer *Voortrekkers* were of course looking after their own interests, and it is unnecessary to attribute to them any loftier purpose. Nevertheless it cannot be denied that, by reclaiming an immense tract of fertile country which had been made desolate, and by giving a chance of recovery to its inoffensive occupants who had been devoured for years by Mziligazi and his pack of human wolves, they had achieved a great forward step in the civilisation of South Africa.

[1] Moffat, *Missionary Labours*, etc., chap. xxxii.

CHAPTER V

THE MANGWATO TANGLE

I. SEKHOME

AFTER their punishment by Uys and Potgieter at Kapain the Matabele were like a swarm of wasps enraged at the destruction of their nest. Their instinct was to hurry away to the north, and thereby put themselves out of range of the Boer sharpshooters, but it was contrary to their nature to move anywhere without stinging, and they did as much mischief as possible on their way, raiding and plundering all the villages within reach. Still they dared not tarry overlong in one spot, and once they had passed did not turn back. Cautiously at first, but gradually gaining confidence the ' crocodile people ' began to creep from their retreats among the hills, to reoccupy their abandoned homes, and take up their old habits. The process was necessarily a slow one. They had lived so long in a state of thraldom that they had almost forgotten what it was like to be free.

The ba-Mangwato were in a worse plight than the rest. They had never had a chance to recover from the demoralisation which followed the defeat and death of their famous leader Khari in 1822. At first they had been exposed to the depredations of Sebitoane and his Makololo—the remnant of the terrible Mantatees—who, after the break-up of the main horde at Kuruman, led a semi-nomadic existence for a year or two, passing from one tribe to another and preying impartially on all. These homeless vagabonds settled for a

brief space in the ba-Kwena country, where they had the
ba-Mangwato on their borders and at their mercy. From
there they were hustled out in the ordinary course by the
Matabele, who kept the ball rolling, and allowed the neighbouring tribes no peace, till they in their turn were forced to
quit by the Dutch trekkers. The harassed ba-Mangwato
were in the thick of all these alarms. For fifteen years they
had been chevied hither and thither, like rabbits bolted and
hunted by ferrets and terriers, and had not some steadying
influence appeared to rally them they must soon have ceased
to exist as a corporate unit, and have become merged—
probably as serfs—in one of the other branches of the
Bechuana family.

The Mangwato Chief Khari left two sons, the elder of
whom, Sekhome, being of inferior birth on the mother's
side, was at first held of no particular account, while the
younger, Khama, having been born to his ' Great Wife ',
was entitled to succeed him. Some years after Khari's
death his great wife, having married again, became the
mother of another son, Macheng, who, by the strange
custom already mentioned, was regarded as Khari's own,
and therefore, next to Khama, his legitimate heir.[1] When
the Matabele began to evacuate the Transvaal the eldest of
these three, Sekhome, was about twenty-three years old.[2]
In early youth he had been captured by the Makololo in one
of their raids, but managed to make his escape, and found
his way back to his own people. As he grew up he proved
to be a man of forceful and ambitious character. He aspired
to become chief of the ba-Mangwato, but knew that he must
first get rid of those with a better title. In the demoralised
condition of the tribe he had no difficulty in procuring, with

---

[1] Mackenzie, *Ten Years North of the Orange River*, p. 364.

[2] Gordon Cumming who visited him in 1844 says that he then
appeared about thirty years of age. (*A Hunter's Life in South
Africa*, p. 323.)

the help of bribed assassins, the death of the elder of his two half-brothers, Khama, who had nominally succeeded his father, and he would doubtless have served the other, Macheng, in the same fashion, but his mother fled with him to Sechele, who, as chief of the ba-Kwena—the senior branch of the crocodile group—enjoyed a sort of suzerainty over the rest, and was ready to give the fugitives an asylum. It was Sechele's first appearance as ' universal protector ', a rôle which he subsequently played more than once with great profit to himself. In this instance he was unable to make much political capital out of his protégé, for Macheng was shortly afterwards carried off by the Matabele, and trained by them as a soldier, with the result that by the time he reached manhood he had acquired all their fierce propensities.

Meanwhile, with both his brothers out of the way, Sek-home was free to pursue his own designs, and at once set to work to reassemble the disconnected particles of his tribe. For some years he applied himself to this task energetically. He was endued with the courage of his father Khari, and his outstanding quality was a strong devotion to tribal traditions. He became known as a successful rain-maker, and as a punctilious observer of all the ceremonial rites connected with the ancestral spirits, whose goodwill he probably cultivated with extra fervour because he knew himself to be an interloper. He fought later on against all innovations which undermined the ancient usages so much abhorred by the missionaries, and in consequence came to be looked upon by them as a dangerous reactionary. Although they were obliged to concede the strength of his personality they shut their eyes to his heroic endeavours to uphold the traditions and restore the fortunes of his own people.[1]

[1] Mr. J. C. Harris, in his *Life of Khama*, calls Sekhome ' an old traitor ' and ' an incorrigible rascal '. Mr. Lloyd (*Three Great African Chiefs*) says he was ' as blind as Pharaoh ', and elsewhere denounces

They always attributed the high position among native tribes attained by the ba-Mangwato to the wisdom and capacity of Khama—and very rightly so. But the credit for first lifting them out of the slough into which they had descended unquestionably belongs to Sekhome, who laid the foundations on which Khama built ; and this the missionaries consistently chose to ignore.

While the ba-Mangwato were still cowering under the parting blows of the Matabele a son was born to Sekhome by his first wife,[1] who had taken refuge in the desert country near the Makorikori salt pans a hundred miles or more to the north, where a portion of the tribe was in hiding. To this son was given the family name of Khama (hartebeeste). He was born in 1837, or perhaps a little later, and was therefore slightly younger than Lobengula, and a few years older than his other notable contemporary—Lewanika, the Barotse king, who lived to be the most powerful ruler of the three.[2]

him as ' a heathen of the heathen ; leader in every heathen custom and ceremony, and a *polygamist of the first water* ', but admits that ' as a general and warrior his military attainments were considerable '. Mr. W. D. Mackenzie, in his life of his father, describes him as ' a very able and quite unscrupulous chief ', and so on.

[1] Harris in his *Life of Khama* (p. 20) says that her name was Keamogetsi, and that she was a Mangwato by birth and died on the Botletli river in 1875.

[2] When Khama was nearing the end of his life there was a good deal of talk among his admirers of his extreme age and the wonderful vigour of his mind for a man of over ninety. This was based on the assumption that he was born in 1827, but there is not the smallest doubt that that date was wide of the mark by at least ten years. The error seems to have originated with the Rev. H. Lewis, who heard from Khama's own lips that the Matabele had passed north before his birth. On referring to some cyclopaedia or other Mr. Lewis found the date of that event given as 1827, and accepted it as correct. (See Harris's *Life of Khama*, p. 26). But the departure of the Matabele did not take place till ten years later, so that on Khama's own statement he could not have been born before 1837. This is confirmed by other evidence. In the first place there is extant his baptismal certificate, which was seen, and has been quoted—though with variations—by several of his biographers. According to this he was baptised in 1862 by the first resident missionary in Shoshong,

The circumstances which surrounded the boy Khama's childhood must have been exceptionally hard and miserable ; but he was endowed by nature with a tough physique and unusual powers of endurance, and was thus enabled to survive the fugitive, hand-to-mouth existence which he and his mother, in common with many others of their tribe, were leading in the bush. And the hour of their deliverance was at hand. Sekhome made rapid progress with the reconstruction of his people, and in less than a year succeeded in reinstating them in their ancestral home at Shoshong, in the Mangwato hills.

By this time the Matabele had reached fresh fields for enterprise beyond the Limpopo river. They still attempted to extort tribute from their former subjects in the south, but were too busily occupied with expeditions against the Makololo and the older tribes they found in the new hunting ground to be able to spare any fighting units to enforce their demands in the old. The distance between the Matopo hills, close to which Mziligazi established his principal military posts, and Shoshong was well over 250 miles, and in the intervening country there were a number of Makalanga villages whose inhabitants were on friendly terms

a Lutheran clergyman, who describes him as then aged twenty-five years. Apart from this the earlier date, 1827, is ruled out by the fact that his father, Sekhome, was then only thirteen years old.

In support of the date 1837 it may be added that Chapman, the explorer, who first saw Khama in 1852, describes him as ' a lad of about 16, of very prepossessing appearance '. The missionary Mackenzie, writing to his sister-in-law in 1865, speaks of Khama as ' really a nice lad '—a term he would hardly have applied to a man who by Lewis's calculation would then have been approaching forty. The Portuguese explorer Serpa Pinto, who saw him in 1879, says he was then about forty, but looked considerably younger. (*How I Crossed Africa*, p. 208.) When the present writer first met Khama, in 1891, he appeared about fifty years of age, and was certainly not as much as fifty-five.

It may therefore be taken for granted that Mr. Lewis was mistaken, but his error has unfortunately misled a number of later writers— among them Mr. Julian Mockford, Khama's latest biographer.

with Sekhome's people, and gave them timely notice of any threatening movement on the part of Matabele *impis*. By 1839 Sekhome had organised a respectable army and when the usual raiding parties approached he was forewarned and ready for them. He even dared to go out to meet them in the open plains beyond Shoshong, and was successful, not only in driving them back with loss, but in recapturing a quantity of cattle which they had collected in the surrounding villages. In the following dry season the Matabele had a second surprise. Mziligazi sent a 'peaceful' deputation of forty men to demand tribute from Sekhome, who promptly had them seized and put to death. This was the only sort of argument likely to appeal to bullies, and it caused Mziligazi to change his tactics. Several times during the next few years he sent messages to Sekhome through Moffat and others to say that he had 'laid his spear in the water', and that no further raids need be feared. But Sekhome was not taking any chances. He kept his regiments trained, and used every means to obtain firearms for them.

Up to this time, so far as is known, no white man had visited the Mangwato country. Roualeyn Gordon Cumming, the elephant hunter, who reached Shoshong in July, 1844, claimed to be the first. This was not strictly accurate, for Livingstone paid two short visits in 1842, but was too much engrossed in his work at Sechele's, where he was just opening a mission station, to pay much attention to Sekhome.[1] At any rate Cumming was the earliest traveller to describe the Mangwato people and their customs, and he has left a very lively and picturesque account of them. His primary object was to trade ivory, of which Sekhome had accumulated a great store. At that time there were elephants in abundance in and around the Mangwato hills,

---

[1] Cumming, *A Hunter's Life in South Africa*, introduction, p. ix. Livingstone, *Missionary Travels*, etc., pp. 10, 11.

but the bulk of his supply was obtained from those killed for meat by the poisoned arrows of the Ngami Bushmen, who were ready to barter the tusks for a few beads. Cumming found Sekhome willing to trade, and expert at driving a hard bargain. Guns were what he wanted, and the hunter complains of the way in which he haggled and cheated. But he really had no great cause for grumbling. He had brought with him a large number of antiquated trade muskets, which had cost him less than £1 apiece in the Colony, and for each of these he managed to purchase upwards of £30 worth of ivory—a very fair profit ! Cumming's general portrait of Sekhome is an unfavourable one. ' His distinguishing feature ', we are told, ' is a wall-eye, which imparts to his countenance a roguish look that does not belie the cunning and deceitful nature of the man '.[1]

Ivory was the first lure that attracted Europeans from down-country, and gradually there set in a stream—hardly a trickle at first, but steady and growing—of hunters and traders making for northern Bechuanaland. Sekhome was quick to grasp the advantages of the business, and anxious to keep it in his own hands. While quite agreeable therefore to the visits of white men he did his utmost to prevent them from going beyond his own domain, and so tapping his sources of supply. He even distrusted Livingstone, and enraged him by extorting payment for allowing him to pass through Shoshong to the districts beyond.[2]

II. SECHELE

In 1843, soon after Sekhome had defied Mziligazi and thereby demonstrated that he was made of better stuff than the other Bechuana chiefs, Livingstone opened his station among the ba-Kwena, for whose intelligent chief, Sechele, he rapidly conceived an admiration as enthusiastic as it is

[1] *A Hunter's Life*, etc., p. 323.
[2] *Missionary Travels*, etc., pp. 46, 146.

hard to understand. Of this man's talents there can be no doubt, and he seems to have made the same favourable impression on Livingstone's colleagues, though outside the ranks of the missionaries—as one of them admits [1]— he was regarded as a clever humbug. There were national and other ties between Sechele and his neighbours at Shoshong. Many years before his father had been murdered as a result of tribal intrigue, and the son had been befriended, and partially brought up, among the ba-Mangwato, who allowed him to participate with their own youths in the circumcision rites. The mutual intimacy thus begotten had been kept up, and there was a frequent interchange of visits between members of the reigning families on both sides. Khama, as a young lad, spent some time at Sechele's town, and acquired there his first knowledge of Christian doctrines, of which the chief, though not going to the length of discarding his harem, or abandoning rain magic, professed himself an ardent disciple.[2] Khama may possibly have been one of Livingstone's actual pupils, though the fact is not recorded.

In 1852, when young Khama was about ready for his *boguera* rite, Livingstone's work among the ba-Kwena came to an end. He was seized with that restless passion for movement which was ever spurring him to explore new fields, and he made up his mind to extend his activities to the Makololo in the north. This decision may have been stimulated by other causes. Livingstone had repeatedly fallen foul of the Boer emigrants, whose numbers had largely increased, and who were exploiting their occupation of the

[1] Mackenzie, *Ten Years North of the Orange River*, p. 105.

[2] Three years after his arrival Livingstone, who found him an apt scholar and a most zealous student of the Bible, induced him to put away his ' superfluous wives ', and then baptised him. The friends of the discarded women took great umbrage at this ; accused the missionary of bewitching their chief, and formed a party which strongly opposed the new religion. (*Missionary Travels*, etc., p. 18.)

Transvaal region with a high hand. He regarded them with a dislike which became an obsession, and lost no opportunity of proclaiming their iniquities from the housetops. The Boers looked on all the Bechuana tribes as specially created by Providence for their convenience as herds and farm labourers, and often resorted to harsh measures to induce them to work. Although Sechele had gained a certain measure of security from outside attack since their advent he had chafed under their jurisdiction, and showed in many ways that he claimed to be an independent ruler. He particularly resented the restrictions which Potgieter imposed on the sale of horses and guns to the natives. In this attitude he received encouragement from Livingstone, who thereby incurred the enmity of the Boer authorities, and built up a good deal of trouble for himself. In 1852 differences were brought to a head, during Livingstone's temporary absence, by Sechele's imprudence in harbouring some refugees from another tribe who had stolen some cattle from the farmers. Pretorius, the commandant-general, despatched a force of 300 or 400 burghers to Kolobeng, where they found Sechele defiant, with his fighting men drawn up to oppose them. There was a hot engagement, in which the white men inflicted severe losses on the natives, and drove off, not only several thousand head of cattle and some horses, but about 200 women and children whom they retained as hostages. It was asserted by Livingstone that the commando then proceeded to wreck his station, and to destroy his furniture, books and drugs. This charge, which was based on Sechele's statements, aroused the most intense excitement and indignation against the Boers at the time, and was the cause of a prolonged controversy. The historian Theal devoted many pages to a discussion of the pros and cons of the case, and arrived at the conclusion that Livingstone's allegations were unproved, and that the outrage, so far from being brought home to the Boers, was

more probably the work of the anti-missionary section—
unquestionably a large one—of the ba-Kwena, whose animosity Livingstone had incurred by 'bewitching' their
chief.[1]

Whatever be the truth the charges stirred up a good deal
of feeling in England, and created a conviction that the
Boers were little more than savages ; and this is another of
those illusions that affected public opinion, and coloured
British policy for many years to come.

III. KHAMA THE CONVERT

In those days tribal distinctions were carefully guarded
among the Bantu, and precedence was strictly respected.
There was no more fruitful cause of discord than an attempt
by any one of a group of chiefs to push himself unwarrant-
ably into a position of ascendancy. Sekhome's growing
influence, and his success in rebuilding the fortunes of the
despised ba-Mangwato were watched with suspicion by his
neighbours, and by none more than Sechele, who was an
officious busybody. On the strength of his traditional
status as paramount he arrogated the right to meddle in
Mangwato politics, and had no intention of allowing his
prerogative to be jeopardised by an upstart. He cast about
therefore for some means of asserting himself, and his

[1] Theal, *History of South Africa*, vol. iv, pp. 381-5. Professor
Eric Walker (*History of S. Africa*, p. 289) after weighing the evidence,
is inclined to accept Theal's view. He dismisses the idea that the
damage—even if the Boers were responsible for it—was done wantonly, and makes light of the looting of furniture found in an empty
house by a party of high-spirited youngsters.

Shortly after the raid Sechele resolved—against Livingstone's
advice—to proceed to England to lay his grievances before the
Queen. He actually got as far as the Cape, but had no money to
continue his journey, and was obliged to abandon his intention.
After his return his ambition was to be regarded as a white man, but
beyond initiating a system of *corvée* among his own people he did not
make any reforms. (Livingstone, *Missionary Travels*, p. 121.
Mackenzie, *Ten Years*, etc., pp. 106, 110.)

thoughts turned to the exile Macheng, who, although he had been living for years under the protection of Mziligazi, and was in fact a soldier in the Matabele army, was still, by native custom, the *de jure* successor of his putative father, Khari.

As early as 1835, when Macheng was only about nine years old, Sechele had begged Moffat, then about to pay a visit to Mziligazi at Mosega, to obtain his release, but the missionary declined at that time to mix himself up in what was purely a tribal matter. Now, twenty-two years later, finding that Moffat was again proposing to visit the Matabele king on missionary business, he once more pressed his request, and this time Moffat unfortunately yielded to his solicitations. He persuaded the king, who was always ready to oblige him, to surrender Macheng, and returned with him to Sechele, in whose custody he left him, thereby sowing a fine crop of troubles for everybody concerned.

On the news of Macheng's release there was a great stir among the ba-Mangwato, many of whom flocked to greet him and to demand that he should assume his rightful place as their chief. Sekhome, finding that popular feeling was so strong, and not daring to flout the law of inheritance, submitted, though with very ill grace, and taking with him Khama and a younger son, Khamani (little Khama), retired from Shoshong, where Macheng was duly installed in his stead. For his disinterested services in re-establishing the legitimate succession Sechele received a valuable gift of ivory and cattle, and at once offered his hospitality to the deposed Sekhome, who, he thought, might be useful to him on some future occasion. In this expectation he was not disappointed.

As soon as he found himself in a position of authority, Macheng, who from all accounts was an offensive blustering bully, began to introduce the methods of tyranny he had learnt from his long sojourn with the Matabele, modelling

his policy on that of his former master Mziligazi, but lacking
Mziligazi's capacity to make it effective.   He essayed to
enforce a harsh system of military discipline, and rode
roughshod over cherished institutions.   He declared that
all cattle and other property belonged to him as chief, and
that nothing could be bought or sold by his subjects without
his consent.   This sort of thing was utterly repugnant to
their ideas and they soon repented of their bargain.   Eventually Macheng overreached himself by ordering the
execution of a popular headman who had incurred his
enmity.   The whole nation took fright, and a plot was
formed by some of the other headmen to rid themselves of
King Stork and get back once more to King Log.   The most
powerful man in the tribe, next to the chief, was Tshukuru
(white rhinoceros), who headed a deputation to Sechele to
beg his assistance in removing the person he had been
instrumental in appointing.   This recognition of his para-
mountcy gratified the 'Kingmaker', who was quite willing
to oblige once more—on terms—and, a substantial reward
having been arranged, sent an armed party back with
Tshukuru to eject Macheng with the object of reinstating
Sekhome.   Macheng, who like all bullies was an arrant
coward, made no show of resistance, but took flight and
went back to Matabeleland, where he sought again the
protection of Mziligazi.   His overtures were rejected, and he
was forced to fall back on Sechele—the very man who had
first procured his restoration and then arranged his downfall.[1]

Once more then, after an absence of less than two years,
we find Sekhome seated at Shoshong in the precarious
position of chief.   He signalised his return to power by
gifts of cattle and other rewards to those who had helped to
bring it about.   He proposed a marriage between his two
eldest sons, Khama and Khamani, and two of the daughters

[1] Mackenzie, *Life of John Mackenzie*, pp. 107, 108.

of Tshukuru, who as the prime mover of the intrigue was of course in high favour. Before his banishment he had urged Khama to take to wife the daughter of another favourite, but she was not to his liking, and for the first time he showed his independence by refusing. He had no objection to the new proposal, and agreed to the match, thereby establishing a friendship with Tshukuru, who in consequence became his firm ally.

During his two years' residence with Sechele Khama had become more than ever attracted by the new teaching, and immediately on his return he begged his father to try to obtain a missionary to live permanently at Shoshong. He wanted to be baptised, and to postpone his marriage until it could be solemnised in Christian fashion. The suggestion was not unacceptable to Sekhome, for it tickled his self-importance. He knew that most of the big chiefs in South Africa now had European missionaries at their towns, who had built churches and opened schools, gave medical treatment to the sick, and were useful in a variety of ways, and he conceived the idea that his own prestige would be enhanced if he too could point to one at his kraal, as a member —so to speak—of his retinue. It never occurred to him that the new teaching was incompatible with the ancestral beliefs of the tribe, or would be likely to cause internal dissensions.

It seems rather strange, in view of the success of their pioneer station at Kuruman, that the London Missionary Society had not already turned their attention to the promising field among the ba-Mangwato, but at this time they were very much under the guidance of Livingstone, who had not taken a fancy to Sekhome, and was more anxious that evangelistic work should be pushed forward in the direction of the Zambesi. Others, however, were ready to step in where they were lagging, and, towards the end of 1859, there arrived a Mr. Schulenborg, a Hanoverian minister of the

Lutheran persuasion, who built himself a house and a school and started classes for religious instruction. In the following May Khama was baptised by him, and a little later married, with Protestant rites, to Tshukuru's daughter, herself a convert to the new faith.[1]

It was about this time also that Khama began his campaign in favour of temperance—afterwards one of the main planks of his life-work, and a potent factor in his success as a ruler. Miss G. Gollock relates [2] that as a young man he accompanied his father to buy a horse from a white trader, who plied the chief with brandy in the hope of getting a better bargain. Sekhome became so drunk that Khama stopped the transaction, ordered his servants to pick him up and take him home, together with the ivory which had been brought to pay for the horse. The incident inspired him with a dread of liquor and a determination to keep it from contaminating his tribesmen.

From the moment of his open avowal of Christianity Khama found himself in conflict with his father. His brother Khamani and many of the younger men had also become converts, and as the new teaching gained ground the tribe came to be divided into two parties—the progressives, who professed Christianity and supported Khama, and the old-fashioned heathen, headed by the chief himself, who strictly maintained their devotion to the ancient cults of rain-making, circumcision, ancestor worship and witchcraft, and looked with horror at any innovation which tended to sap them. The schism waxed in strength and led to constant friction and bickering. Sekhome was distressed and humiliated at the refusal of Khama and some of

---

[1] This woman's name is given in various unpronounceable forms by different writers, but she was generally known as ' Ma-Bessie ', in accordance with the common Bechuana habit of calling parents after the names of their first children. She lived with Khama as his wife for twenty-seven years and had several children by him.

[2] *Sons of Africa*, p. 105.

his brothers to be present at the ceremonial opening of the *boguera,* when custom immemorial prescribed that the chief and the male members of his family should attend in state. There is something pathetic in his outburst quoted by the missionary Mackenzie (who had replaced Schulenborg in 1861) at his sons' contumacy—' What could I say to Khari and the rest of my ancestors if I gave way to my own child?'[1]

Sekhome's behaviour towards his sons has met with violent and unqualified reprobation from all concerned with missionary work. There seems to be some lack of perspective in this view. They appear to have lost sight of the disturbing effect of Christian doctrine on the mind of one to whom it was altogether new and revolutionary. The missionaries knew, of course, that in fighting against heathenism they would have to encounter prejudice and opposition, and this only stiffened their resolution, but it is doubtful if they fully realised how detestable their teaching must have seemed to the older men among the Bantu tribes, brought up from childhood in beliefs which they venerated, and the abandonment of which was to them the rankest heresy. To appreciate these feelings we must picture what our own would be if emissaries from some new iconoclastic community—Russia for instance—were suddenly to descend upon our countryside, try insidiously to undermine our most sacred and venerable ideas of religion, domestic morality and education, and to foist upon our youth of both sexes an entirely new code of ethics. Among the cherished institutions common to all Bantu peoples and condemned by the missionaries were polygamy and the use of magic—which was only a crude form of ceremonial religion—to hasten the rainfall. How should we behave if Bolshevist agents came among us and urged us to replace marriage by promiscuity, and public worship by the deification of Karl Marx ? That they would gain adherents among

[1] Mackenzie, *Life of John Mackenzie,* p. 109.

the younger generation would only make their campaign appear more odious.

That there have been many outstanding cases—Khama is a great example—of Bantu natives who have shaken off their heathenish superstition and become earnest and genuine Christians is beside the point. Their success in these cases is the missionaries' reward, and provides ample justification for their untiring and heroic crusade. But in the first flush of their enthusiasm they were prone to fall into two errors of judgment. They were apt to be taken in by crafty natives who, to serve their own ends, professed the faith, without any real sincerity ; and they were inclined to condemn those who were so strongly rooted in their traditions that they fought honestly against subversive teaching. To those who can see all round the subject the latter class deserves—I will not say admiration, but at least sympathy. If we admit this we must allow that while Khama's espousal of the new morality was a remarkable proof of his own courage, there was nothing very reprehensible in the attitude of his father who regarded it as something monstrous.

IV. SEKHOME'S DOWNFALL

Just when the conflict of the creeds threatened to burst into violence a national crisis arose from outside which for the time being diverted Sekhome's thoughts from the apostasy of his sons, and brought all parties together against a common enemy.

At the close of the wet season of 1862 reports began to get about that Mziligazi, who had given no cause for anxiety for many years, and had pledged his word more than once never to interfere with the ba-Mangwato, was sending *impis* towards the south. Soon a Makalanga fugitive from the border brought more definite information. A strong Matabele force had already swooped down on some of

Sekhome's outlying cattle-posts and killed the herds; had completely destroyed one kraal and murdered its inhabitants, and was now within a day's march of Shoshong. On receipt of this startling announcement Sekhome showed that he was a man of action. He at once sent out heralds to the high points round the town to shout out the recognised signals for alarm. Their calls were taken up and repeated by sentinels on duty on more distant eminences, and in a few minutes the news was broadcasted far and wide. The women and non-combatants were ordered into the hills; the cattle and other stock were hurriedly brought into the kloofs and valleys for safety, and the chief prepared to meet the invaders on the plains outside the town. He held a review and inspection of his fighting men, and, as an ordinary measure of precaution, assembled his witch-doctors to propitiate the spirits and ensure victory. This part of the proceedings gave great annoyance to Khama, who was in command of one of the regiments of younger men, and now begged his father to desist from wasting time on incantations and dice-throwing—in modern parlance 'to cut the cackle and get on with the job'.

Khama was now twenty-five years old. He was a 'fine figure of a man', over six feet in height, lithe and athletic, a swift runner, a great lover of horses and a good rider. His prowess in the hunting field and his strength of will had made him popular with the tribe, and were a powerful influence in attracting the younger ones to his side. His 'regiment' consisted of a hundred of those of his own age, who had been his fellows in the *boguera*, and in most cases belonged to the new school of thought which rejected ancestor worship and its accompaniments of sacrifices and magic. Khamani, his younger brother, who commanded another regiment, was also a professed Christian, and both were staunch admirers of the missionary John Mackenzie who had recently come to live among them. In the present crisis they took the lead, and with their small force of 200, most of them carrying guns, while a few were mounted, they marched out boldly to confront the enemy. Sekhome asked Mackenzie whether he would join the defenders and on being told that as a minister of the gospel he must remain neutral, retorted that the Matabele were unlikely to make nice distinctions, and that the colour of a man's skin was not easily discovered in the darkness of night.[1]

Khama's force met the invaders late in the afternoon advancing leisurely in close formation—a splendid target—and at once opened fire. The Matabele soldiers, who were too young to remember the Boers, at first made fun of the guns and imitated the reports, but when the bullets began to drop among them and some were hit they changed their tune, and on a charge by the mounted men they broke their ranks and took flight. Another party, which had been lying concealed, then made a flank attack on the ba-Mangwato, who lost the advantage of their first success and fled incontinently, leaving a good many dead. For some reason —probably fear of the guns—the Matabele gave up the pursuit, and though they remained in the neighbourhood for several days, took possession of a large number of cattle, and sacked a few villages, they never attacked Shoshong. Among them were two or three of Mziligazi's sons, including Lobengula, who was said to have been wounded in the neck by a bullet fired by Khama himself.

Khama behaved throughout the affair with great gallantry and judgment, covering the retreat with his mounted men and thus averting a rout. His prestige with the tribe

---

[1] This recalls an incident in 1893, just before the Matabele war. The Rhodesian force was joined by Bishop Knight-Bruce, who was careful to inform Dr. Jameson that he was not there as their chaplain, but ' as bishop of the country in which both the contending parties lived.' To this the ' Doctor ' answered that he would be well advised to keep in the background, as some of his flock might not grasp the distinction.

was much increased in consequence. His conduct even made an impression on Mziligazi, who told one of the missionaries that the ba-Mangwato were 'mere dogs', but the son of Sekhome was a man. Sekhome himself, while proud of his son, showed great annoyance at his refusal to follow up the retiring Matabele and endeavour to inflict further losses. He quite failed to appreciate the force of Khama's argument that he regarded all fighting as sinful, except in defence of his country.

In every respect, in fact, the views of father and son were diametrically opposed, and it was impossible for them to settle down comfortably together. Sekhome's irritation gradually rankled and culminated in an open rupture. The history of the ba-Mangwato during the next five years is entirely occupied by the duel between the chief, as bulwark of the old school of thought, and his son, the red-hot champion of the new. In its later stages the quarrel was complicated by the intrusion of two further disturbing elements in the persons of the exile Macheng and his mischievous protector Sechele.

On Khama's side were ranged his second brother, Khamani, also a convert to Christianity, several other brothers who were wobblers, and his father-in-law Tshukuru, who, though not a professed Christian, was his staunch supporter. He had in addition a pillar of strength in John Mackenzie, the missionary, who at times exposed himself to unpopularity, and even to personal risk, by his espousal of the cause of the progressive party. In the old days the feud would have been settled by fighting, which would have gone on till one or other of the principals had been killed or driven out of the country, but Khama refused again and again to be drawn into violence. He maintained a sort of passive resistance, which completely baffled Sekhome, and led him into a course of foolish and discreditable plots.

The first breach occurred through Khama's refusal to become a polygamist. Sekhome was determined that he should take as a second wife the daughter of one of his most influential headmen whom he wished to conciliate—this being the ordinary way among Bechuana chiefs of securing allegiance and cementing tribal unity. But Khama was true to his convictions and rejected the match. In his rage at being thwarted Sekhome attempted to resort to force, and led a body of armed men to attack Khama and his friends who all lived in the same part of the town, but at the critical moment they disobeyed the order to fire, while Khama, with extraordinary forbearance, refrained from any act which might provoke a conflict. Foiled in this first encounter Sekhome retired to nurse his wrath and prepare for a more elaborate effort. In March, 1866, he had that part of Shoshong occupied by the recalcitrants surrounded, with the object of starving them into submission. His animosity was particularly levelled against Tshukuru, who would certainly have been put to death if he had been captured. The two parties held positions on opposite sides of the valley which divided the great straggling kraal, and for more than a month Khama and his adherents were in a state of siege. A good deal of desultory firing took place at long range, but no serious casualties were sustained on either side, and the situation appeared likely to become a stalemate.

Enraged at his failure Sekhome took the strange and insane course of appealing for assistance to Macheng, who, since his banishment, had been a refugee at the town of the arch-plotter Sechele. His overtures did not at first meet with any response, but they had the effect of exciting the interest of Sechele, who once more saw an opening for turning the affairs of his neighbours to his own advantage. He sent messages to Khama offering to harbour him and his supporters—specially mentioning Tshukuru—if they would place themselves in his hands. Khama's position had by this time become critical owing to his water supply having been cut off, and he saw that he must either surrender to his father or accept Sechele's offer. Sekhome was also in a predicament, as he had failed to get help from Macheng or Sechele, and was tired of the useless campaign against his son. He was ready to meet Khama halfway, and assured him that if he and those with him would return to Shoshong they would not be molested and all would be forgiven. The offer seemed to hold out hopes, and was agreed to by Khama and some of his friends, but not by Tshukuru, who mistrusted the chief and preferred to place himself in the hands of Sechele. He accordingly fled by night accompanied by Khamani and a few others, and made for the ba-Kwena country. It was an unfortunate step, for no sooner had he arrived than the treacherous chief, who had schemes of his own on hand, cruelly put him to death. Khama, whose only desire was to live in peace, took the filial course of accepting the olive branch held out to him by his father; descended from the hill-tops, and returned to Shoshong.

At last there appeared some chance of the tribe being at rest. But now Sekhome was to reap the fruit of his folly in approaching Macheng, who, egged on by Sechele, decided to interpret the invitation as an act of abdication, and once more installed himself as ruler of the ba-Mangwato. The old chief, thoroughly broken down by the wreck of his plots, which had alienated most of his own friends and resulted in the resurrection of his rival, slunk away with the few who remained faithful to him, and left Macheng in possession.

The story of the ba-Mangwato has now been brought down to 1867, which stands out in the general history of South Africa as the beginning of a new epoch. That year was marked by an event which heralded a complete revolution in the commercial and political life of the European community, and had a profound effect on the conditions of the native population. Gold was discovered at Tati—a spot in the 'no-man's-land' between the countries of the Matabele and the ba-Mangwato.

The record of the latter may therefore be interrupted in order to bring to the same point that of the other peoples with whom we are dealing.

CHAPTER VI

LIVINGSTONE

I. THE MAKOLOLO

LONG before the affray at Kolobeng, and the wrecking of his mission station, Livingstone had begun to chafe at his position in Sechele's country. The Transvaal Boers were constantly upsetting the ba-Kwena by their persistent demands for labour, and took no pains to conceal their antipathy for the white missionary, whom they looked on as an obstructionist. Apart from this it is clear, from his own admissions, that he had come to regard Kolobeng as a stepping-stone towards wider ministrations. His first thought was that he might be able to induce Sechele to go north with his tribe and settle in a new district beyond reach of the Boers, and, as a preliminary, he resolved to cross the desert and explore the country on the other side. He had been stirred by rumours of a great undiscovered lake and a well-watered tract in the north, and was ambitious to verify them, and perhaps even to extend his journey so as to make the acquaintance of Sebitoane, the Makololo chief, of whose influence and generosity Sechele spoke with much impressiveness.[1] Encouragement came with the opportune arrival of two African travellers, Messrs. Oswell and Murray, the former of whom undertook to make a liberal contribution towards the expenses of a joint expedition to those parts. And then, in 1849, Lechulatebe, the chief of the

[1] *Missionary Travels*, etc., p. 44.

Lake people, sent a deputation to invite a visit, with such glowing reports of the fabulous quantity of ivory to be obtained in his country that the cupidity of the ba-Kwena was excited.[1] Consequently when Oswell and Murray expressed their desire to join Livingstone there was no difficulty in engaging all the guides and carriers they required.

The three white men left Kolobeng in June, and, after an exhausting and hazardous trek through the 'thirst' country, discovered Lake Ngami in August. In the following year (1850) they made a second expedition, accompanied this time by Mrs. Livingstone [2] and her three children, and by the chief Sechele. Livingstone then tried to push on to see Sebitoane, who was said to be settled two hundred miles further north, but was prevented by an outbreak of fever, which attacked his children and native servants, and compelled him to return to Kolobeng.

At the end of June, 1851, again accompanied by his family and by Oswell, he set out for the third time, and after following the course of the river Chobe, and passing through a belt of country infested by tsetse fly, arrived at Linyanti, a village situated in a swampy and malarious district about a hundred miles south-west of Sesheke on the Zambesi. Here Sebitoane came to greet him. It was a meeting fraught with far-reaching results. Livingstone was greatly attracted by the chief, and seems, almost at once, to have made up his mind that a great opening presented itself among the Makololo for future missionary endeavours.

Sebitoane, who was now about forty-five years of age, had taken up his residence in the angle between the Chobe

---

[1] Among other statements made by the deputation was one that the kraals for their cattle were built of large tusks of ivory !

[2] Dr. Robert Moffat's daughter, Mary, who became the missionary's wife in 1844.

and Zambesi rivers,[1] but had extended his sovereignty over an immense stretch of territory ranging from the Barotse valley on the upper Zambesi to the river Kafue on the east, and as far south as the northern margin of Lake Ngami. He had sustained many changes of fortune since the dispersal of the Mantatees at Kuruman by the Griquas, twenty-seven years earlier, when he was little more than a boy. Livingstone, in his *Missionary Travels*,[2] gives a comprehensive account of his career during those troublous years, but without disclosing his sources of information or supplying dates, which makes it probable that most of the story was derived from Sebitoane himself. It must therefore be accepted with reserve, and is only quoted here in outline because it is the sole authority for the events of his chequered life.

We are told that after the affair with the Griquas Sebitoane, who was a Basuto of good birth,[3] left the main horde of the Mantatees with an insignificant party of men and women and a few cattle, and fled northwards. He ravaged a number of the inoffensive Bechuana tribes and settled for a time in the ba-Kwena country near Kolobeng. Here, Livingstone says, ' his people suffered severely in one of those unrecorded attacks by white men in which murder is committed and material laid up in the conscience for a future judgment '. This is a veiled and rather unfair insinuation against the Boers, in keeping with his other strictures on these pioneers. The statement cannot be reconciled with that which immediately follows, which is to

[1] Long afterwards, under the Anglo-German agreement of 1890, this angle was included in German South-West Africa, of which it formed the extreme north-eastern corner. Known as the ' Caprivi strip ', it was occupied by Rhodesian troops at the beginning of the Great War.

[2] Pp. 84-90.

[3] Sir Harry Johnston states that he was actually the son of ' that great crazy woman chief Mantatisi '. (*Barotseland*, by G. W. Stirke, introduction, p. 13.)

the effect that while in this part of the country Sebitoane suffered from raids by Matabele. Beyond an isolated trader or two no white men penetrated so far north until after the expulsion of the Matabele, which took place in 1838, and by that time the Makololo themselves had moved in the direction of Lake Ngami. It seems impossible therefore that Sebitoane could have been the victim of such an attack.

After what could only have been a short sojourn with the ba-Kwena Sebitoane resumed his course of conquest along the Botletle river, eventually reaching the upper Zambesi—then known as the Leeambye. The southern and western shores at the point where he struck it are low, marshy and fever-stricken, but on the north side the country rises into a healthy, undulating plateau, extending towards the Kafue. A robust tribe—the ba-Toka—occupied several of the islands in the main stream, and were spread over the southern part of the plateau, where their descendants still form the bulk of the population. They had reduced brigandage to a fine art. When any fugitive or wandering aliens arrived it was their practice to offer to ferry them and their belongings across the river. They would convey them in canoes to one of the islands, which it was impossible to distinguish from the opposite bank, and leave them marooned to die of starvation, afterwards taking possession of their goods. Sebitoane avoided this fate by compelling the chief to remain with him in a canoe until the whole of his followers and their property were safely landed on the main bank. Once having gained a foothold in the ba-Toka district he proceeded to subjugate the people and to seize their stock. He overran the whole country between the Zambesi and the Kafue, through which the Rhodesia railway now passes, and met with no check until he was obliged to turn round to repel an invasion by his old enemies the Matabele, who, with the assistance of the ba-Toka, fell on him in rear. This attack was beaten off, but others followed, and Sebi-

toane began to think of moving eastward towards the
Portuguese settlement at Tete, much lower down the river.
Livingstone relates a fantastic story of how he was dis-
suaded by the hysterical ravings of a sort of prophet, on
whose advice he turned to the north-west and ascended the
Zambesi as far as the Barotse country. He found the tribe
torn by intestinal troubles. A famous chief, Marambwa,
had died, leaving a number of sons, none of them old enough
to rule. The position of chief had been usurped by their
uncle, Selumelume, but the claims of one or other of the sons
were supported by factions.[1] The nation was divided
against itself, and fell an easy prey to the seasoned Makololo warriors.

Even in the Barotse valley, however, Sebitoane's foot-
steps were dogged by the persistent Matabele, and he only
escaped by copying the ba-Toka trick of decoying a large
body to an island where he left them to perish. In the end
he succeeded in gaining the upper hand by making use of
the local tribes, whose familiarity with the river and skill
in canoe-craft gave them an advantage over Mziligazi's
soldiers, accustomed only to land tactics.

II. THE ZAMBESI PEOPLES

A few words may here be said as to these older tribes,
which Sebitoane brought one by one under his domination.
Chief among them were the ba-Rotse, or ba-Rozi, whose
origin has been the subject of several conflicting theories.
Among themselves no definite traditions have been preserved. Sir Harry Johnston thinks that their name points
to a connection with the ba-Hurutsi, who, it will be remembered, were a junior branch of the crocodile people of

[1] Major Gibbons, *Through Marotseland*, p. 146. Stirke (*Barotseland*, pp. 37, 136) says that Selumelume was Marambwa's son, and
that it was in the reign of another brother, Mbukwano, that the
ba-Rotse were conquered.

northern Bechuanaland, which seceded from the main stock
in the seventeenth century ; others that they are related to
the va-Rozwi, who were early invaders of Mashonaland
from the north.[1]   But the real truth seems to be that the
name ' ba-Rozi ' was conferred on them by the Makololo.
Previously they were known as a-Luyi, and their ancient
language, si-Luyi, though nearly obsolete, and superseded
generally by si-Kololo, is still used as a court dialect among
the chiefs and members of the ruling family.   They appear
to have descended, two or three hundred years ago, from the
Congo basin in the north, and gradually to have gained an
ascendancy over the Zambesi tribes among whom they
settled.   When Sebitoane first encountered them they had
become somewhat degenerate through intercourse with
these tribes, but still preserved a highly developed social
organisation and an advanced form of government, differing
radically from that of the Bechuana and Zulu peoples south
of the Zambesi.   Their position in relation to their neighbours had been achieved by superior strategy and cunning,
but in open warfare they were no match for the Makololo,
and Sebitoane had little difficulty in bringing them to heel.
At the time of Livingstone's arrival on the scene the ba-
Rotse were governed by one of Sebitoane's nominees.   The
partisans of various survivors of Marambwa's family were
squabbling among themselves, and had lost for the time
being all power of combined resistance.   But the succession
was intact.   One party cherished hopes of restoring the
legitimate heir—a youth named Sepopo, who had taken
flight and was living in exile and, somewhere among the
disputants, there was another possible claimant—a lad of
about ten years old, who was destined to make history later
on.   This was Robosi, afterwards known as Lewanika, a
grandson of Marambwa, and a lineal descendant of the
ancient a-Luyi chiefs.

[1] Stirke, *Barotseland*, p. 39.

Before Livingstone no white man had visited the ba-Rotse. All they knew of Europeans was derived from the periodical arrival of Mambari slave-dealers of mixed Portuguese and native blood, who regularly came over from Bihé in Angola to purchase ivory—black as well as white. Livingstone never stopped long enough among the ba-Rotse to study their habits or history in any detail, but from later travellers—Serpa Pinto the Portuguese explorer, Emil Holub an Austrian scientist, and F. S. Arnot a Scottish missionary in particular—we have accounts which show that, in spite of their comparatively high mental and social development, they were addicted to hideous cruelties and totally devoid of the elementary principles of morality as we understand it. Human sacrifices were an everyday occurrence. Some form of trial by ordeal was invariably employed for the detection of sorcery. Usually the accused person was forced to plunge his hands into boiling water, and if, as generally happened, the skin peeled off his guilt was established, and he was burnt alive. Another punishment which, according to Arnot, was common as late as 1888, was to place the victim, with hands and feet bound, on a nest of black ants, there to meet a lingering and horrible death. These conditions are worthy of record in view of the extraordinary change which has been wrought among the ba-Rotse since the advent of missionary influence, which paved the way for British rule.

Up to the time of Sebitoane's invasion the ba-Rotse were the aristocracy among the Zambesi tribes, and the only people accounted free. By right of conquest they treated all others (with one exception to be noted presently) as slaves, and exacted an annual tribute from them. There were about twenty of these subject tribes altogether, but only a few of the more outstanding ones can here be mentioned.

The ba-Toka, a strong and virile race of uncertain antecedents, occupied, as before mentioned, the country immediately north of the Victoria Falls, and had affinities with tribes living on the other side of the river. Apart from their predatory habits they were an industrious community, engaged in agriculture and, in parts not infested with the tsetse fly, in cattle-raising.

The ma-Totela, who dwelt in the central area, between the Zambesi and the Kafue, were boat-builders and smelters. Both iron ore and a special kind of hard red wood were plentiful in this district and they enjoyed what was practically a monopoly in the manufacture of assegais and hoes, and of dug-out canoes. They shared with the ba-Toka the peculiar habit of knocking out the two upper front teeth of males in childhood.

The ma-Subia, who lived on both sides of the Zambesi round about Sesheke, were canoe men, fishers and pottery makers. In the wet season, when the rising waters drove quantities of big game to seek refuge on patches of elevated ground, they surrounded them in their canoes and slaughtered large numbers at their leisure.

The ma-Mbunda, on the east and west banks of the upper Zambesi, had voluntarily accepted the ba-Rotse as overlords from the outset, and were in consequence regarded as free subjects, exempt from tribute. They were skilled in medicine and the occult arts, and provided all the official magicians of the nation. In addition they were proficient in the manufacture of mats and baskets—some of the latter so finely woven as to be capable of holding four or five gallons of water.

At the bottom of the scale came a remarkable people living on both sides of the Kafue river—the ba-Ila, more generally known by their nickname—Mashukulumbwe. The people of this tribe—if tribe it can be called, for it was more a collection of semi-independent septs speaking a common language—had no industries, and though their country swarmed with game were too lazy to hunt. The men went stark naked, and were distinguished, up to quite recent times, by their bizarre method of training their hair, with the aid of wax, fibre and the hair of their women and cattle, into a spiky cone two or three feet in height. Selous, Gibbons and other travellers have left vivid records of the intractable and treacherous character of these wild savages. In consequence of their evil reputation they were given a wide berth until the opening of the present century, when they came gradually under the influence of courageous missionaries, who took their lives into their hands and began their reclamation. The Mashukulumbwe have now, under British administration, been transformed into a community as peaceful as any of the tribes of Northern Rhodesia.

Such were a few of the peoples that Sebitoane had brought under his sway at the time of Livingstone's visit, and it is a striking proof of his capacity for government that he was able to extort obedience—albeit unwilling in most cases—from so heterogeneous a mass.

III. LIVINGSTONE AND SEBITOANE

As Sebitoane had control of the high grazing grounds in the ba-Toka country, and must have known that the Zambesi was his best line of defence against the Matabele, it is not clear why he preferred to skulk in the reeds and swamps round Linyanti, where Livingstone found him. The latter realised that it would be hopeless to plant an English mission in such pestilential surroundings, and would probably have endeavoured to induce the chief to return to the healthy plateau ; but any ideas he may have formed in this direction were frustrated by the death of Sebitoane himself, who fell a victim to inflammation of the lungs a few days after their first meeting. Bearing in mind the shortness of their intercourse one is left to wonder at the force of the affection which the missionary conceived for this native despot, who had spent twenty-five years in preying on every district he passed through, and whose record as a marauder is only a degree less black than those of Tshaka and Mziligazi. Not long before their first contact he had departed from ba-Suto tradition by dealing in slaves. During his invasion of the ba-Rotse he had come across some Mambari, who were regular purveyors of human flesh. Finding that they were ready to supply him with Portuguese guns in exchange for boys of about fourteen years of age Sebitoane had opened business with them. On the other side of the country he had done the same thing with a party of Arabs from Zanzibar—in each case bartering children of captive tribes for firearms. It was only a small beginning, and its expansion was cut short by his death, but it is worthy of note that in his case Livingstone seems to find palliating circumstances for what was in his eyes one of the most odious of practices.[1] Other instances of Sebitoane's enormities are related by Livingstone, and yet, in summing up his character, he says ' He was the best specimèn of a native chief I ever met. I never felt so much grieved by the loss of a black man before'.[1]

That Sebitoane was a powerful autocrat and a capable administrator, and that he could act generously when it suited him may readily be conceded, but any one less likely to captivate a man of Livingstone's principles it is difficult to imagine. Still more strange is it that he afterwards entertained a similar regard for his son and successor Sekeletu, who was an adept in double-dealing and perfidy. A possible explanation is that in both these men he thought he detected leanings towards Christianity. Like Sechele, the ba-Kwena chief, they were astute enough to pretend sympathy with the mission work. In those days such professions were a sure passport to the favour of the missionaries, who rejoiced in the hope that they might pluck brands

[1] *Missionary Travels*, etc., p. 92.

from the burning. For others, like poor blundering Sek-home, who openly and honestly clung to their old beliefs, they could find nothing but reprobation.

The favourable impression which Livingstone formed of the chief was extended to the people, whom he described as ' the most intelligent and enterprising of the tribes he had met '. As far as can be gathered from the reports of other travellers they had no more humane traits than the Mata-bele, but, being of Suto origin, and therefore on a somewhat higher mental plane, they were inclined to attain their objects by strategy rather than brute force.

Shortly after Sebitoane's death Livingstone, with Oswell, pursued his wanderings northward. At the end of June, 1851, he reached Sesheke, where he was rewarded for two years of arduous exploration by the discovery of the great river Zambesi, the course of which had previously been supposed to lie far to the east. Keeping in view the dual purpose he had formed—of starting mission work among the Makololo, and providing a means of access for British trade in this part of Africa—he determined to investigate the possibility of opening up a route by way of the west coast. He took his family to the Cape and placed them on a home-bound ship, and in June, 1852, set out on the first of his more famous journeys—to St. Paul de Loanda, the capital of Portuguese West Africa, travelling by way of Kuruman [1] and Kolobeng. The account of this expedition, of his return *via* the Zambesi to Linyanti, and of his sub-sequent achievement in reaching Quilimane, on the east coast, fills 600 of the 700 pages of his book *Missionary Travels*. Two years—from June, 1852 to June, 1854—were spent in reaching Loanda, where he made a long stay, and a further twenty months in crossing Africa from west to

[1] It was during his short stay at Kuruman that the Boers made their attack on Sechele, and wrecked and looted the mission station at Kolobeng. (See chap. v.)

east. Nothing can be said here of this prodigious effort except in so far as his journeys throw light on the conditions of the Makololo and the river tribes of the Zambesi, which must be briefly referred to.

At Linyanti he found Sekeletu installed as chief of the Makololo. The late chief Sebitoane had wished his favourite daughter Mamochisane to follow him, and had publicly proclaimed her as his successor long before his death. Among tribes of Suto origin women chiefs, though by no means uncommon, occupied a peculiar position. Sebitoane had intended that his daughter should choose any man she wished as her husband, and that he should be regarded as her ' wife '. But the arrangement, besides leading to intrigue among other members of the family, was distasteful to Mamochisane, and after a short reign she insisted on abdicating in favour of her brother, Sekeletu, a man entirely deficient in his father's redeeming qualities and possibly the most unpleasant of all the native rulers we have so far encountered. James Chapman, the first explorer, after Livingstone's party, to visit the Makololo, states that, immediately after his accession, he began to put to death, one by one, the councillors and friends of Sebitoane, and that murders or massacres, disguised as executions, took place almost daily by his command.[1] Shortly after Livingstone's return, and almost in his presence—for they were travelling together—Sekeletu had one of his brothers, Mpepe, treacherously killed on the ground that he was conspiring to assassinate him. Livingstone apparently took a tolerant view of this act. He had already begun to show a friendly interest in the man, and relied on him for canoes and porters for his journey.

With the object of searching for a suitable site for a mission he made a preliminary excursion by way of the river as far as the ba-Rotse valley, but was disappointed to

[1] Chapman, *Travels in the Interior of S. Africa*, p. 168.

find that belts of tsetse infested country and the prevalence everywhere of malaria made the neighbourhood of the river unfit for white occupation. Accordingly he turned to the second part of his plan—that of pushing his way to the west coast. For the time being he deferred consideration of the missionary project, and did not seriously revert to it until his arrival in England, two years later.

CHAPTER VII

' THE OPEN DOOR '

I. THE MAKOLOLO MISSION

THE obscure Scottish minister, who had left his native land unnoticed in 1840, returned sixteen years later to find himself the most famous man in Great Britain. Before his arrival Livingstone had been awarded the gold medal of the Royal Geographical Society, and immediately the public realised that he was in their midst he was overwhelmed with invitations to show himself and let his voice be heard. He was presented with the freedom of cities and boroughs in England and Scotland. He was made a Fellow of the Royal Society, an Honorary D.C.L. of Oxford and an LL.D. of Cambridge. The British Association, the London Missionary Society, and various Chambers of Commerce vied with one another in fêting him. The Prince Consort granted him an interview and the City of Glasgow voted him a testimonial of £2,000. It is a striking proof of his mental poise that he never allowed these honours to turn his head or to distract him from his self-imposed task of throwing light on the dark places of Africa. He had ceased to be a missionary in the narrow sense, but a fuller life had opened in front of him. It was his purpose to blaze an ineffaceable trail along paths yet untrodden, and no pioneer ever followed a purpose more unswervingly.

One of his public appearances—notable because of the results which flowed from it—was at a reception by the

University of Cambridge, when he delivered a rousing address to an audience largely composed of undergraduates. A single phrase from this became classic : ' The door of Africa is now open. Do you carry out the work which I have begun. I leave it with you '.

This, and other appeals in the same vein, rekindled in an extraordinary manner the public zeal for the redemption of black humanity, which had died down a little since the glowing triumph of the emancipation campaign twenty years before. They stirred the crusading spirit which is always latent in British hearts. There is—and it can be said without the slightest disparagement—an element of the sporting instinct in the yearning felt so often by the youth of our country for a missionary career. Livingstone knew this, and was careful to stress the adventurous side of work in the interior of Africa. ' The missionary', he said in his Cambridge lecture, ' can earn his living by his gun—a course not open to a country curate. I would rather be a poor missionary than a poor curate'. It was the sort of pointed shaft that in after years Cecil Rhodes was wont to let fly ; and, like so many of Rhodes's sayings, it hit the mark.

Unfortunately, in the first outburst of enthusiasm, the schemes set on foot for keeping open Livingstone's door were prepared in a hurry and without sufficient regard for the perils of climate, the extreme difficulties of transport, and the dangerous character of the native populations in the regions half disclosed by his explorations. With the initial failure of the Universities' mission, whose objective was the country round Lake Nyasa and the Shiré highlands, we are not here concerned ; but the fortunes of the expeditions organised to work up from Cape Colony to the Zambesi must be dealt with in some detail. They created the first obstacle to the aspirations of the Boers to lock up South Central Africa for their own primitive and unproductive methods of colonisation, and, though hampered by a series of unforeseen mischances on the spot and by injudicious handling at headquarters, they ultimately provided the foundations upon which was erected the edifice of British supremacy.

One of the effects of Livingstone's call to arms was to thrust the Makololo tribe into an exaggerated prominence. The personal services they had rendered to him and their sufferings at the hands of Matabele raiders combined to focus interest on them. The jingle of their name caught the popular fancy. This handful of aliens, the remnant of a vagabond invasion from the south, began to figure as the most important tribe in Africa, and it was to them that the first efforts of the London Missionary Society were directed. By some queer process of reasoning it was also decided that a mission ought simultaneously to be despatched to their bitter enemies the Matabele. The influence which Moffat had gained with the king of that truculent people seems to have inspired the hope that the presence among them of a few earnest workers would wean them from their habit of persecuting the Makololo, who might then come out of their swamps and settle down peacefully in the healthy uplands. Or it may be that the very reputation of the Matabele for ferocity acted as a magnet.

Early in 1858 the L.M.S. arranged to send out an advance party of four young married men to open the dual campaign. They were to be reinforced at the Cape by two others who had already gained some knowledge of up-country conditions, and the small body thus augmented was to be divided into two groups. One was to make for the upper Zambesi, where Livingstone, who had left England a little earlier, would be ready to introduce them to the Makololo chief, and the other to proceed to Matabeleland under the guidance of Moffat, who would secure their favourable reception by Mziligazi.

The danger of sending with their families small detachments of Englishmen utterly strange to the exigencies of
African bullock transport, inexpert in the use of firearms
for their own protection, and unacquainted with the ways
of the natives to whom they were expected to minister, to
isolated posts in the wilds of the interior, with no support
nearer than Kuruman six or seven hundred miles in their
rear, did not seem to weigh very heavily with the L.M.S.,
nor did it damp the spirits of those selected, whose apostolic
zeal compensated in some degree for their inexperience.

For nearly a year they were delayed in the Colony by one
cause or another, and it was not until the middle of 1859
that they were ready to start from Kuruman, where they
assembled before setting out on the final stage of their
journey. The party for Matabeleland,[1] after the usual
mishaps incidental to waggon travelling through a district
where there was no regular track, where they were never
sure of getting water, and were frequently exposed to
attack from lions and other dangerous beasts, reached their
destination towards the end of the year—eighteen months
from the date of leaving England. They were received with
moderate civility by Mziligazi. After keeping them waiting
about in their waggons for several weeks he finally gave
them permission to establish themselves at Inyati, one of
his kraals a few miles north of the main town of Mhlahlanhlela,[2] and there for the present we will leave them.

The Makololo missionaries left Kuruman about the same
time, but had a far more difficult route to follow, through
country where water was sometimes unobtainable for days
at a stretch, and where there were occasional belts of tsetse

---

[1] It consisted of the Revs. John Smith Moffat (Dr. Moffat's son),
and Thomas Morgan Thomas, with their families, and William
Sykes, whose wife died at Kuruman before the expedition started.
Dr. Moffat also went with them for the purpose of securing the consent of Mziligazi to the opening of a mission station in his country.

[2] See below, p. 105.

fly. This party consisted of the Rev. Holloway Helmore with his wife and four young children, and the Rev. Roger Price, his wife and one child. The Rev. John Mackenzie, the third member of the expedition, remained with his family at Kuruman, the intention being that he should follow with supplies a year later. Their journey across the inhospitable desert-like district north of Shoshong was one of extreme hardship, but they were buoyed up by the assurance that Livingstone would be in the Makololo country to receive them. In this they were disappointed, for when they reached Linyanti in February, 1860, he had not arrived. It transpired later that his own plans had fallen through. The steamer which he had bought to convey him up the Zambesi from its mouth had broken down, and while waiting for a substitute he had taken advantage of the delay to make further explorations in the direction of Lake Nyasa. Helmore and Price were compelled therefore to confront Sekeletu without introduction, and to wait on his convenience.

Since Livingstone had left him, four years before, Sekeletu had been stricken with leprosy. He attributed this loathsome affliction to witchcraft, and had caused a number of his subjects to be put to death to counteract imaginary spells. His reception of Helmore and his companions was the reverse of cordial, and he refused point blank to entertain their suggestion that he should move with his people to the north of the Zambesi. It is possible that owing to their inexperience the proposal was made without the tact which Livingstone would have employed, but the very fact that it was made at all roused suspicion and resentment in the king's mind.

There were at his kraal some Mambari slavers, with whom he was on friendly and intimate terms. These men were alive to the opposition which their business would meet at the hands of the English missionaries, and without doubt instigated Sekeletu to get rid of them. With native guile he then affected to treat them more hospitably, and sent them gifts of beef and beer. Within a few days the whole party, including their Bechuana servants, were attacked by some acute gastric complaint. By the middle of April Helmore, his wife and two of his children, Price's little girl, and several of the native servants were dead, and Mrs. Price was in a critical condition. The rascally chief then proceeded to appropriate the waggons, guns, clothing and stores brought up by the expedition. Reduced to desperation Price, who had been very ill himself, sought permission to leave the country with his dying wife and the two surviving Helmore children. To this Sekeletu agreed, and after robbing them of their remaining valuables, supplied them with guides; but the latter—no doubt by arrangement—led them into a belt of tsetse fly and then deserted. The few oxen Price was allowed to keep were 'fly-stuck', and all perished but two. He managed somehow to struggle across to the country of the Lake people, and there his wife died and he was left stranded with the two children.

On September 9 he was found in a state of physical and mental collapse by Mackenzie, who was on his way north to join the mission, and providentially arrived at the Mababe river just in time to save him and the young Helmores. Mackenzie had repeatedly heard from natives encountered on his journey that the whole of the party had been killed by Sekeletu, but refused to believe that a man held in such high estimation by Livingstone could be guilty of such a fiendish crime. When sufficiently recovered from his breakdown, however, Price assured him that they had been deliberately poisoned, and this was corroborated by his surviving Bechuana servants, who had learnt the truth from one of the Makololo headmen.

Two months after Price had escaped, but before he had been rescued by Mackenzie, Livingstone at long last reached Sesheke, where he was warmly welcomed by the

hypocritical Sekeletu. From Makololo sources he learnt
the pitiful fate of those who had responded to his call, and
who had expected to meet him on the river. A brief
account of the tragedy afterwards appeared in *The Zambesi
and its Tributaries*, which was compiled from the journals of
David Livingstone and his brother Charles, who had accompanied him. With our knowledge of the former it seems
impossible that the passage in which this episode is described could have emanated from his pen, for it is so
matter-of-fact as to be almost callous, but as it sets out the
case for Sekeletu it is only fair that it should be quoted :

' Our information was derived entirely from the natives of the
different tribes, which now form the Makololo. They are
generally truthful, unless they have some self-interest at stake ;
and they cannot be made to combine to propagate any down-
right falsehood. Taking their statements as probably true, the
whole party consisted of twenty-two persons, of whom nine
were Europeans, and thirteen people of colour ; of these five
Europeans and four natives perished by fever in less than three
months. The missionary associate of Helmore was then left in a
somewhat trying position. Four out of the nine Europeans had
succumbed to the disease, and his own wife was lying ill, and
soon to be the fifth victim. He had been but a short time in
Africa, his knowledge of the native was of course limited, his
influence small, and he had no experience : accordingly he took
the wise course of leaving the country ; his wife died before he
reached the healthy desert. The native servants from the south,
who had never seen the fever in their own country, thought that
the party had been poisoned by the Makololo ; but although
they are heathens, and have little regard for human life, they
are not quite so bad as that. The spear, and not poison is their
weapon. There is no occasion for suspecting other poison than
malaria, that being more than enough. We have witnessed all
the symptoms of this poison scores of times, and, from the
survivors' description, believe the deaths to have been caused
by severe African fever, and nothing else. We much regretted
that, though we were on the same river lower down, we were
not aware of their being at Linyanti till too late to render the

ROGER PRICE

(Survivor of the Makololo Mission)

(face p. 100)

medical aid they so much needed. It is undoubtedly advisable that every mission should have a medical man as an essential part of its staff.' [1]

Mackenzie, from whose books and letters the details of this lamentable affair have been mainly gathered, is also at great pains to clear Sekeletu from the charge of murder, which he thinks arose through his subsequent conduct in stealing the property of Price and his colleagues.[2] But others who were near the spot at the time, or collected first-hand evidence from native witnesses, had no doubt as to the chief's guilt. It is also worthy of note that the victims were reported to have suffered during their illness from acute internal pains—a symptom not generally observed even in the most violent cases of malaria.[3]

Sekeletu's leprosy ended fatally in 1863. After his death the Makololo régime, which, owing to his incapacity for government, had for some time been crumbling, began rapidly to break up. His younger brother Mpololo, who succeeded him, was even less capable of holding it together, and made himself obnoxious by petty cruelties. Intrigues and internal quarrels precipitated the ruin of the tribe. The fear of assassination drove some of the principal men to migrate to Lake Ngami, and others even sought refuge among their old enemies the Matabele. By 1865 the numbers of the Makololo had become so reduced that the river tribes were emboldened to revolt. Headed by the ba-Rotse they rose simultaneously and, in a single night, murdered in cold blood every member of the tribe they

[1] Livingstone, *The Zambesi and its Tributaries*, pp. 279, 280.

[2] Mackenzie, *Ten Years North of the Orange River*, p. 194.

[3] Whether Sekeletu was responsible for these murders or not his other crimes were notorious. Some of the missionaries, however, seem to have shut their eyes to his real character, and to have considered that as a friend of Livingstone he must have been impeccable. An American lady (Georgina A. Gollock) has gone to the length of including him in a book entitled *Eminent Africans*, in which he is described in favourable terms.

could find except some of the marriageable women, whom they appropriated as wives. A few of the men had warning, and fled across the Mababe river, but these were treacherously killed not long afterwards by Lechulatebe, the chief of the Lake people. The devastating career of the Makololo had lasted for forty years, and Africa was well rid of them.

The Missionary Society at home were so disheartened by the disastrous result of their first attempt to found a settlement north of the Zambesi that they made no effort to repeat it. In fact with the extermination of the Makololo all inducement to do so had vanished. Livingstone was not within reach to advise them. After his brief visit to Sesheke in 1860 he had left those parts for good and was pursuing his explorations in the Lake districts. He had never awakened special interest in the other tribes of the upper Zambesi, and very little was known about them. The whole enterprise was dropped, and, so far as missionary labour was concerned, the ground lay fallow for more than two decades.

II. THE MATABELE MISSION

When John Moffat and his colleagues Thomas and Sykes came to Inyati the Matabele were firmly established as masters of the country. If we treat their periodical raids upon the neighbouring tribes as part of an ordinary routine —as in fact they were—there had been only two episodes since their arrival which can be said to have interrupted their progress or affected the course of history. The first of these occurred shortly after they entered the land, and before they had conquered it. On his way north from the Transvaal Mziligazi had divided his followers into two forces, one of which, with the women and children, was left in the rich pastoral country of the ma-Kalanga, or that part of it lying immediately north of the Matopo hills, while the other, under the king's personal command, took a north-

westerly course, in the hope of waylaying and crushing
Sebitoane, against whom he cherished an inveterate hatred.
We have seen how he succeeded in crossing the Zambesi, and
how, in the long run, he was worsted by the superior tactics
of the Makololo, who had the assistance of the river tribes.

Mziligazi was engaged in this expedition for two or three
years, and during his prolonged absence the southern portion of the tribe, as was natural, grew restless. Such scraps
of information as filtered down from time to time through
the agency of wandering Bushmen pointed to an intention
on Mziligazi's part to settle in the country north of the
great river. Deprived of a controlling authority those left
behind became unruly. The leading men were divided in
council, some having a strong desire to follow their king,
while others feared he had shaken them off for good, and
that they would have to shift for themselves. Eventually
reports began to circulate of Sebitoane's coup in enticing a
part of the Matabele army to an island and leaving them
there to perish. This was magnified by rumour into the
destruction of the whole expeditionary force, and the
indunas and headmen fell into the rash error of presuming
the death of the king himself. Obviously the next course was
to elect a successor. They proceeded in a perfectly orthodox fashion and chose Nkulumane, the son of Mziligazi by his
great wife, herself the daughter of a Zulu chief. But he was
still a lad of tender years, and it became necessary to appoint
a regent to govern the tribe until he should arrive at matur-
ity. This question led to rivalries and intrigues, and before a
definite conclusion was reached there came a rude awakening.

News of their intentions reached Mziligazi, who was
actually on the return march, and had arrived at the Makorikori salt pans, about ten days' journey to the west of the
Matopò hills. Without a moment's delay he descended on
the king-makers, who were taken utterly by surprise, and
too terrified to resist. In Mziligazi's eyes they had been

guilty of treason—the most heinous of all crimes, and one for which death was the inevitable penalty. Short indeed was their shrift. By the king's orders one and all were hurled over a precipitous cliff on the neighbouring hill, which, in memory of the event, has ever since been known as *Ntaba-z-Induna* (Hill of the Indunas).

But Mziligazi was nothing if not thorough. To make sure that there would be no recurrence of plots to supplant him all who might provide a rallying point for disaffection must be removed. His next step therefore was against those of his sons who were of royal birth. He gave orders to Umnombate, his principal councillor, that Nkulumane, the boy selected as his successor, should be put out of the way, and with him Ubuhlelo, son of another wife of Zulu lineage, and Lobengula, whose mother was the daughter of a Swazi chief, and who was therefore a possible focus of future mischief. In the case of the first two the order was executed. They were taken away very secretly by a confidential servant, bound to trees and done to death.

The king was careful to allow no suspicion of this murder to leak out. The two men privy to it were instructed to spread the report that the lads had been sent to Zululand, the home of their ancestors, to be kept in safety until their time should come, and this explanation of their disappearance was accepted by all.[1]

[1] The real facts were afterwards given by Uhabai, the servant who carried out the order, to the missionary Thomas, and are recounted in his book *Eleven Years in Central South Africa* (pp. 227, 228).

Thomas Baines, the explorer, was in Matabeleland in 1869, shortly after the death of Mziligazi, when the question of the succession was before the heads of the nation, and the truth was officially disclosed for the first time by the same servant. Baines (*Gold Regions of South Central South Africa*, pp. 32, 33) spells his name Gwabaiiyo—showing that he got his information independently of Thomas—and says that he was a ba-Suto. In order that the body of a royal child might not be disfigured by spear or club wounds he was directed to twist Nkulumane's neck, but he departed from his instructions by garotting him with a bark rope.

The other boy, Lobengula, was smuggled away to a hiding place by his mother's friends, and escaped the fate of his brothers. He was kept concealed till long afterwards, when, the king's suspicions having abated, it was thought safe to produce him.

These matters having been disposed of to the king's satisfaction he decided to settle down and attend to the legitimate business of state. He gave up all idea of seeking a better land and from that time forth ceased to lead his armies personally in the field. Near the head-waters of the Khami river and about fifteen miles south-west of the spot where Bulawayo now stands he founded a large town, which he called Mhlahlanhlela ('road clear'), after the name of a military kraal in Zululand. He then set to work to consolidate the tribe, with a view to extending his dominion over as much of the surrounding country as he could encompass by raids.

The second episode—the only other which threatened to disturb Mziligazi's peace of mind—occurred in 1847, a few years after the events just recorded. The Transvaal Boers had not forgotten the two white girls carried off by the Matabele in their attack on Erasmus's camp ten years before, and learning through native reports that they were still alive organised an expedition to rescue them. Doubtless also they coveted the desirable country which rumour said the Matabele were now occupying, and having succeeded in driving them out of the Transvaal were not unwilling to try conclusions with them a second time.

Hendrik Potgieter, known to the Matabele as Enteleka—a corruption of his Christian name—was chosen to lead a commando of about a hundred well-mounted men, with some allies recruited from the Bechuana, to attack the Matabele at their main town. Knowing from past experience that mobility was their chief advantage they left

all waggons at the Shashi river, a hundred miles to the
south, and advanced on horseback through the Matopo
hills which were thinly occupied by Makalanga. On their
way they captured a large number of cattle which were left
in charge of the Bechuana, but this was a blunder, for it got
abroad, and reached the ears of Mziligazi, who made his
preparations. Before they reached Mhlahlanhlela several
strong *impis* pounced on them. In the engagement which
followed the Boers were obliged to fall back before superior
numbers, and were lucky to escape without loss of life.
The Bechuana levies were not so fortunate. The Matabele
stole on them in the early dawn of the following morning,
and slaughtered them to a man, recovering at the same time
all the captured cattle.

This was the last organised attempt made by the Boers to
challenge the Matabele by force of arms. In some ways it is
a matter for regret that it failed, for it might have precipitated the break-up of a tyranny which was to last for another forty years. If on the other hand it had succeeded
the high veld of Southern Rhodesia, with its immense
mineral and agricultural resources, must have become an
annexe of the Transvaal, and a permanent barrier against
British expansion in the north.

The Matabele now entered on a long period of unbroken
prosperity, and were free to devote themselves whole-
heartedly to the marauding expeditions which were at once
their profession and their pastime. The tribes scattered
over the plateau on their north and east were easy victims.
The ma-Kalanga, the ba-Nyai, the va-Roswi and others had
for a century or more formed one loosely organised nation
under a succession of paramount chiefs known by the
dynastic name of Mambo, the inheritors of the great kingdom of Monomotapa. Even before the Matabele settled on
their flanks they had gained some experience of Zulu
oppression, for more than one of the fierce hordes which

fled to escape from the terrible Tshaka had stopped to harass them. Most of these after cutting a track of desolation and massacre swept on to the north, but a few Swazis remained under a woman chief, Nyamazana, and were still in the country when Mziligazi appeared on the scene. He was shrewd enough in fact to secure them as allies, and to cement the bond added their chief to his regular harem. In one of the Swazi raids the reigning Mambo had been killed at his principal stronghold (Ntaba-si-Mambo), after which his people had become broken up into their component groups and had lost the power of combined resistance.

All previous persecutions endured by these unfortunate tribes were as nothing, however, compared with their sufferings at the hands of the Matabele. At the commencement of each dry season Mziligazi sent out one or more divisions of his army to round up cattle and bring back women. Some of the weaker clans were absolutely wiped out, others reduced to slavery, and many of their young boys were absorbed into the Matabele fighting machine as an inferior class of soldiers, termed by them *ama-Holi*. The raids were gradually extended until, within a radius of 150 miles north and east of Mhlahlanhlela, no part of the plateau was left unravaged.

The fiendish cruelties indulged in by the Matabele on their forays would hardly be credited were they not vouched for by so many authorities. The missionary writers were usually reticent about them. Their calling, and the inhibitions imposed by nineteenth-century conventions no doubt made them reluctant to describe in detail what they knew. The elder Moffat and Mackenzie alone speak out. The former—most restrained of chroniclers, and always on the look-out for good traits in the savages around him— makes no attempt to palliate the devilish practices of Mziligazi's *impis*.

'They were not', he tells us, 'satisfied with simply capturing cattle ; nothing less than the entire subjugation or destruction of the vanquished could quench their insatiable thirst for power. Thus when they conquered a town, the terrified inhabitants were driven in a mass to the outskirts, when the parents and all the married women were slaughtered on the spot. Such as dared to be brave in the defence of their town, their wives, and their children, are reserved for a still more terrible death ; dry grass, saturated with fat, is tied round their naked bodies, and then set on fire. The youths and girls are loaded as beasts of burden with the spoils of the town, to be marched to the homes of their victors. If the town be in an isolated position, the helpless infants are either left to perish with hunger, or to be devoured by beasts of prey. . . . Should a suspicion arise that these helpless innocents may fall into the hands of friends, they will prevent this by collecting them into a fold, and after raising over them a pile of brushwood, apply the flaming torch to it. . . .' [1]

The same story is told by all other white men who penetrated the interior during the heyday of the Matabele.[2]

In their terror of the raids the wretched inhabitants took permanent refuge in the clumps of granite boulders dotted over the country, and their life only differed from that of the baboons which shared these retreats in the fact that they still built huts and grain-bins and crept out to cultivate their scanty crops.

There was, however, one small body of the Makalanga which enjoyed from the outset exemption from persecution. The inaccessible fastnesses of the Matopo range were the abode of a strange group of creatures known as ' Children of the Mlimo '—an ancient hierarchy possessing a knowledge of thaumaturgy, and practising a cult which had been handed down in the same familes for many generations.

---

[1] *Missionary Labours*, etc., chap. xxx.

[2] See, among others, Oates, *Matabeleland and the Victoria Falls*, p. 79 ; W. Montagu Kerr, *The Far Interior*, p. 102 ; Selous, *Travel and Adventure in Africa*, p. 81, and Rev. J. Mackenzie, *Ten Years North of the Orange River*.

They were expert rain-makers, and professed to hold converse with a supernatural being—a sort of God—whose
oracular utterances issued from the caves, and who could
only be approached through their agency. They were also
accomplished humbugs, and made a rich living by their
chicanery, but they were held in superstitious awe by their
own tribesmen, and with a certain amount of respect by the
invaders. Probably with some idea that they might be
useful in seasons of drought or in time of war they were left
unmolested by Mziligazi, and were even consulted on
occasion—if not by him, by some of his people.

It was due entirely to Mziligazi's genius that his subjects
did not become indolent through prosperity. He took
measures to guard against any such relapse, and kept them
constantly strung up to concert pitch. Each village was a
military cantonment in charge of an *induna*, and its occupants were trained to hold themselves at all times ready for
war. The young soldiers were not allowed to take wives
until they had proved their capacity in the field, though
permission to marry was often given to a whole regiment at
the same time as a reward for success in battle. This led to
a perpetual emulation to win the king's favour by some act
of bloodshed, for a man's prowess was measured by the
tally of his victims. The King, although he ceased, after his
return from the Zambesi, to lead his troops into action, was
careful to keep in close touch with every unit by frequent
surprise visits to the various posts, and a large part of his
time was spent in a travelling waggon. On such occasions
contests of a warlike character—gymkhana meetings, in
fact—would take place ; numbers of oxen would be killed
to provide feasts, and prodigious quantities of beer consumed. At each military kraal there was a bevy of the
King's women ranking as lesser wives. In all there were
about three hundred of these ladies, chosen from the
daughters of the principal men of the tribe, who considered

it a high honour to establish a family connection with their king. Mziligazi, for his part, besides finding it politic to bind his *indunas* to him by domestic ties, used the women as spies, and through their agency was kept informed of all that went on at their kraals in his absence. No detail of increase or casualty among the cattle or the people themselves was hidden from him, and it was an offence punishable by death to attempt concealment. He was also chief magistrate, and sat daily in judgment to determine disputes and try criminals. In practice all crimes resolved themselves into offences against his person, and again the invariable penalty was death.

By these autocratic measures Mziligazi succeeded in maintaining his position as the central figure in the tribe, and the whole life of every individual was consecrated to his service. With absolute assurance, and perhaps with greater justice, he could have used the boast attributed to Louis XIV : ' *L'état c'est moi* '.

His relations with white men did not at first cause him any serious concern. After the arrival of the missionaries a few were allowed to enter the country from below—always through Shoshong—with beads, blankets, guns and other trade goods, for which they found a ready market. Occasionally there came others who sought permission to hunt, or buy ivory, and these were not discouraged provided they brought satisfactory gifts. But all were compelled to enter the country by the one road, and to halt at a fixed spot at a distance from the king's own town while their business was enquired into, and leave asked to proceed. In course of time there were some who made regular trips to Matabeleland, and even two or three who were granted permission to cultivate a patch of land and build camps for trading, or as centres for hunting expeditions, on the outskirts of the country. But their position as squatters was precarious ; at any moment they might be ordered to withdraw, and they were obliged to curry favour not only with the king, but with his wives and the *indunas*, who were insatiable in their demands for presents.

After what has been said it will be seen that the lot of the pioneer missionaries was by no means an easy one. For years they had to plough a lonely furrow without the slightest tangible result. It is true that their elementary knowledge of medicine and their willingness to act as interpreters ensured them a certain amount of consideration, but their lives were drab and unprofitable ; their surroundings sordid and repulsive ; they were conscious of standing always on the edge of a precipice ; in spite of patient efforts they failed to gain a single convert, and they must often have been at a loss to understand why their Society did not transfer them to a more fruitful field. Could they have peeped into the future, however, they might have taken heart, for this little group of British men and women proved to be the thin end of a mighty wedge.

CHAPTER VIII

THE DAWN OF A NEW ERA

I. EXIT MZILIGAZI

THROUGHOUT all this turbulent period, and in face of the risks of entanglement in the raids and wars which kept the Bechuana and their neighbours in a state of ferment for forty years, British explorers were steadily advancing further and further into the interior. By 1860 the routes to Lake Ngami and the upper Zambesi were becoming fairly well known, and as far as Shoshong there was almost a beaten track. It is interesting to remember that in the north of Africa, just about the same time, Burton, Speke and Grant were pushing southwards towards the sources of the Nile. The two thrusting points of British exploration were beginning to approach one another like the carbon pencils of an arc light, though it was many years before they met to irradiate the gloom which enveloped the heart of the continent.

Apart from Moffat the pioneer in the Limpopo-Zambesi region was David Hume, who started his wanderings in 1825, and spent the next few years in constant trading and hunting trips in Bechuanaland, penetrating as far as the Macloutsie river, then regarded as the limit of the Mangwato territory. He was the first white man to visit Mziligazi at his original settlement in the Marico district, and was there when Moffat reached it in 1829. Sam Edwards, another noted elephant hunter, who was still alive ten years ago,[1]

[1] Edwards died in the Cape Province, at the age of ninety-five, in 1922.

followed some time later. He accompanied Gordon Cumming to Sekhome's town in 1848, and afterwards made
many journeys to Lake Ngami and the Zambesi. He and
Moffat were the earliest arrivals at Mziligazi's kraal in
Matabeleland, where in the course of time Edwards took up
his residence, and so far gained the confidence of the old king
and his successor that he was made an *Induna* of the
nation.

Hume and Edwards were followed by James Chapman,
an Englishman, Jan Viljoen, a Boer, and a number of
others, who gradually established a recognised highway to
the Zambesi, and more or less permanent trading stations
at Shoshong, at Pandamatenka, sixty miles south of the
Victoria Falls, and at other places along the route where a
water supply could be counted on.

Soon after the work of the London Missionary Society
was inaugurated at Inyati some of the bolder spirits ven ·
tured into Matabeleland, and in the early 'sixties George
Westbeech, Henry Hartley, George Phillips and two or
three other hunters were well known to Mziligazi, who
found them worth encouraging for the sake of the trade
goods—more especially firearms and gunpowder—which
they brought with them, but although they enjoyed comparative freedom to shoot and barter for ivory in the
immediate vicinity of his own kraals, where their movements could be kept under supervision, they were never
permitted to trespass upon the king's cherished raiding
grounds in Mashonaland, for fear that they might supply
arms to his subject tribes. It was common knowledge that
immense troops of elephants and other large game roamed
over the high veld on the eastern side of his domain, and
year after year the king was beset by demands for leave to
go in that direction, but all to no purpose. The embargo
was maintained, and Mashonaland long remained a sacred
preserve.

But Mziligazi's vitality was beginning to fail. Even such an iron constitution as his could not hold out for ever against the constant guzzling of beef and beer in which he indulged, and when the missionaries saw him first in 1859 he had already had several attacks of gout. His mental faculties were alert, and he kept up the practice of travelling round his country in an ox-waggon, but the malady had obtained such a hold on him that in the winter season he was unable to use his swollen feet, and had to be carried about in an arm-chair by four of his wives. Mackenzie, who saw him in 1863, describes him as an old, frail and helpless man, though his features indicated the intelligence and force of character he once possessed. Clearly his spirit must have deteriorated, or he would never have tamely submitted to the rebuff which his *impis* had sustained in their expedition against Sekhome in the previous year; nor would he have tolerated the importunities of the Europeans who were more than ever pressing him to allow them greater freedom in their movements.

In 1865 he was at last prevailed upon to grant permission to a select and limited number of these to hunt in Mashonaland, and by consenting sealed, unwittingly, the death warrant of his nation. The first to set out for the newly-opened field of adventure was Hartley, who, as a child, had come out to Cape Colony with the 1820 emigrants and had engaged in many hunting trips in the interior. He was at this time over fifty years of age and a man of unwieldy build, but in spite of these drawbacks, and the additional handicap of a club foot, he was wonderfully active, and could jump on and off his horse like a circus rider.[1] He was credited with having shot 1,000 elephants, and was held in high favour by Mziligazi, to whom physical strength and prowess in the hunting field always made a strong appeal.

[1] G. Lacy, *South African Exploration*, series 4, p. 24, series 8, p. 18. Mohr, *Victoria Falls*, pp. 201, 202.

Nevertheless, in granting him permission to enter Mashona-land he insisted—as he did in all other cases—on sending with him one of his headmen, nominally as a guide, but in reality to keep an eye on his movements, and to report any suspicious action. Hartley hunted as far as the Umfuli river in 1865, and again in 1866, and on both trips was struck by the shallow excavations, dumps of rock and other indications of a bygone mining industry, which he noticed in various parts of the country. He made up his mind to seize the first opportunity of getting expert advice for a scientific examination of these remains. On his way south he happened to fall in with a young German geologist named Karl Mauch, who was looking for a job and gladly accepted an invitation to join the hunter on his next trip. In the winter of 1866 Mauch accompanied Hartley, who had with him two of his sons, to the Umfuli river, where he soon satisfied himself that the whole district was intersected by gold-bearing quartz reefs. His examination of the old workings and dumps was necessarily perfunctory, and had to be conducted with extreme caution, as spies were with the party, and there was a danger that if the king heard that the white men were looking for gold instead of hunting he might prohibit further expeditions.

In the following year Mauch transferred his activities to Tati, which lay in territory claimed both by the ba-Mang-wato and the Matabele, and was often raided by the latter. Here again he found a promising gold formation, and a second visit on his own account to Umfuli confirmed his impression that he had there lighted on one of the most important auriferous deposits in the world.

On his return to the Colony Mauch announced his dis-coveries in the most extravagant language. He described one of the gold-fields as eighty miles in length and two or three in breadth, and in a letter to the press related how he was ' so transfixed at their beauty and extent that at a particular spot he stood riveted to the place ; struck with amazement and wonder at the sight and unable for some minutes to use the hammer '.   He added that thousands of persons might find ample room to work in these extensive fields without interfering with one another.[1]   Specimens of his quartz were sent to England for examination and were found to yield from three to fifty or more ounces of gold to the ton.[2]   The people of South Africa were dazzled by the prospect of wealth so close at hand.   Just about the same time some stir had been caused by the report of diamonds having been found near the Vaal river—not yet in sufficient numbers to lead to a rush, but enough to tickle their palate and whet the appetite for further sensations.   Mauch's reports were the very thing.   Whatever might be the truth about the diamonds the gold appeared a certainty.   His samples had been exhibited locally and showed specks and nuggets of the precious metal plain for all to see, and there was eager competition to reach the spot where they had been found.   Syndicates were formed and parties of individual diggers made preparations to set off for Tati, which, being nearer than Umfuli—though in the general ignorance the two localities were not precisely distinguished—became the first goal.[3]

The question of the ownership of the Tati area did not cause any particular concern in the minds of these adventurers, but it was not long before it began to bulk large in the politics of those in the more immediate neighbourhood —the ba-Mangwato, the Matabele and the Boers of the young republic of the Transvaal.

[1] Letter to *Transvaal Argus*, December 3, 1867.

[2] On September 11, 1868, the London *Times* published an assay of some of Mauch's specimens furnished by the Bank of England, showing 1185 ounces of gold and 60 ounces of silver per ton !

[3] Baines (*Gold Fields of South East Africa*, p. 3) gives a list of nine parties that had reached Tati by 1869, including one of thirty-five Australians equipped in Natal.

For some years after their first migration the Boers had failed to obtain recognition from the British authorities, but in 1852, as a result of constant pressure, they had secured the right of self-government. A meeting took place at Sand river between the Cape Governor and Pretorius, the Boer Commandant-General, and an agreement was concluded whereby the Transvaal was guaranteed independence and Great Britain was pledged to make no encroachment north of the Vaal river. Unfortunately this document was silent as to the western limit of Boer influence. The Boers at once assumed the right to control the native tribes as far as the Kalahari desert, and, as we have seen, attempted to exercise it by repeated aggressions against Sechele and other chiefs. They also sought to restrict the movements of Moffat, Livingstone and their missionary colleagues, and to close the route through Bechuanaland, on the pretext that the natives were obtaining firearms by this channel. In short, although they were not strong enough to make effective occupation, they acted as if the whole of Bechuanaland belonged to them, and the British authorities took not the slightest trouble to challenge the assumption.

On the discovery of gold at Tati the Boers laid plans for acquiring that area also, but Mziligazi claimed it by right of conquest, while Macheng, the Mangwato chief, protested that from time immemorial his people had herded their cattle in the district, and that the Makalanga tribes inhabiting it were his tributaries. Macheng tried to emphasize his authority by demanding a tax of £1 from each white prospector passing through Shoshong, but lacked the courage to enforce the impost. Although he seemed outwardly to have established himself as chief he was despised and cordially detested by travellers, partly because of his inveterate propensity for begging drink and presents, and also on account of his unpleasant manners and appearance. He was a huge corpulent man, six feet in height, with a gloomy, sensual face, and an insatiable thirst; an arrant coward, who would never have dared to put forward a claim to the ownership of the Tati strip had he not been aware of the feeble condition of his former master Mziligazi, and outside the circle of his few satellites he was held of no account.[1]

The Boers—the remaining party in the triangular contest —had never seriously interfered with the ba-Mangwato, and had learnt to their cost from the experience of Potgieter in 1847 that the Matabele were better left alone. Their present policy was to obtain a foothold in the disputed area—not by force, but by negotiation with both the other claimants, and with this object they made use of the elephant hunter Viljoen, who stood well with Mziligazi, and could probably square Macheng by bribery. The first bait held out to the latter was the promise of protection from the expected invasion of unruly diggers from the south and against attacks by the Matabele, but it entirely failed owing to the alertness of Mackenzie, the resident missionary, who induced the besotted chief to appeal to the Governor at the Cape (Sir Philip Wodehouse) for help, and to make a voluntary offer to place himself and his people under a British protectorate. Wodehouse referred the matter to the Cape Parliament, and a sum of £2,000 was voted for a commission to enquire into the value of the gold fields and the whole question of their rightful ownership. Though it never led to anything this decision had some slight effect in restraining the activities of the Transvaal Boers.

Viljoen's negotiations with Mziligazi took the form of an offer to buy the Tati district, and as the old king was by no means sure of his ground this may have presented some attractions to him. But he mistrusted the Boers instinctively, and doubted their capacity to pay. After consulting

[1] Baines, *Gold Regions of S. E. Africa*, p. 18. Mohr, *Victoria Falls*, p. 137.

with his *indunas*, and, like Macheng, taking the advice of the missionaries, he replied that a sale of any part of his dominions was out of the question, and that no permanent settlement of white men could be permitted so close to his own people. He would allow them to come for the temporary purpose of digging gold,[1] and for this privilege he would of course have expected payment. But a temporary settlement for mining made no special appeal to the Boers. They had not yet learnt the opportunities which such a grant would provide for enriching themselves by traffic in concessions and monopolies. What they coveted was the freedom of the hunting veld and the rich pasturage of Matabeleland, and this they saw would be lost for ever if the country was overrun by miners and prospectors from England and the colonies.

Viljoen next fell back on a favourite Boer device. He endeavoured, by a discreditable intrigue, to engineer a Matabele attack on the ba-Mangwato to settle the ownership of the bone of contention, hoping that war between the two tribes might afford an opportunity for Boer intervention on humanitarian grounds, and pave the way for annexation. But this plot was exposed before it had time to mature. As a last resort the Transvaal Government audaciously issued an official announcement ' proclaiming ' sovereignty over the whole of Bechuanaland—a piece of bluff which they were not strong enough to carry through by force of arms, and which therefore fell completely flat.

The three-cornered tussle eventually subsided owing to the disappointing results of the mining operations. Shafts were sunk at various points on the reef, and batteries and engines erected, but the cost of dragging machinery and stores over the long route from the coast was prohibitive, and throttled all prospects of profitable mining. The small community of diggers, who had braved sickness and untold

[1] Thomas, *Eleven Years*, etc., p. 395.

hardships in the first outburst of enthusiasm, lost heart and melted away. The exodus was accelerated by the counter-attraction of the diamonds—now definitely proved to exist in quantities in the south, and the much advertised Tati gold fields were soon practically abandoned. One company, which had been formed with influential backing in London, and was represented on the spot by Sir John Swinburne, survived, and began to make preparations for exploring the more distant reefs found by Mauch near the Umfuli river, but all steps in that direction were suddenly made impossible by an event which threw Matabeleland into a state of violent unrest, and caused all ideas of mining development to be indefinitely postponed.

In August, 1868, Mziligazi, who was well over seventy years of age, and for some time had been little more than a helpless log, died of a complication of diseases. During the last weeks of his life he allowed the Rev. Morgan Thomas to attend him, but he had submitted too long to the ministrations of his own quacks and witch-doctors, whose foul concoctions probably aggravated his complaints, and he was past human aid when the missionary came on the scene.

Though his long tyranny may not seriously have retarded the advance of civilisation, it was a constant menace to Europeans, and a sore affliction to all native tribes that came within his reach. He is remembered chiefly for his persecutions, and will go down to history as a monster of inhumanity. But it is irrational to judge Mziligazi by our own standards, and if we make allowance for his racial temperament, his upbringing and his environment we may find something almost admirable in his career, and at least admit that he was a very great ruler. His cruelty was neither immoral nor fanatical. He was not a Caligula, who revelled in insensate murder ; his excesses were not inspired by vindictiveness, like those of 'Butcher' Cumberland ; nor were they the fruit of spiritual aberration, as were those of Torquemada. Mziligazi was cruel because cruelty was the only weapon by which he could enforce discipline among his fiery soldiers, and preserve control over those he had conquered. He practised and encouraged plunder, slavery and bloodshed because these things—so far from being looked on as crimes—were, to the Zulu comprehension, an essential part of the business of existence. There was nothing petty or underhand about his misdeeds ; they were absolutely open and above board, thorough and consistent. He never wavered in his policy, or faltered in its execution. He had set himself to build a nation out of the most unpromising and unmanageable material, and he achieved his purpose by the sheer force of his personality.

By white men in general Mziligazi was justly regarded as a troublesome pest ; by the missionaries as the personification of Satanic evil. Moffat alone among the latter had sufficient discernment to detect some spark of humanity in his composition. It was there no doubt. Had he lived fifty years later it is conceivable that contact with civilisation would have taught him—as it did other notable Bantu rulers—the value of milder methods of government, and he might have gone down to posterity with a reputation equal to that of Khama.

II. ENTER LOBENGULA

Although they must have been aware for some time that their king's life was ebbing, his death, when it actually occurred, threw the *indunas* on the spot into a state of consternation. There was no one in the country ready or eligible to step into the kingship, and they were at a loss to know how to proceed. To guard against the uproar and disturbance which they feared would break out when the people discovered that they were without a head they tried at first to keep the matter secret, but the truth was known of course to the members of the late king's household and to

some of the royal wives, who were alarmed for their own
safety, and found it convenient to disappear. This aroused
suspicion and the news gradually leaked out. Meanwhile
the leading councillors anxiously debated the question of a
successor, and their thoughts turned to Nkulumane, who
was supposed to be living in Zululand. They were taken
aback when it was revealed for the first time that both he
and his brother Ubuhlelo had been strangled to death by
the king's order nearly thirty years before, and many refused to credit the story.

At this juncture the veteran Umnombate, the man who
had stood highest in Mziligazi's confidence, and who had
been employed by him on several weighty errands—among
others the mission to the Governor at the Cape—took the
lead. Being one of the two or three who knew the facts
about Nkulumane—having indeed been responsible for
carrying out the order for putting him away—he was
determined that the succession should fall to Lobengula,
whose interests he had long watched over ; but he knew
that the tribe would never accept him contentedly as long
as any doubt existed in their minds as to the fate of the
rightful heir. And Lobengula, when suddenly confronted
with Umnombate's proposals, took fright. Like the others
he had assumed that one or other of his absent brothers
would reappear at the proper moment, and never contemplated the prospect of himself filling the position of king.
He foresaw plots against his life, and was so scared that he
fled from his kraal and took refuge with the missionaries,
who had some difficulty in persuading him to return.

The situation was one calling for all Umnombate's diplomatic craft, and he was equal to the occasion. He undertook to send a deputation of headmen to Zululand to make
enquiries as to Nkulumane, and nominated as members his
own son Mhlaba [1] and a natural son of the late king,

---

[1] In later years Chief Councillor to Lobengula.

Mangwana, who was the commander of a military kraal, and, though not regarded as of the blood royal, had already begun to throw out hints suggesting that he aspired to fill the vacant throne.[1] Pending their return Umnombate contrived to get himself appointed as regent, and occupied the time of waiting publicly in organising on a grand scale the obsequies of Mziligazi, and privately in coaching Lobengula, whose nervousness he had managed in some degree to allay, in the duties of kingship.

Upon Mziligazi's death his body was sewn up, according to Zulu custom where great chiefs were concerned, in the freshly-flayed hides of two oxen, and was guarded in the royal quarters at Mhlahlanhlela by twelve of his widows until it became so decomposed that removal was imperative. The corpse was then placed on a waggon, which with infinite pains was dragged—in some places by a human team —into the heart of the grim and trackless Matopo mountains, and deposited in a cave, known as Ntumbane, hidden among the granite defiles. Fifty black cattle were slaughtered as an offering to the ancestral ghosts, and the spirit of Mziligazi himself formally introduced and commended to them. A second waggon was loaded with the chief's private possessions—his spear and shield, his skin rugs and chair, his eating and drinking vessels and everything he had used in his lifetime, all of which were placed in an adjoining cave. After the sacrifices and ritual observances were over the mouths of both caves were blocked with boulders. There, with the grey and ancient peaks towering

---

[1] The despatch of this embassy and its official reception in Natal were facilitated by Sir John Swinburne, then working at the Tati gold fields, who, as a reward, was granted exclusive permission by Umnombate to take an expedition to Matshayangombi's town in the Umfuli district of Mashonaland, to satisfy himself as to the gold discoveries made there by the German Mauch. (Thomas, *Eleven Years*, etc., p. 398.) Later on, owing to the disturbed condition of the country, all whites were recalled and, excepting the missionaries, ordered to leave the country. (Mohr, *Victoria Falls*, etc., p. 190.)

above as sentinels, the remains of the famous despot were laid to rest.[1]

In due course the deputation of headmen returned from Zululand with the announcement that they had failed to find any trace of Nkulumane or his brother. This enabled Umnombate to point publicly to Lobengula as the proper successor to his father, and to proceed with preparations for his formal investiture. But there was still a strong party which clung to the belief that the missing heir would be found, and refused to acknowledge any other king. The leader of this section was one Mbigo, the powerful *induna* of the Zwang-Indaba division of the army, 5,000 strong, to which Nkulumane had formerly belonged. Their opposition to Lobengula gained encouragement on the receipt of a report—which must rather have puzzled Umnombate— that Nkulumane had turned up in Natal, and was on his way to take up his inheritance. It transpired that a native known as Kanda, who had for some years been in the employ of Mr. (afterwards Sir Theophilus) Shepstone, the Natal Secretary for Native Affairs, had suddenly announced that he was the man for whom search was being made;

[1] Long afterwards—during the Matabele rebellion of 1896—the caves were discovered by some white soldiers, who thoughtlessly dragged their contents to light. This act of desecration caused intense anger among the rebel chiefs, and nearly led to the breakdown of the negotiations for peace, which had then reached a critical stage. The situation was saved by the prompt action of Cecil Rhodes, who went to the spot, ordered the remains to be carefully replaced, and appeased the wounded feelings of the chiefs by providing them with ten black oxen as a propitiatory sacrifice. The incident is related in Sir James McDonald's *Rhodes—A Life* (pp. 259-63).

The present writer was informed by Mr. Rhodes that the skeleton of Mziligazi had been found in a sitting position on a throne of stones, with the empty sockets of the eyes turned towards an opening in the granite barricade at the entrance of the cave, as if his eyes were to gaze for ever on the land over which he had reigned so long. This made a great impression on Rhodes, and may have inspired him with the thought of choosing the Matopo Hills for his own last resting-place.

that he had hitherto concealed his identity through fear of the Zulus, who still bore a grudge against Mziligazi's family and would have killed him, and that he could produce incontrovertible proofs of his claim. His pretensions were to some extent supported by the Governor of Natal, who appears indiscreetly to have accepted his *bona fides.* Kanda started up country and, in July, 1869,[1] reached Shoshong where he claimed hospitality from Macheng. He seems to have taken it for granted that he had only to show himself in Matabeleland for the whole tribe to rally at once to his standard and welcome him as their king, and his confidence so impressed Macheng that he lent him a considerable force of armed men to act as an escort.

But he had reckoned without Umnombate, who heard all about his movements and promptly despatched a force to meet him. The escort of ba-Mangwato, who had been sent out without their proper commander, Khama, and in his absence had no stomach for a fight with the Matabele, deserted, and the pretender was compelled to beat an ignominious retreat. He remained for some time an unwelcome guest at Shoshong and ultimately retired to his former obscurity in Natal.

The road was now clear for Lobengula, who, on March 17, 1870, was formally installed at Mhlahlanhlela as King of the Matabele. The inaugural functions, which lasted for several days, were of a most imposing character, and were attended by upwards of seven thousand warriors. A full description of the barbaric ceremonies is given by Thomas, who was present, but it is too long to be repeated here.[2] In accordance with Zulu precedent the king then built himself a new town, at first known as Gibixegu, but afterwards renamed Bulawayo, and settled down to the unenviable task which had been thrust upon him.

[1] Mohr, *Victoria Falls,* etc., p. 138.
[2] *Eleven Years,* etc., pp. 231-40.

From a life of comparative seclusion, occupied mainly in hunting, with occasional interludes of service in the national army, Lobengula had suddenly been exalted to a position which bristled with dangers and embarrassments. He succeeded a man who was the father and creator of the tribe, and had held it together by his military genius and inflexible will-power. He, with no outstanding exploits of arms to his credit, with no experience of statecraft, was called upon to undertake the control of a body of obstreperous hotheads who only respected force and an iron discipline. He was surrounded by his father's old councillors, who would be quick to detect any sign of weakness, and would resent the slightest deviation from established procedure, and he was confronted in addition with a problem which in the past had been little more than a vague threat—the problem of the growing stream of white adventurers, attracted by the gold, whose intrusion would speedily become troublesome if they were not kept within rigid bounds.

But if Lobengula lacked the arrogant self-confidence which had enabled Mziligazi to carry matters with a high hand he had more than an ordinary share of natural subtlety. Among his people he could count on no friends— with the possible exception of Umnombate—and outside them no well-wishers save the missionaries, who seem to have cherished hopes that they might influence him to abandon at least some of the objectionable practices which had made the name of Mziligazi a terror in the land. These latter he made it his policy to conciliate. He saw that their aims were entirely disinterested, and in certain respects opposed to those of the trading and gold-seeking class, and he was intelligent enough to grasp the importance of making them his allies. At the outset of his reign he attended their religious services ; offered them sites for additional stations, and, while not committing himself to

the relinquishment of the annual raids, professed a desire to
abolish the enslavement of the subject tribes. He gave the
missionaries an assurance that no one accused of sorcery
should be put to death without a proper trial, and he
avowed the intention of limiting his harem to a few necessary wives in place of the multitude of concubines maintained by his father.[1] Most of these fair promises were
afterwards broken, but at the time they served his purpose.
Morgan Thomas, who left Matabeleland within a few
months of Lobengula's accession, was convinced of his
sincerity, and felt that a new era was dawning.[2]

With his own people the young King was equally successful in creating a good impression. He had for one thing the
advantage of immense physical bulk, and was outwardly a
far more commanding figure than Mziligazi. But an imposing outward mien would not by itself have been sufficient
to secure the respect of such a tribe as the Matabele, who
looked for deeds, and whose animal passions could only be
satisfied by fighting and feasting. Some achievement of
arms was demanded, and very early in his reign fortune
placed in Lobengula's hands the opportunity of proving his
mettle. Mbigo, the *induna* of Zwang-indaba, persisted in
treating him as a usurper ; swore that he would never submit to him, and gained the support of a considerable section
of the army. The King at first tried conciliation, and sent
messengers inviting him to come and thrash the matter
out, but these overtures elicited nothing but scornful and
insolent replies. Umnombate was then sent to mediate,
but was fired on and driven away. It was imperative for
Lobengula, if he wished to retain his position, to resort to
force, and he led the loyal regiments of his army to attack
Mbigo at his military kraal, which lay some forty miles
north of Gibixegu. It was the first time that Matabele had

---

[1] Thomas, *Eleven Years*, etc., pp. 411-13.

[2] Thomas, *op. cit.* p. 415.

fought Matabele ; the two forces were fairly well matched, and their tactics were alike. The fiercest battle in the history of the tribe ensued, and there was heavy slaughter on both sides. At last Mbigo himself fell, mortally wounded. This turned the scale in the king's favour, and discouraged the rebels, who fled in disorder. The Zwang-indaba kraals were burnt and the women seized—with additional zest because they were of the same blood and kin as their captors. Lobengula marched back with his victorious *impi* drunk with carnage, chanting their songs of victory, acting again in pantomime their exploits with assegai and knob-kerrie, and driving before them a great mob of looted cattle. These Lobengula distributed to the regiments to provide them with an orgy of beef.

Such a triumph had a powerful effect on the tribe, and raised the new king to a pinnacle of popularity. He had proved himself a valorous warrior and a generous pillager—a man after their own heart. All opposition died down completely, and all talk of Nkulumane was silenced for ever.

CHAPTER IX

BLACK DESPOTS AT THEIR WORST

I. THE STORY OF MACHENG

IT was fortunate for the Matabele that, when the critical moment came, they had, in Umnombate, a man with a definite purpose; a man who, when he saw the quicksands and breakers ahead of his tribe, took the helm and steered it into smooth water. With the ba-Mangwato the case was very different. Their strong man had not yet appeared and they were destined to be tossed about for a long time to come in a maelstrom of troubles.

When we last took a look at them Sekhome's plots against his sons, the outcome of his hatred for their new-fangled ideas, had recoiled on his own head. Once again he found himself an exile, supplanted by his detested brother. If he cherished any affection for his tribe—and from the careful way in which he had built it up and nursed it through its troubles we may give him the credit for some such feeling—there was the added bitterness of expectation that in the feeble hands of an incompetent drunkard, who was moreover in all essentials an alien, it would soon slip back into chaos. And in this expectation he would not have been deceived. In every way Macheng proved himself a useless drone. He paid little attention to tribal observances. He had none of Sekhome's skill as a rain-maker, and took no trouble to keep up the customary ceremonies of sacrifice to the ancestral spirits; he was slack in the exercise of his

judicial powers ; disputes were left unsettled and crimes
went unpunished. There was no security of property. The
white traders found themselves robbed and could obtain no
redress. The more reputable among them were disgusted
at the general laxity, and made preparations to pack up and
quit. Shoshong, once the principal up-country trading
centre, the established mart for ivory from the far interior,[1]
got a bad name with Europeans, and only a few of the riff-
raff remained there.

Khama and Khamani, though now free from the persecutions of their father, were in no better plight. They were
leading a miserable existence, watching matters go from
bad to worse, and powerless to stop the rot. They were
sustained by their devotion to the new religion and occupied
much of their time in trying to bring others to their way of
thinking. Without actually making many converts they
did succeed in attracting a large following among the
younger generation, who disliked Macheng's Matabele ways,
and would have welcomed Khama as their chief. But the
ba-Mangwato as a tribe were apathetic, and disinclined for
revolution or violence. Loyalty to the rules of descent—a
characteristic of most Bantu peoples—was in them peculiarly developed. They accepted Macheng, the legitimate
heir of the great Khari,[2] as their chief by right of birth, and
however much they might resent his misrule were too supine
to strike a blow to end it.

If Macheng had been content to remain quiet, and to
refrain from mixing himself up in matters which did not
concern him, he would probably have retained his position

---

[1] The missionary Coillard estimated that more than 150,000 lbs.
of ivory, representing the tusks of over 12,000 elephants, passed
through the hands of the traders at Shoshong in the year 1877, but
by that time business had resumed its normal flow. (*On the Threshold
of Central Africa*, p. 49.)

[2] The irony of the fact that he could not have had a drop of
Khari's blood in his veins was lost on them. (See chap. v, p. 60.)

until, in the natural course of events, he died of drink, but
he brought about his own downfall by his folly in espousing
the cause of the pretender Nkulumane.

It has already been mentioned that he sent a body of
fighting men to escort this pretender to Matabeleland.
One of the regiments so despatched was 'Khama's Own',
and by rights Khama should have led it in person. But it
was contrary to the principles he had absorbed from his
Christian teaching to engage in any aggressive expedition,
particularly one that was concerned with the politics of
another nation. Apart from this Macheng had no love for
Khama whom he consistently ignored, and he attempted to
supersede him by giving the command to one of his own satellites. This put up the backs of the whole corps, which
mutinied and left Nkulumane in the lurch, stating that they
would obey no one but their regular captain. The chief was
greatly incensed, and from that moment took every opportunity of irritating Khama, and of making his position and
that of his partisans intolerable. For some time Khama,
together with his staunch ally Khamani, exercised the
utmost forbearance, and though the tribe was split into
two factions they carefully avoided an open breach. They
were engrossed in their religion, and all they wanted was to
be left alone. Finding that he could not goad Khama into
any overt act which would provide an excuse for attacking
them Macheng resorted to sorcery, and began to work
secretly with spells in the hope of compassing their death.
When these failed he resolved on a direct attempt to poison
them. He secured the help of a disreputable white man,
who undertook, in return for a heavy bribe of ivory, to
procure a few doses of strychnine, which was kept by one of
the store-keepers for the purpose of destroying wolves. In
due course he handed a small bottle to Macheng, who then
invited Khama and his brother to his house to a meal,
hoping to induce them to partake of some coffee, which he

would carefully doctor. But this unusual access of hospitality put them on their guard, and they declined the invitation. It afterwards came to light that the storekeeper's suspicions had been aroused, and that instead of strychnine he had supplied Macheng's accomplice with a bottle of ordinary marking ink ! The story was too good to be wasted, and the chief found that he had made himself the laughing stock of the whole community.

It was not, however, a laughing matter for the two young men concerned, and when, a few days later, they discovered that another of Sekhome's sons, Raditladi, had been suborned by Macheng to murder them their patient endurance broke down. They realised that there would be no peace for them or for the tribe unless the author of these odious plots was finally removed. They were still loth to act on their own responsibility or otherwise than in a constitutional manner. Once more therefore they appealed to their patron Sechele—that 'remarkably intelligent chief', as Livingstone calls him—who had first helped Macheng to oust their own father Sekhome ; had then removed Macheng to restore Sekhome, and had finally egged on Macheng to reassume the chieftaincy. Three times he had put his finger into the Mangwato pie, and he was perfectly willing to oblige again for a fourth time on the usual commission terms. In August, 1872, he despatched a strong force of ba-Kwena in charge of his principal son Sebele. In three days they reached Shoshong and camped for the night in the bush outside the town. At the first streak of dawn they drew in close without being observed and suddenly opened fire on Macheng's quarters. The chief, startled out of his sleep, hurried from his hut, and as he stepped into the *kothla* found himself surrounded by Sebele's troops, with whom were Khama and a few of the ba-Mangwato. A sorry figure he cut, trembling with fright, crapulous from the previous day's potations, and shivering in the chilly

morning air, for in his agitation he had not stopped to dress,
and had no clothes to cover his corpulent nakedness.
Sebele was for putting him to death at once, but Khama,
whose missionary training made him recoil from bloodshed,
begged that his life might be spared. He was therefore
released, and roughly told to quit the town forthwith, an
order he lost no time in obeying.

In the confused hurly-burly of the first assault about
twenty of Macheng's friends, including six of his councillors
and some of the Matabele youths who formed his retinue
and shared his debauches, were shot dead. Most of the
common people, who had been taken by surprise, slunk out
of sight, and concealed themselves in the labyrinthine
passages between the groups of huts, which afforded abundant hiding places ; but Sebele's men started a fire, which
spread rapidly through the dwellings of wood and thatch
and drove them into the open. In their consternation and
uncertainty as to what their fate might be they fled after
their chief into the hills round Shoshong, whence for some
hours an intermittent fire was directed on the wells from
which the tribe drew their water, but towards evening
Khama took out a party of horsemen and dispersed them.
This gave them a clue to the position and a lead. They
grasped the fact that the struggle was between Khama and
Macheng, and their sympathies at once veered towards the
former. In the course of the night they crept back to the
half-gutted town, and Macheng was deserted. He sought
refuge in one kraal after another, but he had no friends
among the neighbouring petty chiefs, and found himself an
outcast. Eventually he made his way to southern Bechuanaland, where in a few months he drank himself to death.

On the day following his successful coup Sebele sent out
orders to the Mangwato headmen to assemble in the *kothla*,
and as soon as a sufficient number overcame their panic and
answered the summons he called upon them, in the name of

his father, to adopt Khama as their chief. In their agitated
condition of mind they were ready to agree to any course
which seemed to promise peace. The only dissentient was
Khama himself, who disclaimed any idea of aspiring to the
doubtful honour, and recommended the recall of Sekhome,
but on being informed that this would not be allowed by
Sechele, and receiving assurances that his own acceptance
was the desire of all the headmen, he somewhat reluctantly
gave his consent.

One source of mischief was fortunately removed. The
soi-disant Nkulumane thought it wise to save his skin, and
disappeared in the general confusion, leaving behind him a
herd of cattle which he had collected on his abortive expedition to Matabeleland, and these were promptly im-
pounded by Sebele, and carried off to his father.

II. KHAMA COMES INTO HIS OWN

It might have been thought that after the flight of
Macheng and Nkulumane, and with Sekhome safely out of
the way, Khama would have entered upon his new duties
with a certain amount of confidence. Such, however, was
far from being the case. Owing to a conflict between his
conscientious respect for parental authority and his yearning for reform he brought upon himself a regular pack of
troubles. He earnestly desired to put a stop to the superstitious cults so dear to the tribe, and one would have
expected that the last thing in his mind would be the return
of Sekhome, who had always been a stickler for their strict
observance. Added to this Sekhome had bullied him, con-
spired against him and more than once threatened his life.
He had every justification therefore for keeping him at a
distance. Yet one of the first steps he took was to send an
invitation to Sekhome to come back to Shoshong. The only
credible explanation of this suicidal action is that at this

period of his life Khama's religious zeal had inspired him with a morbid sense of filial responsibility. His humility and forbearance amounted to an obsession, and he seems to have thought that there would be something noble in suffering the martyrdom of his father's presence. Towards the end of 1872—within a few months, that is, of Khama's accession—Sekhome responded to the call, and on his arrival in Shoshong immediately began to stir up mischief. But this time he made use of new tactics. Hitherto Khama and Khamani had lived together in perfect brotherly harmony ; both were enthusiastic Christians, and both were pledged to repress the heathen rites and practices to which the ba-Mangwato were addicted. But Khamani was apparently the weaker vessel. It was to him that Sekhome now addressed himself, and by cajolery and subtle insinuations he gradually succeeded in arousing in him feelings of jealousy and in alienating his affections from his brother. He threw out hints that he could manoeuvre Khamani into the position of chief, and went so far as to arrange that he should assume the control of one of the subject tribes of Bushmen, a dignity which had always been the prerogative of the eldest of the royal sons of the reigning chief, like that of Prince of Wales with us. It was a terrible blow to Khama, and he was still more distressed when he realised that Khamani had become his father's tool and was deeply involved in a conspiracy against himself.

This trouble Khama had unquestionably brought on his own head by his insane anxiety to play the part of the dutiful son. There were others which arose from his attitude towards the traditionary customs of the tribe. As chief he was expected to act as Master of the Ceremonies in all the old-fashioned rites. As a devout Christian he had been taught to regard them as devilish and accursed. It happened that the year 1873 was marked by a severe drought. In former days the chief would have resorted to rain-making magic, and the duty now devolved on Khama. The older men of the tribe demanded that he should propitiate the ancestral mumbo-jumbo and conduct the prescribed sacrifices, and were greatly disappointed—if not shocked, when they were met by a point-blank refusal. Their alarm was fomented by Sekhome, and public feeling ran so high that Khama thought it prudent to compromise. He informed the agitators that if they were determined to have their ceremonies they could get them performed by someone else. He would not forbid them, but would take no part in them, nor would he provide cattle for sacrifices. This answer, while by no means allaying the prevailing uneasiness, threw the malcontents into the arms of Sekhome. It also put a weapon in the hands of Khamani, who accused his brother of hypocrisy, and reported to the missionaries that while openly denouncing the rain-making business, he was secretly encouraging—if not actually practising it.

Finally Khama's burning ambition to put down the traffic in drink created strained relations with some of the white traders. Shortly after he assumed the reins of government he called them to a meeting, at which he stated that he would allow no liquor to be sold to his people or even to be brought into the country. His decision was received with mixed feelings. The better class of traders saw its wisdom and promised compliance, but a certain number caused bitter indignation in Khama's mind by continuing to smuggle in brandy, secretly purveying it to the kraal natives, and indulging among themselves in noisy carousals.

From all this it may be seen that Khama found the task of ruling according to his own ideals anything but an easy one. He was not so firmly in the saddle as to feel confidence in his capacity to keep his seat, and his moral courage was not yet strong enough to tempt him to use coercion to force the pace. The constant pressure of public opinion for the resumption of the ancient magic-mongering ; the carking anxiety caused by the plots of that old man of the sea Sekhome ; the treachery of his brother, and the covert attempts of low white men to evade his prohibition policy proved too strong a combination of forces. He lost heart, brooded over his troubles, and concluded that he was a failure. He decided to leave Shoshong, and to move, with as many of his friends as chose to follow him, to some place where he would no longer have to maintain the uphill struggle. Sekhome and the other reactionaries could be left at Shoshong to stew in their own juice. He would wash his hands of the place, and of them.

With these ideas he first migrated to his own private cattle post at Serowe, about forty-five miles to the north-west, where there was an abundant and perennial stream of good water. He let it be known that this would be his head-quarters, and that he was prepared to welcome any of his fellow-tribesmen who cared to join him there. Somewhat to his surprise, and greatly to his satisfaction, a large portion of the tribe at once flocked out, and for several weeks the exodus went on, until Shoshong was nearly deserted— only Sekhome, Khamani, and a few of the older men remaining behind. But Serowe was an exposed and defence-less spot, too close for safety to the Matabele border, and the responsibility of looking after so large a number of the people, including many women and children, convinced Khama that a further move was imperative. He resolved to push on towards Lake Ngami, and thereby to ensure freedom from attack, while increasing the distance between his followers and their old associations. It was an unfortunate decision, as the route lay for 150 miles across a stretch of desert country, and he was unable to find sufficient water or pasture for his cattle, or to keep them together. Some stragglers fell into the hands of a Boer hunter, and were claimed and taken over by Sekhome, who also seized and forced back to Shoshong a number of women who had become separated from Khama's main body. This outrage seems to have been too much even for Khama's patience, and to have put an end to his irresolution once and for all. Feeling that he had at his back what was practically the whole tribe he made up his mind to recover the women and cattle, if necessary by force, and with this intention he returned with an armed party to the hills round Shoshong. He reconnoitred the position, and satisfied himself that he could count on the allegiance of the subject tribes, and after a slight skirmish with a few of Sekhome's scouts went back to rejoin his own people and to make ready for an organised attempt at a later date to reoccupy the capital of the country of which he had been appointed chief. His short sojourn in the Lake district had proved that it was unsuitable in every respect for a permanent settlement, and he was as eager now to leave it as he had before been to reach it.

In January, 1875, he marched on Shoshong with his whole force, leading them in person, but keeping the women and children well in rear. Shoshong (or ' Old Mangwato ', as it was sometimes called) was described by one who visited it in that year as a collection of huts at the edge of a dry sandy plain under the shadow of the mountains, which afforded an easy refuge in time of warfare. The huts and stores of a few English traders, built of wood or clay, were grouped together at one extremity of the town. The only water in the dry season was got from a small stream up a gorge behind the town some distance away, whence it was carried to the dwellings in gourds and earthenware vessels on the heads of the women. In this gorge stood the church and houses of the missionaries. The level ground below the town was cultivated to a depth of two or three miles, but no attempt had been made to irrigate it. In spite of its unfavourable situation Shoshong—abandoned in 1889 in favour of a much more desirable site at Palapye, forty miles

to the north-east—was by far the biggest native kraal
south of the Zambesi, and contained about 30,000 souls.

On arrival at the outskirts Khama sent messages to his
father to announce his intention of asserting his rights, and
to let him know that he would give battle if his entry was
disputed. Sekhome was defiant. He had been prepared
for some such move, and had taken great pains to consolidate his forces. He was, however, outmanoeuvred by
Khama, whose first step was to seize the springs from which
the water supply was obtained. He then lined the hills
overshadowing the huge sprawling town with his sharpshooters, and with his mounted men proceeded to clear the
valley. For what followed we have only the confused
accounts of the missionaries, Mackenzie and Hepburn, who
were too busily occupied in looking after the wounded to
give more than a general idea of the course of the fighting.
But it is certain that Khama's forces won all along the line.
Most of Sekhome's men were commandeered from the subject tribes round about, who lost heart after the first few
casualties, and made haste to get out of range. The remnant that stood their ground were hunted out of the kloofs
and ravines and driven into the open, where their losses
were heavy. Sekhome and Khamani, seeing that the day
was going against them, took flight, and no effort was made
to follow them. Khama then entered the royal *kothla* and
was once more—and this time finally—acclaimed as chief.

Some time later, when he thought that his father's capacity for mischief was exhausted, Khama allowed him, on
promise of good behaviour, to return to Shoshong. After
all his previous experience it was a risky step, but it was
unattended by bad results. Though not a very old man
Sekhome had outlived his times, and his own folly and
vacillation had entirely destroyed his prestige with the
tribe. He lingered on a few years as his son's pensioner, and
died in 1883.

III. BAROTSE POLITICS

South of the Zambesi the principal tribes were now beginning to settle into the conditions which existed within the memory of Englishmen still living. Little more than a generation ago the names of Lobengula and Khama were household words in South Africa, and were linked with those of intrepid British pioneers who left a permanent mark on history. Prominent among these was Frederick Courtenay Selous, who made his first journey to the Mangwato and Matabele countries in 1872. He did not aspire to be regarded as a historian, but he kept careful journals, and his straightforward narratives of hunting adventures contain many notes which throw a vivid light on the state of the native tribes, and the manner in which they reacted to the first contact with civilisation. He draws, for instance, a sharp contrast between the evil condition of Shoshong on his first visit, when Macheng was chief, and the improvement which had been wrought by Khama, when he was once more there seven years later.

The railways and telegraphs were of course still a long way off, but individual natives were travelling on foot in increasing numbers to work at the diamond diggings in the south, and when they came back to their kraals spread reports of their experiences among the white men ; of their shops and wonderful machinery ; their soldiers, engineers and doctors. The kraal natives were shedding their cloaks and kilts of skin and developing an absurd mania for white men's coats, hats and trousers, and especially for discarded uniforms, for all of which there was a steady demand, and the traders found it a profitable business to buy shoddy and second-hand European garments for retail. Unfortunately with the clothes the natives adopted bad habits as well, and drink and syphilis threatened to sap the vitality of peoples whose lives had formerly been free from any destructive agencies other than the wars and raids which with primitive races are nature's means of preventing overpopulation. One of the more satisfactory results of the freer intercourse between the whites and the natives was the growth of an intense interest in that distant woman ruler whom the British obeyed—Queen Victoria, and her name became invested with a sort of mysterious reverence, akin to, but even stronger than the feelings which the Bantu races entertained for their own departed chiefs. The ' Great White Queen ' soon became a symbol of the white man's power—something which, although in the background, stood for motherly protection and an all-embracing security.

North of the Zambesi, however, there was little sign as yet of an improvement in the conditions. The tribes had not shown the least tendency towards an emergence from their primeval barbarism, and were still struggling in a confused turmoil of upheavals and bloody strife. For a long time after Livingstone's departure and the tragic end of Helmore's expedition no missionaries dared to approach these dangerous regions, and, up to the middle seventies, only one white man, whose name is now almost forgotten, succeeded in establishing any sort of foothold among the ba-Rotse and other tribes on the river. This was George Westbeech, whose career was crowded with adventure and romance. Between 1863 and 1868 he was trading and hunting in Matabeleland, where he gained a high reputation with Mziligazi and his people for straight dealing. Just before the old king's death he was shooting near the Mazoe river in Mashonaland, being the first to penetrate so far. He was bold enough to remain in the country when, owing to its unsettled state, all other white men left it, and he was present at the accession and investiture of Lobengula. In 1871 he struck out for Barotseland, and obtained leave from the King—it was during the short reign of the tyrant Sepopo —to ascend the river to parts where only Livingstone had

preceded him.   Later on he made his permanent head-
quarters at Panda-ma-Tenka, south of the Zambesi, and for
some years made regular trips to Lialui, where by honest
and fair trading he did much to counteract the evil influence
of the rascally Mambari half-breeds, whose primary object
was the purchase of slaves.   He reaped a rich reward, for
between 1871 and 1876 he sent away from his station no
less than 30,000 lbs. of ivory.   When other hunters, explorers and missionaries began to make their way to these
fields of enterprise where Westbeech had so long laboured
alone they found him anxious to befriend them and to
smooth their path with the difficult chiefs, and his generous
hospitality and ungrudging support won their universal
regard.   His iron constitution broke down at last under
repeated attacks of fever.   He died at the Jesuit mission
station on the Zambesi in 1889—just before the arrival of
the first expedition sent there by Rhodes—having done
more to open up the river area than any individual pioneer.

Unfortunately Westbeech left no written journals, and
for what befel the ba-Rotse during the twenty years which
followed their successful revolt against the Makololo we
have once more to rely mainly on the statements of natives
collected and recorded by missionaries and others.

The revolution left them dominant but without a head.
There were, however, several descendants of their old royal
line with claims to the succession.   The last of the hereditary chiefs of the tribe had been Marambwa, whose death
had given Sebitoane the opportunity of stepping in and
establishing his own authority.   This man left a number of
sons, one of whom, Sepopo, was still alive when the Makololo dominion came to an end.   He had for many years been
living in exile among the ma-Mbunda, a tribe scattered over
a large district three hundred miles or more to the west of
Sesheke, and he was now brought back by the ba-Rotse
headmen and proclaimed their king.   As a race the ba-

Rotse were addicted to revolting cruelties beside which
the murderous exploits of the Matabele appear almost insignificant, and Sepopo, by all accounts, was true to the
national character. He was fertile in the invention of new
methods of torture. One of his favourite diversions was to
fling live babies into the Zambesi at Sesheke so that he
might watch their struggles from the bank, and listen to
their dying screams as they were fought for by the crocodiles which infested the sluggish stream. Occasionally he
would vary the amusement by having the helpless children
dismembered first and throwing them bit by bit to the
greedy monsters, as one feeds ducks in a pond.[1] After he
had reigned about five years his brutalities brought him
into conflict with some of his headmen, who organised an
armed revolt against him. He fled for safety to an island
on the river, but was shot in the back by one of his own
servants, and perished miserably.

At his death there were three young men—all grandsons
of Marambwa—with about equal claims to succeed—
Ngwana-Wina, Akafuna (also known as Tatira) and Robosi.[2] The choice of the tribe fell on the first named, but
his reign was brief and ignominious. His cousin Robosi, a
forceful man in the prime of life, who had on his side a good
many of the pure-blooded ba-Rotse from the districts
higher up the river, headed another revolution. He had
little difficulty in driving away the young king (of whom no
more was ever heard) and in getting himself accepted as his
successor. But to hold the power he had thus usurped was a

---

[1] Coillard, *On the Threshold of Central Africa*, p. 57. Mackintosh,
Coillard of the Zambesi, p. 270. The crocodiles of Sesheke seem to
have retained a lively memory of these feasts, for until quite recently
they were peculiarly bold and voracious, and levied a constant toll
from the women and children who went to the river-side to fetch
water or wash clothes.

[2] Robosi afterwards adopted the name of Lewanika, by which he
is much better known.

very different matter, for of all the Zambesi tribes the ba-
Rotse were the most fickle and the most addicted to secret
conspiracies.   Had not Robosi himself been possessed of
unusual strategy and statecraft he would speedily have
shared the fate of his predecessors.   Even so he had a
stormy time in front of him, and many ups and downs of
fortune, the narration of which must be left to a future
chapter.

NOTE.—The relationship of Marambwa's descendants is
differently stated by various authorities, but the following table
is an attempt to reconcile the particulars as far as possible.
The names of those who actually became chiefs are printed in
capitals :

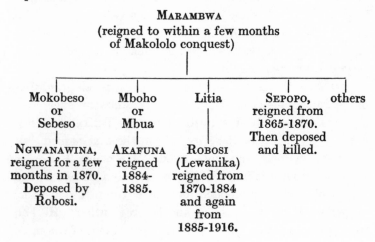

MARAMBWA
(reigned to within a few months
of Makololo conquest)

Mokobeso or Sebeso	Mboho or Mbua	Litia	SEPOPO, others reigned from 1865-1870. Then deposed and killed.
NGWANAWINA, reigned for a few months in 1870. Deposed by Robosi.	AKAFUNA reigned 1884-1885.	ROBOSI (Lewanika) reigned from 1870-1884 and again from 1885-1916.	

CHAPTER X

THE BRITISH PROTECTORATE

I. THE BOER PERIL

DOMESTIC feuds, wars of mutual rivalry and wars of pillage had been keeping these Bantu tribes in a ferment for upwards of fifty years. About 1875 there seemed to come a lull. Three black monarchies were left standing like rocks. The angry waters of internal strife were stilled and the horizon around looked clear. Khama, Lobengula and Robosi (Lewanika), the autocrats of the dominant tribes, were unaware, or at any rate unapprehensive, of the forces which were gathering strength outside their kingdoms—forces working at first imperceptibly and independently, but always in the same direction, and gaining by degrees a momentum which was to shake the foundations of the native body politic from Cape Colony to the Congo.

One source of danger—the first to become manifest—was the restlessness of the Transvaal Boers, whose roving and land-grabbing propensities had for years menaced the independent tribes of southern Bechuanaland, and before long began to cause uneasiness further afield. An influence, at first insidious, but in the end overwhelming, was the competition among civilised races to acquire tracts of Africa for colonising purposes. This had its origin in H. M. Stanley's explorations in the Congo basin in 1875, and was brought into the sphere of European politics, from motives the reverse of altruistic, by Queen Victoria's dis-

solute cousin Leopold, King of the Belgians. In the scramble
that ensued the Boers were not conscious participants, but
their insatiable greed for territory precipitated the activities of other Powers.   As far as our own Government is
concerned it is as well to remember that although it con-
nived at the annexation of Griqualand West, on account of
its valuable diamond deposits, the idea of a general forward
movement of British expansion was not conceived nor
favoured in Downing Street.   It was a slow growth, prompted by the trend of outside circumstances, and fostered by
the exertions of a few Englishmen—notably Sir Bartle
Frere and Cecil Rhodes—whose vision was longer and
clearer than that of their contemporaries.

A third agent in the undermining of the native autocracies was the rapid development of the diamond and gold
industries, which brought upon the scene a swarm of prospectors, diggers and speculators from all parts of the world,
attracted first to Kimberley, later on to de Kaap and
Witwatersrand, and ultimately to the almost forgotten
reefs found by Mauch in the far north.

To take the Boers first—it was apparent from the outset
that no conventional frontier lines could keep them within
bounds.   They were for ever trying to ' burst their kraal '
by encroachment on the native territories lying to their
east, west and south.   For some of these excursions their
government was directly responsible, while others were
bare-faced, plundering forays on the part of lawless and
ill-controlled burghers.   In the north they were more
cautious.   Their previous encounters with Mziligazi had
taught them a wholesome respect for the cold blades of
Matabele assegais, and forced them to curb their lust for
the grazing and hunting veld beyond the Limpopo river.
The milder Bechuana peoples were easier victims, and
hardly a year passed without a raid on one or other of the
border tribes by marauding parties on the look-out for

cattle and labourers. The Boers did not seem to find such conduct inconsistent with their narrow religious creed. From a long course of struggles with Hottentots and Bushmen they had come to regard the coloured races of all kinds as their natural enemies and lawful prey. Their only use was as herds and workers on the land, provided by Divine Providence for the express convenience of white men.[1] As human beings they were of small account. In deference to outside prejudices the Boers hypocritically described this servitude as 'apprenticeship', but actually it differed very little from slavery.

Two of the chiefs most sorely afflicted—Montsioa, of the ba-Rolong tribe and Mankoroane, of the ba-Tlapin—sent repeated appeals for assistance to the Cape authorities, but without avail. Within a year of his accession Khama wrote the following letter to Sir Henry Barkly, the High Commissioner : [2]

' I, Khama, King of the ba-Mangwato, greet Victoria, the great Queen of the English people.

' I write to you, Sir Henry, in order that your Queen may preserve for me my country, it being in her hands. The Boers are coming into it and I do not like them. Their actions are cruel among us black people. We are like money ; they sell us and our children. I ask Her Majesty to pity me and to hear that which I write quickly. I wish to hear upon what conditions Her Majesty will receive me and my country and my people under her protection. I am weary with fighting. I do not like war, and I ask Her Majesty to give me peace. I ask Her Majesty to defend me as she defends all her people. There are three things which distress me very much—war, selling people and drink. All these things I shall find in the Boers, and it is

---

[1] Time has by no means eradicated this view. Since these words were written the Member of Parliament for Hoopstad (Orange Free State) is reported to have stated publicly that he was totally opposed to the education of natives, for *God had placed them in Africa to serve the Whites*. (*South Africa*, Nov. 20, 1931.)

[2] Printed in *Blue Book*, C. 1748, p. 251.

these things which destroy people to make an end of them in the country. The custom of the Boers has always been to cause people to be sold, and to-day they are selling people. Last year I saw them pass with two waggons full of people whom they had bought at the river at Tauwane'.

The burdens of the luckless Bechuana were made heavier by other intruders. The opening-up of the diamond fields drew to South Africa a stream of adventurers, some of them of a reckless and disreputable type—unsuccessful miners from California and Australia ; fugitives from justice in England or other parts of Europe ; men of decent birth who had come to grief, and men of low origin who were birds of prey by nature. Some of this flotsam and jetsam drifted up to the Transvaal border. The majority started as traders, and a few stuck to legitimate business, but others belonged to a class that could not resist the opportunities for cattle-lifting and horse-stealing. The shady element predominated. There was no authority to check robbery and crimes of violence, and southern Bechuanaland became a sort of Alsatia.

Khama's moving appeal, like the others, fell on deaf ears. The truth was that the grievances of the Bechuana chiefs were dwarfed by the more pressing problems which now began to exercise the officials both in South Africa and at home. The Transvaal was threatened with reprisals from Zulus, Basutos and other tribes goaded into anger by border incursions ; its Government was in a hopeless state of insolvency, and the only course which could save the country from ruin was annexation. This step was taken in 1877. The burghers accepted the transition to Imperial control with sullen resignation ; the Bechuanas hailed it with relief, for they were confident that their obnoxious neighbours would henceforth be kept under lock and key.

Their satisfaction was shortlived. Within the next few years the British floundered in a regular morass of trouble.

In rapid succession came the Zulu War, the Basuto revolt—both the outcome of Boer quarrels—and finally the rebellion in the Transvaal, which brought disaster to our arms at Majuba, and was terminated by a humiliating evacuation.

In their anxiety to rid themselves of responsibility for the Transvaal the Gladstone Ministry took no precautions to safeguard the natives on its western borders, who were left once more to their fate. The Boers were not slow to take advantage of this neglect, but they were becoming more sophisticated, and were at some pains to clothe their designs with the outward garb of legality. On the pretext of settling a dispute between two rival chiefs living close to the frontier a number of burghers entered southern Bechuanaland and, as the price of mediation, obtained the grant of a large tract of land. Having thus secured a foothold they invited others to join them and in due course proclaimed the area so acquired a ' republic ', under the name of ' Stellaland '.[1] So successful was this stroke that it was repeated farther north, where a second republic—' Goshen ' —was founded, and both these upstart states became the resort of a reckless class of freebooter. One of the chiefs involved—the above-named Mankoroane—renewed his appeal to the Cape Government for assistance in maintaining order, and went so far as to offer to accept annexation. The House of Assembly responded by appointing a commission to enquire into the question of Mankoroane's boundaries—a trifling matter in itself, though it contained the germ of vast developments.

II. THE FREEBOOTER PERIL

One of the members of the Mankoroane commission, appointed to it at his own request, was Cecil Rhodes, who

[1] This name is said to have been chosen because the occupation took place at the time of the great comet of 1882. (*Blue Book*, C. 4643, p. 202.)

saw in it a chance of sowing the seed of a greater South
Africa, and so arranged matters as practically to usurp the
whole of its functions.   He had not then reached his
thirtieth year, and had only been a member of the Cape
Parliament for a few months, but he had already given
close study to the racial competition for supremacy between
English and Dutch, and knew that enormous issues were at
stake.   He saw that the design of the leading spirits in the
Transvaal was to interpose a barrier which should shut out
Cape Colony for ever from the territories north of the
Limpopo river, where the expeditions of hunters and explorers had proved the existence of an immense healthy
plateau eminently suited for white occupation, and where
gold reefs of fabulous richness were said to abound.
Bechuanaland itself was of no great value for colonisation,
but if Bechuanaland were seized a wall would be built
across the route to the north.   And Rhodes's intuitions
pictured a still more sinister prospect.   He was aware that
German missionaries and traders were settling on the coast
of south-west Africa—in Damaraland and Namaqualand,
where the Imperial Government, on the strength of an
insignificant strip of country held round Walfisch Bay,
complacently regarded British influence as established and
unassailable ; he knew that one of the reasons that prompted the annexation of the Transvaal in 1877 had been the
discovery that its Government, faced with insolvency and
dreading the prospect of having to submit to British rule,
had been coquetting with various European Powers—
Germany in particular—with the object of securing financial support and protection.[1]   He saw clearly and appre-
hensively the possibility of Germany, under Bismarck's
guidance, first appropriating some portion of the west coast,
and then stretching inland across the barren wastes of the

[1] Letter from Sir Bartle Frere to Mr. J. M. Maclean, quoted in
Pratt's *Leading Points in South African History*.

Kalahari to join hands with the Boers. If that came about it would only be a matter of time before a belt of German territory barred the way from the Atlantic to the Indian Ocean. Good-bye then to all hope of British expansion northwards !

Full of these thoughts Rhodes entered on his mission to the disturbed area, and in a few weeks came back with a petition from the Chief Mankoroane for annexation to the Cape and a cession of his territory as an earnest of good faith. To his intense chagrin the Ministry, nervous of giving offence to their Dutch constituents, whose sympathies were with the Transvaal, would have nothing to do with it. Rhodes then urged the Home Government to accept the proposal, and they agreed to do so if the Cape would bear half the cost of administration. But this also was more than the parochial minds of the local Ministry would entertain. Ultimately the Colonial Secretary (Lord Derby) caused Mankoroane to be informed that the Government would not interfere on his behalf, but that should he, or his neighbour Montsioa, be driven from their countries Great Britain would consider what pecuniary or other help could be given to them in the Colony !

Why, after this rebuff, the Bechuana chiefs continued to rely on Great Britain passes comprehension. The only conceivable explanation is that they were sustained by their almost superstitious trust in the ' Great White Queen '— an invisible presence, but a real one.

Just in the nick of time, however, the Home Government were startled out of their exasperating indifference by the very event that Rhodes had foreseen. The Germans occupied Angra Pequena, on the west coast,[1] in what was known as Namaqualand, and soon afterwards proclaimed sovereignty over the whole sea-board of seven hundred miles from Cape Frio in the north to the mouth of the Orange river in

[1] Now the chief centre of the recently discovered diamond field.

the south, completely enveloping the small British port of Walfisch Bay, and implying of course claims over the immediate *hinterland* as well.

With belated anxiety the Gladstone Ministry realised that something must be done to save their face in Bechuana-land, and instructed the High Commissioner to take the necessary action. Early in 1884 John Mackenzie the missionary, as being the person most thoroughly to be trusted, and the best acquainted with local conditions, was invited to proceed as Deputy Commissioner to the region of the new republics and to establish the Queen's authority there.

Mackenzie was a man of great courage and rigid con-scientiousness, but he was no tactician, and was, moreover, suspicious of the Cape politicians, regarding them as under the thumb of the newly-formed Afrikander Bond, whose aims were anti-British. There was more than a grain of truth in this supposition, but it was nevertheless unfor-tunate that he should have allowed such prejudices to in-fluence him at a time when racial feelings should have been kept out of sight. To him all Dutchmen, whether of the Transvaal or the Cape Colony, were tarred with the same brush. All were oppressors of the natives, and he felt it as much his duty to protect the Bechuana against government from Capetown as from persecution by the Transvaal. In his eyes only direct rule from Downing Street could save them. Immediately on arrival he entered into arrange-ments with the leading chiefs to accept British sovereignty ; proclaimed the whole of southern Bechuanaland British territory, and hoisted the British flag at Vryburg, the capital of Stellaland. But these demonstrations failed to impress the squatters, who, since Majuba and the retro-cession of the Transvaal, had ceased to entertain any pro-found respect for British authority, and were not in the mood to be dragooned by an ex-missionary with no armed force behind him. In fact Mackenzie only succeeded in irritating them, and his proposals were met with defiance. The two republics were soon in open rebellion, and the attacks on the natives went on as wantonly as ever.

Mackenzie was then recalled, and Rhodes, whose policy was to humour the Cape Dutch by annexing the country to the Colony, was appointed to succeed him. But Mackenzie had ' queered his pitch ', and although he managed, by guaranteeing their titles, to effect a favourable settlement with the Stellalanders, he failed as completely as his predecessor in Goshen, where, during his visit, and almost in front of his eyes, the freebooters attacked the Chief of Mafeking, and proceeded to divide up his land.

Providentially the Government at Pretoria, convinced that the fruit was now ready for plucking, lost their heads. Paul Kruger, the President, issued a proclamation taking the territories of the invaded chiefs under the protection of the Transvaal ' in the interests of humanity ', and thereby raised a storm which brought his whole house of cards tumbling to the ground. Indignation meetings were held in Capetown, and resolutions passed calling upon the Home Government to fulfil its obligations to the natives, and to assert control over the trade route to the interior. Once more the Cabinet was shaken into direct action. Colonel Sir Charles Warren was appointed Special Commissioner, and ordered to take an expeditionary force to the disturbed districts, to remove the filibusters, to reinstate the natives on their land and to hold the country until its destiny should be decided. He carried out his instructions promptly and vigorously. With a well-equipped column of 4,000 regular and colonial troops he swept away the republics and cleared out the intruders. Taking it for granted that he had a free hand he stretched it as far as he could. He proclaimed the whole of Bechuanaland to be under the protection of Her Majesty the Queen. With a squadron of his force he visited Shoshong and held a conference at which Khama, Sechele and other principal chiefs accepted the protectorate and signed a treaty acknowledging the queen's supremacy.[1] He had accomplished his mission without firing a shot, and one cannot help regretting that the terms of his settlement should have given umbrage to Rhodes, who accused him of breach of faith on account of his refusal to ratify the pledges given to the Stellalanders that their titles should be respected. No doubt Rhodes felt that this was calculated to impair the goodwill of the Afrikander party, whose support he was anxious to secure for his larger schemes of expansion. The matter was afterwards adjusted and the squatters appeased. Rhodes had no reason to be dissatisfied, for he had now in front of him a clear corridor towards the door which Livingstone had opened thirty years before.[2]

III. THE DRINK PERIL

The Bechuanaland freebooters died hard. The small force of mounted police enrolled after Warren's withdrawal had all their work cut out to sweep the seven hundred miles of border clean of the collection of riff-raff that had been littering it for four or five years, and though the expedition had made a temporary clearance it had also ren-

[1] The term 'protectorate' has since been employed in cases where no protection was either requisite or desired, as for instance in Rhodesia, where it led to misunderstandings, and in Basutoland, where the natives were well able to take care of themselves. In these and other cases it was really intended as a warning against trespassers. With Khama and the Bechuana chiefs, however, it meant what it said. They wished to be protected against Boers and other freebooters, and obtained a permanent military force for the purpose.

[2] The southern portion of Bechuanaland, which included Vryburg and Mafeking, was constituted a Crown Colony a few months later, and eventually became part of Cape Colony. The 'Protectorate' then comprised all territory north of Mafeking and west of the Transvaal and Matabeleland as far as the Zambesi river.

KHAMA TRYING A PRISONER, 1890

Photo ✒ *W. Ellerton*

dered the country easier of access from the south, whence
new adventurers were steadily dribbling in. Khama soon
found that the protection of the British Crown carried with
it serious disadvantages.

He had employed the years since his final return to power
prudently and profitably, and had immensely increased the
standing of the ba-Mangwato tribe. Shoshong, which was
still his capital, was becoming overcrowded, and would
probably have been abandoned by Khama but for its
strategic position. In 1885 there were about twenty
resident Europeans and six permanent stores at which an
important trade was carried on in ostrich feathers, ivory
and skins. In the palmy days of this business one firm alone
was reputed to have an annual turnover of £50,000, but
ostrich farming in Cape Colony and the gradual retreat of
elephants into less frequented parts had considerably reduced the trade.

Khama could put into the field an army of 2,000 men
trained in the use of firearms, and three hundred of these
were mounted. He had a well-devised scheme for defending
the town against the Matabele—the only enemies, apart
from the Boers, of whom he had any fear. Shortly after his
accession he had sent friendly messages to Lobengula, and
had received reassuring replies, but the ownership of the
Makalanga country between the Macloutsie and Shashi
rivers was still a bone of contention, and might at any time
provide an excuse for war. The ba-Mangwato were not by
nature a fighting race and in spite of their guns and horses
could not be depended on to withstand the rush tactics of
the Matabele.

For the moment, however, the Matabele were quiescent,
and a domestic problem was filling Khama's mind with far
greater misgivings. His passionate anxiety—amounting
almost to a monomania—to keep his people from contamina-
tion by drink brought him into constant difficulties with

some of the unruly white men, who resented the restrictions which he placed on the importation of liquor. At first they were allowed to introduce it for their own consumption provided it was not brought up in casks for sale to natives ; but as Khama found that this concession was abused he made an order that no spirits should be introduced into his country under any circumstances, and thereby created still more trouble. A decision to expel certain Englishmen who defied this prohibition led to a series of misdeeds which were made the subject of an official enquiry. To avoid burdening the text with details of an episode of no definite historical importance the account of this is relegated to an appendix (II). The facts are unsavoury, and are not related for the sake of disinterring a forgotten scandal, but because they expose in a striking manner the recklessness of some of the white men who frequented Bechuanaland in the early days of the Protectorate, and incidentally shed light on the character of Khama himself.

CHAPTER XI

THE MATABELE UNDER LOBENGULA

I. LOBENGULA THE MAN

LOBENGULA did not feel the pressure of 'civilisation' so early as Khama. From the outset of his reign he kept up the rigid surveillance over the entry of white men which had been instituted by his father. Military posts were established near his frontier, where all newcomers were stopped and interrogated as to their business. They were detained while a report was submitted to the King, who discussed it with his councillors, and, if satisfied, sent back—perhaps after a delay of a week or more—formal leave for them to proceed—in his own phrase 'gave them the road'. He was not always able to discriminate between the *bonâ fide* hunter or trader and the less desirable type of adventurer, and it was inevitable that some of the latter class should find their way into Matabeleland, but they were fully alive to the risks they would incur by misbehaviour, and had every reason to avoid giving offence to the King or his aggressive soldiers.

When the Bechuana chiefs in the south accepted a British protectorate Lobengula had reigned for fifteen years, and the best proof of his capacity was the entire absence of the discordant elements which were making Khama's life a nightmare. No border raids, no freebooters disturbed Lobengula's peace of mind. His word was law, and the white men were as careful to keep on the right side of that law as were his own subjects. Apart from the half-dozen resident traders at Bulawayo, and the missionaries at Hopefountain and Inyati each dry season brought to Matabeleland a certain number of visitors from outside who came up to shoot big game or to attempt the difficult journey to the Victoria Falls. In every case they were made to feel that they were in the country on sufferance, and were expected to pay for the privilege of admission by coming provided with costly gifts for the King himself and beads, blankets, brass wire and the like for distribution as baksheesh among the ' queens ' and smaller fry. Well aware that all who took the trouble to make the long waggon journey from the south were seeking favours Lobengula responded by squeezing as much as he could out of them, and his example was followed by the rank and file of the tribe, who developed into the most inveterate beggars. In course of time the royal store house became the repository of an immense collection of valuable rifles, saddlery, furniture and other European goods, few of which were ever made use of. The men and women of the tribe learnt to regard all white people as objects of plunder, and their constant demands for presents and pilfering habits were a source of endless annoyance.

Many of those who sought sport or adventure in Matabeleland in the 'seventies and 'eighties afterwards wrote accounts of their travels, but the casual impressions of men who pass rapidly through a country are not of great value in revealing the true character of its ruler or people, which can only be learnt from the experiences of more settled residents, and of these, unfortunately, only two or three have left records. One naturally turns to the books of Selous who spent several seasons in elephant and big game hunting in Matabeleland and adjacent territories, but Selous was always on the move, and his narratives, though vivid and free from any taint of exaggeration, are consequently disconnected.

Of Lobengula's personal appearance we have many im-
pressionistic pictures, so strangely inconsistent that they
might be taken to refer to different men. Frank Oates, one
of the first Englishmen to visit him (1873), speaks more than
once of the intense blackness of his colour, and says he was
one of the darkest complexioned natives he had seen,[1]
whereas Sir Sidney Shippard, who paid him an official visit
some years later tells us that his skin was ' of a fine bronze '.[2]
Oates again refers to the ' benignant smile ' which generally
illumined Lobengula's face, and this is corroborated by the
French missionary Coillard (1878).[3] On the other hand
Mr. E. A. Maund, in an official report (1885), speaks of him
as ' a gross fat man, with a cruel restless eye '.[4] When he
first received Selous he was dressed in a greasy shirt and a
dirty pair of trousers,[5] and when Oates saw him he wore
' a broad-brimmed hat, an unclean cotton shirt, unbraced
baggy trousers and large clumsy shoes '.[6] These sketches
suggest that he was slovenly, and lacking in the dignity
usually associated with savage potentates. Yet Coillard
and many others tell us that he was generally naked, except
for a kilt of blue monkey skins ; Shippard that in spite of
his obesity he had ' a most majestic appearance ',[7] and a
still higher flight of admiration is reached by the noted
French explorer Lionel Décle, who thought him ' the most
imposing monarch he had ever seen, except the Tzar
Alexander '.[8]

Probably the most trustworthy picture of all is that

---

[1] *Matabeleland and the Victoria Falls*, pp. 103, 111.

[2] *Blue Book*, C. 5918, p. 124.

[3] ' A corpulent but pleasant-faced man, with smooth hands and
nails of exaggerated length '. *On the Threshold of Central Africa*,
p. 33.

[4] *Blue Book*, C. 4643, p. 114.

[5] *A Hunter's Wanderings*, p. 29.   [6] *Op. cit.*, p. 115.

[7] *Blue Book*, C. 5918, p. 124.

[8] *Three Years in Savage South Africa*, p. 142.

drawn by Mr. J. Cooper Chadwick, who was in almost daily intercourse with the Matabele king from 1887 to 1890 :

' Lobengula stands over six feet in height, but is so enormously fat that it makes him look smaller, though his proud bearing and stately walk give him all the appearance of a savage king. His features are coarse, and exhibit great cunning and cruelty ; but when he smiles the expression completely changes, and makes his face appear pleasant and good-tempered '.[1]

From these conflicting accounts we may infer that Lobengula was a man of many moods, and that his countenance had a mobility not common among ordinary Matabele, whose expression is usually stolid and often vacuous. We have practically nothing in the way of portraits to help us. He refused, on superstitious grounds, to be photographed, and such few sketches of him as have survived were apparently drawn from memory, for they bear little resemblance to one another.[2]

Lobengula's chief kraal, and the seat of government, was Bulawayo (' the place of killing '), which in his later years, after one or two changes of site, occupied an extensive area

[1] *Three Years with Lobengula*, p. 90. This little book contains a graphic description of the daily life at Bulawayo during the last few years of Lobengula's supremacy. It has a further interest in that it was written after the author had lost both hands in a gun accident. He had to use a pen fastened to one of the stumps.

[2] In the library of the South Kensington Museum there are two water-colour paintings of Lobengula from the brush of Thomas Baines, and one of these (rather crudely reproduced in Thomas's *Eleven Years in Central South Africa*, p. 236) depicts him as he appeared at his installation as king, wearing a European hat and jacket, and with his bare legs streaked with blue paint. There is a thumb-nail sketch of his head and shoulders in M. Décle's book, drawn twenty years later. A most striking photograph of a native, purporting to be Lobengula, forms the frontispiece to a small book by the late Mr. Carnegie, of the London Missionary Society (*Among the Matabele*, published by the Religious Tract Society), but the present writer was assured by the Rev. Charles Helm, Carnegie's colleague at Bulawayo and a missionary of the highest standing, that this was not a portrait of Lobengula, but of some other native, and that he had protested against its use for illustrating the book.

on rising ground overlooking the Umgusa river, about three miles north of the modern town of the same name. Here he had two brick houses, built by an English sailor who had wandered up from the coast, and behind them were arranged the huts of a score or more of his wives, constructed neatly of poles and cowdung cement, with thatched roofs like beehives, each tenement being enclosed by a palisade of reeds. Hard by were the courtyard for meetings and interviews, and the goat-kraal, where the king presided over the mysteries of rain-making and other magic rites. The latter was closely guarded, and could not be entered by the profane. The whole of the royal precincts (known as the *si-Godhlo*) was surrounded by a strong zareba of tree-trunks, while a further area was cleared of bush and marked off for military parades and ceremonial dances. Outside these reserves were the huts of the common people, closely packed in groups which were fenced off for privacy. In his latter years Lobengula used generally to sleep in an ox-waggon, drawn up inside the central enclosure, and was in the habit of making sudden and unannounced journeys to his other royal kraals, of which there were several within a few days' journey.

The accounts given by various writers of Lobengula's character differ almost as widely as those of his physical appearance. Most of those who came into contact with him were content to judge him by externals, and lay great stress on the cruel and ever-recurring executions which formed the groundwork of his system of discipline. Had they looked deeper, and reflected on the peculiar difficulties with which he had to contend from the moment when he first accepted the duties of kingship, they would have recognised that he was distinguished by a farsightedness and diplomatic ability which lifted him to the front rank among African potentates—to a position surpassed perhaps only by Moshesh, the enlightened chief of the Basutos.

He had started his reign with severe handicaps. He had
to live down the prejudice arising from his inferior birth and
to follow a king who for forty years had been the central
object of an almost fanatical devotion. The system which
Mziligazi evolved had deprived his subjects of independent
volition, and upon his death the tribe was left a headless
trunk. In the hands of a less capable successor it would
have become uncontrollable, and would speedily have gone
to pieces. Lobengula's intelligence told him that with such
a people as the Matabele ' not Amurath an Amurath suc-
ceeds ', and that he must adopt new methods if he wished
to hold them together and retain his own ascendancy. He
had little of his father's military genius, and his victory over
the partisans of Nkulumane was largely a stroke of luck,
but it carried him at once into popular favour and gained
him a reputation for courage in the field and good general-
ship which he was far from possessing. As, however, after
this initial triumph he ceased to lead his armies in person it
was necessary for him to resort to other devices for en-
trenching his sovereignty and surrounding himself with an
aura of infallibility. Early in his reign he discovered that
an accusation of illicit sorcery was the surest means of
removing an enemy or potential rival, and one against
which there was no defence. Such a crime could only be
detected by the official witch-doctors, who gradually be
came the supreme instruments of his government. By their
agency he was able, without loss of dignity or danger of
opposition, to rid himself of all whom he suspected of dis-
loyalty or ambition. Did one of his *indunas* appear to be
growing too rich, or acquiring an undue influence in the
tribe ? A hint to his terrible myrmidons and a charge of
practising secret and seditious magic was brought. There
was no possibility of escape, for evidence of evil designs was
readily manufactured and as readily accepted by the gul-
lible common folk. With a pretence of formal investigation

the selected victim was ' smelt out ', and publicly denounced.
In most cases he made no defence or resistance, and was
hurried away to be strangled, clubbed to death or hurled
to the crocodiles in the Umgusa river, according to his rank
or the degree of his guilt.   The sentence was frequently
extended to include his wives and slaves.   Blood relationship to the king gave no protection—rather the reverse.
Mindful of the plots which had centred round Nkulumane
Lobengula regarded all his father's offspring as possible
conspirators.   Several of his half-brothers were put out of
the way on trumped-up charges of wizardry, and one of his
blackest deeds was the murder of his sister Mncencengi, the
child of his own mother.   This woman—generally known by
Europeans as Ningi—was for years his favourite, and the
acknowledged mistress of his household, taking precedence
even over his wives.   She had shared her brother's exile and,
after his accession, often accompanied him on his travels.
She was consulted in his matrimonial affairs and wielded a
powerful influence in matters of state.   She was also popular with the white traders and visitors, who loaded her with
presents in the hope of securing through her the favour of
the king.   On all these grounds she incurred the enmity of
the magicians, who were bitterly jealous of her influence
and sought about for an excuse to destroy her.   At last they
accused her of casting spells over a girl recently added to
the royal seraglio, and the malicious suggestion so preyed on
Lobengula's mind that in a fit of passion he had her put to
death.

II. LOBENGULA AND WHITE MEN

By degrees the bogy which Lobengula had created to
serve his political ends assumed a reality.   Even his keen
intelligence was not proof against the poison constantly
dropped into his ears by his crafty satellites, and in imagination he felt himself surrounded by intriguers.   Europeans

were not exempt from suspicion, though he was careful in their case to refrain from overt acts of violence. He had a premonition that any rough treatment of white men —especially Englishmen—might recoil on him by setting in motion forces whose strength he was astute enough to realise. Apart therefore from accepting their presents— and even demanding them if they were not spontaneously offered—he cultivated their goodwill, and although he made no effort to check the exasperating importunities of the rank and file of his people he let it be clearly known that any active molestation of white men would be severely punished.

The majority of the traders and others who came to Matabeleland were men whom the king could respect—who besides being straightforward in their dealings never stooped to servility in their demeanour towards him. There were, unfortunately, a few of a different type. These sought to curry favour by pandering to the King's vanity. They lowered their dignity by squatting on the ground in his presence, by obsequiously shouting out his titles, and in other ways behaving as if they were his subjects.[1] In some cases they descended to the native level by adopting black ' wives '. Except in this last respect it may perhaps be urged in their defence that they were living at the King's mercy, and might have incurred his dislike or provoked the wrath of his subjects if they had taken up a bolder or more dignified attitude. Without belittling the risks of the position in which the traders in Matabeleland had volun- tarily placed themselves it may confidently be stated as a

---

[1] Oates, *Matabeleland and the Victoria Falls*, p. 115. Cf. also the report by Sir Sidney Shippard printed in *Blue Book*, C. 5918, p. 124 ; ' Some of the old white inhabitants (of Bulawayo), and even some of the new concession seekers, actually grovel before the ama-Ndebele [Matabele] chief with their hands on their knees, . . . sidling up to their places in the circle in the crouching attitude of the natives who are fawning on him for boiled beef and Kaffir beer'.

general principle that Bantu natives—be they kings or common folk—are more impressed by an assumption of superiority and aloofness on the part of white men than by affability. The slightest approach to complaisance—an excess of courtesy even—is interpreted by them as weakness and they are not slow to take advantage of it. In Lobengula's case it is undeniable that the men for whom he had the highest regard were Dr. Jameson, Sir Sidney Shippard, Selous the hunter and a few others of the same class, who preserved their pride of race and never condescended to kowtow to him.

Lobengula's relations with the missionaries were on a different footing. The high hopes which they had founded on his apparent sympathy with their labours at the opening of his reign were doomed to disappointment. He kept on good terms with them and was tolerant of their presence, as his father had been before him. In Mziligazi's case this amiability was due no doubt to the fact that they had been introduced by Dr. Moffat, for whom he had a strong affection. But Lobengula was inspired by other motives. At the outset he was glad of their support, and in return displayed a certain amount of interest in their work ; but this feeling, whether genuine or assumed, soon evaporated, and as far as their spiritual labours were concerned they gained no ground, either with the King or his people. Very little was to be made out of them in the way of presents, and their attempts to wean the natives round them from their brutal and heathenish practices met with absolute failure. Abstract morality was meaningless to savages whose whole scheme of existence was based on robbing and killing the weak ; who regarded lying as a praiseworthy accomplishment—provided it was not detected—and a plurality of wives as the ideal of human welfare. The rewards of virtuous conduct as depicted by Christian teachers—vague promises of a life hereafter ; Paradise, as the abode of eternal peace ; a land flowing with milk and honey—offered no attractions to people who could comprehend no greater joy than an abundance of beer and beef, cattle to be looted at their pleasure, and girls to be seized to gratify their carnal desires. The missionaries would have found their position insupportable had they not been favoured by Lobengula, who recognised the advantage of having at his elbow men who could read and write letters for him and, having no personal axe to grind, could be trusted to give him disinterested advice in his dealings with other whites. The common folk were apathetic ; they were ready to avail themselves of the missionaries' willingness to attend without reward to the bodily ailments of themselves and their livestock, but regarded them as more or less mad. They never made a solitary convert to Christianity, and it is difficult to imagine a more unpromising field for religious work than that in which they were engaged.

With the Boers from the Transvaal Lobengula was always on his guard. Two or three regular elephant-hunters by decent conduct gained his goodwill to the extent of being allowed to squat and graze their cattle on the outskirts of the Matopo hills, but these were exceptions, and the entry of any considerable party would have been refused or even repelled by force.

On the whole it may be said that whatever his real feelings might be towards white men, when once he had permitted them to cross his boundaries Lobengula dealt with them justly and considerately. This was markedly the case with those of British origin, whom he seemed to trust more than others, and treated with a kindliness which, if somewhat rough, and marred by occasional outbursts of ill-temper, was apparently sincere. They knew that they had nothing to fear from the king himself ; what kept them in a state of anxiety was the possibility that he might be unable to keep a whip hand over his less discerning subjects, who, more than once during the last critical years of his reign, clamoured for leave to fall upon the *amakiwa* and ' wipe them out '. Had Lobengula then lifted his finger in assent there would have been a general massacre, and it must be recorded to his credit that he stood firm, and never betrayed those who trusted him.

Of actual treachery only one charge has been definitely laid at Lobengula's door, and although the evidence against him is black it is not conclusive. In 1877 Captain Paterson, a British officer, presented himself at Bulawayo in company with a Mr. Sargeant (son of a former Colonial Secretary of Natal), to ask leave to visit the Victoria Falls. They innocently brought with them a letter from Sir Theophilus Shepstone, and this created a bad impression, for the memory of the Natal pretender—the self-styled Nkulu-mane—who had been in Shepstone's employ, was still fresh in the king's mind. Possibly, however, no harm would have befallen them had it not been for a rumour—spread, it was said, by a malicious Boer—that Paterson and his companion were spies, and that behind them was an army of Natal colonists who were preparing to invade the country. Lobengula tried to induce them to return to Natal, and was strongly opposed to their being accompanied to the Zambesi by one of the sons of the missionary Morgan Thomas, whom they proposed to take with them as guide. In the end, however, he gave way and allowed the whole party with their colonial kaffir servants to proceed, sending with them some of his own people. Two or three weeks after their departure the latter returned with the news that the three white men and their servants had died of drinking water which had been poisoned by Bushmen. David Thomas, another of the missionary's sons, suspecting foul play, endeavoured to ascertain the true facts, and obtained from certain Matabele statements that the poison story was an invention, and that the Paterson party had been assegaied by order of the King. He made efforts to persuade the authorities in the south to institute an official enquiry, but was himself unfortunately murdered by natives near the Zambesi river, and the matter was allowed to drop. So far as Lobengula was concerned therefore the charge must be regarded as not proven.[1]

III. LOBENGULA THE KING

Besides acting as his agents for detecting and removing obnoxious subjects there were other ways in which the witch-doctors were useful for strengthening the King's prestige. The nation was taught to look on him as vested with supernatural powers of control over the rainfall, upon which depended the success of the crops. He was the Great High Priest and Master of the Ceremonies held every year towards the end of the dry season, and if the much needed showers were delayed he was supplicated by the people to exert his gifts to hasten them. There were special magic-mongers who studied the weather conditions, of which they were shrewd judges, and when they deemed the moment propitious they conducted, under Lobengula's supervision,

[1] Mr. Walter Montagu Kerr, who travelled through Matabeleland in 1883, and spent some time at Bulawayo, gives a detailed account of the tragedy in his book *The Far Interior*. According to this the prejudice against Paterson and Sargeant was due to the indiscreet tone adopted by them in their conversations with the king and to the contents of Shepstone's letter, which complained of alleged grievances among the white traders in Matabeleland. A copy of ' these transactions ' came into the possession of Mr. Kerr, who formed from them the impression that they were calculated to excite the suspicions of the *indunas* and the doubts of the king. He also had access to David Thomas's journal which contained, he says, voluminous evidence that the members of the party were assegaied by order of the king, acting in accordance with the wishes of his *indunas*.

The late Rider Haggard, who was a Government official in the Transvaal at the time of the incident, was of the same opinion. In a chapter contributed to *The Downfall of Lobengula*, by Wills and Collingridge, he expressed his firm conviction that the King ' did plan and execute this most wicked murder '.

a series of secret and nauseous rites in the pretence of aiding him to bring about the desired result. Goats were cut open and their warm and smoking entrails examined for omens ; cattle were sacrificed to conciliate the spirits, and all sorts of herbs and other nostrums were brewed into a mysterious concoction—known to Europeans as ' hell-broth '—with which the fields were sprinkled as ' rain-medicine '. When, as usually happened, this hocus-pocus was followed by a welcome downpour the credit was attributed to Lobengula's occult influence.

Similar observances were practised before the annual raiding expeditions. Nungu, the great ' war-doctor ', who advised the king on military matters, was responsible for the preparation of special ' medicine ' to render the troops invulnerable and to ensure their success in battle. He was rewarded by a share in the loot, and was one of the few men in the country, apart from Lobengula, allowed to accumulate cattle.

It may here be mentioned that the ownership of all cattle in the realm was, in theory, vested in the king, who could dispose of them as he willed. It was his custom to make presents of breeding-stock from time to time to deserving subjects, who retained the progeny, and to this limited extent private ownership was recognised, though never allowed to attain undue proportions. Numbers of the cattle were also handed over to the custody of the *indunas* of the principal districts, their inhabitants being permitted to use the milk, which was curdled into a sort of junket, known as *amasi*, and in this form constituted an important item in their diet. None of the beasts so farmed out could be slaughtered without the king's authority, but the meat for the soldiers in training, for sacrifices and ceremonial feasts, and for the consumption of the king and his household had to be provided from the royal herds, which would have been insufficient to meet the constant drain had not their natural increase been supplemented by the spoils of war. Hence the periodical raids, besides supplying an outlet for the bloodthirsty instincts of the Matabele warriors, were a necessary adjunct of the national economy.

The land was on a different footing. In accordance with the almost universal custom among Bantu races it was the property of the tribe. Its allocation for particular purposes was in the hands of the King, and no new ground could be brought under cultivation, or new kraals erected, except by his direction. He could not, however, make grants of land to outsiders without the concurrence of the national council, which included Mhlaba (the ' regent ', who had succeeded his father Umnombate, and would take control in the event of the King's demise until a successor was appointed) ; Nungu, the chief war doctor, and several of the leading generals and *indunas*. This was the only limitation on the King's dominion. In all other respects he was an absolute autocrat, with power of life and death over every one of his subjects and vassals.

Lobengula was scrupulous in keeping up all the outward pomp of barbaric majesty. Whenever he showed himself in public he was attended by posturing heralds and court officials who shouted out sycophantic compliments, and vied with one another in a continuous display of grovelling obeisance. He sat in state daily to try cases, hear petitions and receive reports. When he was so engaged the strictest etiquette was demanded ; no one could stand erect before him ; all arms had to be laid aside at a distance, and the only concession permitted to white men was that they were excused from crouching and stooping as they approached the presence. He was kept informed of every detail of what happened outside Bulawayo—casualties or births among his herds of cattle ; domestic incidents among his people ; the arrival of white men at his border outposts, and their movements on their hunting or trading expeditions. He had an exceptionally retentive memory, which was of great assistance to him in guiding his decisions and policy. At his court great quantities of beer and stewed beef were provided, and white men who had business with him were invited, and in fact expected, to share in its consumption, and rather looked down upon if they failed to prove themselves good trencher-men. The absence of shelter from the baking sun and the myriads of flies attracted by the meat and the hides and skulls of oxen littered about the royal premises rendered an audience with Lobengula a trying test of endurance for Europeans, but it had to be faced if favours were sought.

The term 'nation', as applied above to the Matabele, is perhaps somewhat of a misnomer. In reality they were a comparatively small warlike clan, which by force of arms had reduced to subjection a wide tract of country, and compelled its original inhabitants to become its tributaries. Lobengula's military organisation was modelled on the Zulu system, under which all boys were trained from their earliest years for warfare, and all adults were active soldiers until they became too old for service in the field. There were four main divisions of the army, each composed of a number of regiments occupying military kraals in the same district, and commanded by a leading *induna*. A regiment consisted of from 700 to 1,000 men of about the same age. The *amatjaha*, or young soldiers, were obliged to remain bachelors until they had earned experience and distinction in the field of battle. When they had 'blooded their assegais' to the King's satisfaction he would give permission to a whole regiment at once to take wives, to build a new town and to wear the head-ring, which was the badge of the married estate. They then became veterans (*amadoda*). The chief division was the 'Ikapa', which was quartered in the towns of the Bulawayo area, and contained several famous regiments, notably the Imbezu (king's bodyguard), a *corps d'élite* of picked young men. West of Bulawayo were the kraals of the ' Mhlope ' division, commanded by Gambo, a relative by marriage of the King, and including, among others, the Mhlahlanhlela regiment of veterans (Pioneers) and the Nyamandhlovu (' Elephant's meat '). These are mentioned because they figured conspicuously in later encounters with the British. Others with a similar claim were the Induba, Enxa and Insukamini. The total strength of the army was estimated in 1885 at about 15,000, but only a small proportion of these belonged to the original Zulu stock, the remainder being partly or wholly descended from tribes conquered in the Transvaal before the anabasis of 1837, and in a few cases from slave mothers, captured later from the neighbouring Makalanga people. The first named were styled *abe-Zanzi* (' men from down-country ', *i.e.* Zululand), and were the aristocracy of the tribe ; those of the imported strains were the *abe-Nhla* (' men from above ', meaning the Transvaal high veld). There was a third class—the *ama-Holi*—composed mainly of youths captured from the Makalanga, Mashona and other tribes of the Zambesi-Limpopo districts, who went through a course of military training, but never rose above the status of slaves.[1]

Every year, at the season for the garnering of the first crops—that is in February—a grand ceremonial review was held, for which fully half the army was assembled at Bulawayo and inspected by the king. The proceedings included elaborate war-dances, and the spectacle of so many thousands of warriors, arrayed in full panoply, with heavy capes and head-dresses of black ostrich plumes, all carrying the long shields of ox-hide of distinctive colour for each regiment and moving in perfect unison to the chant of their war songs, was magnificent and even awe-inspiring. At a certain stage in the display the King announced, with

---

[1] In a wider sense the term ' Holi ' was applied, in a somewhat contemptuous way, to all the local subject tribes.

solemn ritual, his war policy for the winter months, hurling an assegai in the direction of the proposed invasion. During the review the witch-doctors were allowed publicly to denounce any persons suspected of covert plots, who were promptly led off to execution. The formal parades and dances were followed by the slaughter of large numbers of cattle, and by an orgy of feasting and drinking which lasted for several days. The period of the ' great dance '—*in-Xwala*, as it was called—was one of intense excitement in the tribe, and of some danger to any Europeans present, who were dependent on the King for their safety.[1]

By 1885, when the establishment of a protectorate in Khama's country began to awaken men's interest in the comparatively unknown region beyond, the fiery blood of Mziligazi's old Zulu stock had been diluted by the steady infusion of alien elements, and there were signs that the morale of the Matabele army was degenerating. Their method of fighting too was becoming obsolete. They still relied on the stabbing assegai as their main weapon of attack and their long shields for defence, despite the fact that most of the tribes to the south and west of them had acquired firearms and some skill in the use of them. Except against the feeble Mashona clans it was becoming increasingly difficult for Lobengula's *impis* to employ their rush tactics and engage their enemies at close quarters. A few years previously they had surprised the ba-Tauwana, who dwelt on the shores of Lake Ngami and were agriculturists rather than warriors, sacked many of their villages and run riot in carnage. Although the Matabele lost 600 men from fever, thirst and privation they returned to Bulawayo with 15,000 cattle and many captives, and the remnant of the ba-Tauwana fled to the impenetrable marshes north of

---

[1] A detailed description of the *in-Xwala*, taken from the accounts of several English eye-witnesses, is given in the author's *Making of Rhodesia*, pp. 38-42. See also *Eleven Years in Central South Africa*, by T. M. Thomas, pp. 301-3.

the lake. In 1885 Lobengula sent another *impi* to the same part ; but the ba-Tauwana had in the meantime obtained breech-loading guns and prepared a warm reception for the raiders. They concealed themselves in the patches of reeds on the banks of the Okavango river, and from these and from canoes kept up a well-directed fire on both flanks of the Matabele as they attempted to cross and compelled them to retreat with heavy loss. Only about 1,000 emaciated men returned to Bulawayo to report the disaster. They had taken no loot, and had even lost their arms and shields.[1]

Lobengula began to realise that the days of the assegai were passing by. By strenuous efforts he collected a large number of guns of various patterns, but he was hampered by the difficulty of obtaining ammunition, and never succeeded in getting his army reliant in the use of them. Still there remained a wide field for pillage on the east, where the tribes were of poorer mettle, and had no firearms, and in this direction the annual raids were carried on with undiminished ferocity. The inhabitants of Mashonaland had long ceased to dwell in the open, and sought security by building their villages among the granite kopjes which were scattered profusely over the plateau, forming natural fortresses. To the inaccessible parts of these, when danger threatened, they escaped by means of rope ladders which they drew up after them. Only by starvation or the lack of water could they be forced to emerge, but their crops and stock were at the mercy of the raiders. Those nearest the Matabele naturally suffered most, but even such distant parts as Lomagunda and Matoko were visited by marauding parties in quest of cattle. Some of the petty chiefs bought an uncertain immunity by paying heavy tribute ; others fled for safety with their people across the Zambesi, but all who held out were subject to incessant persecution and their lot was little better than that of hunted animals.

[1] *Blue Book*, C. 4643, p. 117.

Up to the beginning of the nineteenth century the natives of Mashonaland had been banded together in a loose federation and their relations among themselves had been fairly peaceful. They were industrious agriculturists and cattle-breeders, and many of them were skilled in weaving, gold-washing, iron-working and other handicrafts. They carried on a brisk trade with neighbouring tribes in rice of excellent quality and other cereals, rubber and tobacco, and were among the most prosperous native inhabitants of Africa. With the coming of the Matabele and the other fugitives from Tshaka's tyranny these happy conditions became a thing of the past. Repeated massacres had thinned their numbers and caused their utter disintegration. Over an immense expanse of country they were scattered about in families and broken fragments of tribes, afraid to move from the protection of their rocky fastnesses, fearful even of each other, and with no power of combined action.

The Matabele hegemony south of the Zambesi was a veritable curse to all around them, and on humanitarian grounds alone their complete extermination had become a crying need.

CHAPTER XII

THE CREEPING TIDE

I. BOERS AND MATABELELAND

A HANDFUL of miners and prospectors still clung to Tati, though their work was intermittent and desultory. They suffered no interference from Lobengula, who was loth to part with the annual subsidy of £50 which he received from Sir John Swinburne's company for allowing the concession to remain open. The diggings were in a part sparsely inhabited by poverty-stricken Makalanga, and on that account were outside his regular raiding grounds; these people too were claimed by Khama as his subjects, and it was not worth Lobengula's while to stir up trouble by sending his *impis* in their direction. Elsewhere in his dominions he discouraged—indeed prohibited—any search for gold reefs. It is true that soon after his accession, when he was not so confident of his powers, he had thought it judicious to ratify a licence granted, verbally and informally by Umnombate during his regency, to Thomas Baines, to prospect in the Mashona country between the Gwelo and Hanyani rivers. But nothing came of this. Baines had no private means, and although he made valiant efforts to turn the concession to account he died before he could raise sufficient funds to carry out any serious work.[1]

---

[1] Baines's concession passed into the hands of a group of Kimberley speculators, and for twenty years remained dormant. It was, like several others, dragged to light when Rhodes's negotiations for a charter gave it a bargaining value.

For the first fifteen or sixteen years Lobengula was not troubled by other gold-seekers. The Boers, as we know, had no particular interest in mining, and shortly after the failure of their intrigues to secure possession of Tati the internal affairs of the Transvaal became so involved that they had no time to pursue their designs of gaining access to the land of promise beyond the Limpopo. They had by no means forgotten it, however, as is proved by an illuminating piece of evidence which came to light long afterwards in the shape of a letter, written to Lobengula less than a year after the retrocession of the Transvaal, by Piet Joubert, the Commandant-General of the newly constituted republic. This effusion, which is couched in insinuating language, professes the ardent desire of the Transvaal Government to live in amity with Lobengula, as they did with his father, who is described as ' our old friend Umzilikatse ', and to maintain the peace ' which is so strong that the vile evil-doers were never able to destroy it, and never shall be able to, as long as there shall be one Boer that lives, and Lobengula also lives '. Joubert lets loose a flood of invective on the iniquities of the English (whom he compares to ' a monkey, that has its hands full of pumpkin seeds—if you don't beat him to death he will never let go '), and proceeds to assure Lobengula that ' when the stink which the English brought is blown away altogether ' he will ride up to Bulawayo and pay him a special visit to cement the long-standing friendship.[1]

Joubert's protestations of affection must have fallen rather flat, for had Lobengula sent a favourable reply it would most certainly have been made use of by the crafty

[1] Joubert's letter is stated to have been handed to the custody of James Fairbairn, one of the permanent traders at Bulawayo, who was often consulted by the king as to his correspondence with white men. Fairbairn showed it to F. R. Thompson, one of Rhodes's agents, and allowed him to take a copy of it. The full text is quoted in Fitzpatrick's *Transvaal from Within* (p. 44, Popular Edition).

Commandant-General, whose nickname of ' Slim Piet ' had not been earned for nothing.   No such reply was ever heard of, and in all probability none was sent.   The king was far too wary to be beguiled by oily references to a long-standing friendship which never existed.   However, the letter strengthens the presumption that Matabeleland was one of the directions in which the Transvaal leaders, elated by their recent grant of independence, were looking for fresh fields of enterprise.

During the next two or three years the Boers were largely taken up with the affairs of the mushroom republics of Goshen and Stellaland.   But the clearance effected there by Warren's expedition, while shutting out hope of further escapades on the west, gave them a fresh incentive to possess themselves of the more desirable uplands of the north, and evidence that this was in their minds was not long in forthcoming.   Towards the close of his operations Warren received authentic reports that numbers of Boer families had begun to trek along the south bank of the Limpopo under the pretext of hunting, but without doubt watching for an opportunity of crossing if they could manage to elude the vigilance of the Matabele.[1]   Rumour indeed said that a force was actually being raised, under the leadership of Commandant Ignatius Ferreira (a well-known and seasoned campaigner, who had earned a British decoration for services rendered in the Zulu war) to invade Mashonaland.   Such preparations were consistent with Boer tactics.   Their method was to stalk their quarry, whereas the British generally waited until it was driven up to them.

Significant movements were also reported from other quarters.   A party of Germans under one Tripmacher visited Khama, with the professed intention of going on a hunting expedition to Lake Ngami.   They were observed to be carrying out a careful survey of the route, and from this,

[1] *Blue Book*, C. 4643, p. 124.

and from the nature of their enquiries as to the suitability
of the interior for white occupation, it was inferred that
they had more permanent objects than a mere shooting
trip. In fact it was positively affirmed by persons in a
position to know that Tripmacher was an emissary of the
German Government.[1] It was quite natural that Germany
should be looking about in these parts for opportunities of
establishing settlements, without which her acquisitions on
the coast would be comparatively valueless. So far as
European nations were concerned the whole of the region
lying to the north and east of the British Protectorate was
open to the first who could bring forward a reasonable
excuse for occupying it. Germany was passionately eager
to found new colonies in Africa. Her statesmen were not
restrained by the same scruples about interfering with
native rights as those which exercised the British Government, and they were ready to give warm encouragement to
any adventurer from the Fatherland bold enough to push his
way into parts not definitely appropriated by other Powers.

Even the Portuguese, who for three centuries had been
drowsily content with a few trading stations on the lower
Zambesi and the Mozambique coast, were beginning to be-
stir themselves, and were said to be making friendly advances to some of Lobengula's subject chiefs in the east of
Mashonaland.

All the above reports were duly communicated by Warren
to Sir Hercules Robinson, the High Commissioner at the
Cape, and it is hardly possible that they should not, directly
or indirectly, have come to the ears of Rhodes. But Rhodes
was mistrustful of anything which emanated from Warren.
He had not recovered from his disgust at the high-handed
manner in which that officer had over-ridden his own project for extending the territorial influence of Cape Colony,
and he was disinclined to come again into the open until

[1] *Blue Book*, C. 4643, p. 124.

Warren was safely out of the way. Added to this he was absorbed, between 1885 and 1887, in his great scheme for consolidating the various diamond companies at Kimberley. He had conceived the idea that he might weld them into one powerful corporation, which should not only control the industry but should be so constituted as to support him, when the time was ripe, in his wider purpose of northward expansion.

As for Lobengula, whose country was now becoming the focus of so much attention from outside, his main pre-occupation was with the Boers. He had welcomed the Protectorate in Bechuanaland because it showed him that Britain was not disposed to allow them to overstep their borders. His only grievance was that the northern boundary line was so drawn as to cut across a district which he claimed by right of conquest—the ' Disputed Territory ', over which Khama also asserted rights—and he persisted in declaring that Khama had been responsible for ' fixing the line ', thereby cheating him out of a valuable strip of country. But while he grumbled a good deal, and sent several protests on this point to Sir H. Robinson, he showed no intention of making it a *casus belli*. None of the Matabele were settled in the strip in question, and its loss only meant a small curtailment of their raiding grounds. Mashonaland was on a different footing. There he was determined to allow no intrusion. He knew well that the Boers were prowling along their side of the Limpopo, but his spies were keeping a sharp look-out on their movements, and they would never catch him napping.

II. MOFFAT'S TREATY

This uneasy state of mutual watchfulness went on— Boers and ba-Mangwato watching Matabele ; British watching Boers, and Lobengula watching all parties—until the end of 1887. The administration of the Protectorate had been placed in the hands of Judge (afterwards Sir Sidney) Shippard, and Mr. John Smith Moffat, son of Robert Moffat of Kuruman, had been appointed as his principal assistant. It will be remembered that the latter had been one of the members of the first party of missionaries sent to Matabeleland. Later on he had relinquished missionary work, and had held an official post in the Transvaal during the short-lived British administration. This of course he had vacated after the retrocession, but before leaving he had been exposed to harsh treatment at the hands of the Boers, and had even been threatened with death. On his appointment to Bechuanaland it had been arranged that he should take an early opportunity of paying a visit of courtesy to Lobengula, to reassure him as to the intentions of the British, and to pave the way for friendly relations. His previous knowledge of the Matabele, and a moderate acquaintance with their language, made him well qualified for such an errand, and his experience of the Transvaal Government was not likely to prepossess him in its favour.

Moffat started on this mission at the end of 1887, and was still on the road when news suddenly reached Rhodes at the Cape from a responsible informant in Pretoria that Lobengula was on the point of concluding—had possibly already concluded—a ' treaty ' of alliance with Paul Kruger, the Transvaal President. To Rhodes, with his imperfect knowledge of the state of Lobengula's feelings, there was nothing inherently impossible in this. Had he been in communication with anybody in Matabeleland conversant with the circumstances he would have been assured that the Transvaal Boers were the last people with whom Lobengula was likely to ally himself, but he had no means of knowing this. All he saw was that any such treaty would be a fatal bar to his dream of extending British influence to the Zambesi.

In his concentration on the diamond industry he had temporarily withdrawn his eyes from the more distant horizon, and now he realised all at once that he must act vigorously or others would snatch the fruit from his mouth.

Without a moment's delay he tackled Sir Hercules Robinson. He pressed him to send urgent and supplementary instructions to Moffat to offer a definite British alliance to Lobengula, which might, he thought, be more attractive than one with a small nation like the Transvaal Boers. But Robinson scented difficulties. He had grave doubts as to the propriety of risking further entanglements in the affairs of uncivilised tribes—especially one with the sinister reputation of the Matabele, whose arrogant and quarrelsome tendencies would inevitably land the British Government—if it assumed responsibility for them—in awkward situations. The Warren expedition had cost the tax-payers at home more than a million of money, and what was there to show for it ? An immense tract of half-desert territory, useless for colonisation and inhabited by savages who were perpetually in trouble with one another or with lawless white men. The maintenance of order in this unwanted protectorate was involving an annual outlay of many more thousands, and there was not the faintest likelihood of any adequate return. All this was in Robinson's mind, and made him loth to commit Great Britain to new obligations in the remote interior.

But Rhodes would not be put off by paltry considerations of cost. By this time his mining investments had not only brought him great personal wealth, but had placed him at the head of the leading financial group in South Africa. He had acquired large interests in the new gold-fields at Witwatersrand, and was on the verge of completing his amalgamation of the whole of the diamond companies. He had made up his mind that the trust deed of the gigantic corporation which was shortly to be launched should be so

framed as to permit its profits to be used for projects of
northern development, and he and two or three of his
chosen allies would virtually be able to dictate its policy.
On the question of expenditure therefore he was in a position to reassure the hesitating representative of the Queen's
Government, and, as a beginning, he offered to defray the
expense of keeping Moffat, if he succeeded in the object of
his special mission, permanently at Bulawayo as the representative of Great Britain. It may be assumed that
Rhodes also impressed upon the High Commissioner that
if Britain stood by and did nothing, thereby allowing Lobengula to drift into the embrace of the Transvaal, the Government would have to face a repetition in Matabeleland of the
disorders and scandals which had made Bechuanaland a
byword, and had so recently, and with such difficulty, been
brought to an end.

The upshot was that he prevailed upon Robinson to give
a qualified consent to his proposals. It was agreed that
Moffat should be directed to ascertain the truth about the
alleged Transvaal treaty, and that he should sound Lobengula as to his willingness to enter into an exclusive one with
Great Britain. The necessary instructions were sent
through Shippard, who was thoroughly in accord with
Rhodes's policy and took upon himself to despatch them to
Moffat by special messenger.

This decision put a new complexion on Moffat's mission,
which had previously been entirely non-committal. Providentially when the instructions reached him his conversations with the king had been purely formal, and, as the time
was now approaching for the Great Dance, when a large
portion of the army would be assembled at Bulawayo, and
the king would be busily engaged in reviewing his regiments,
in settling his war policy for the coming winter and in
superintending the mysterious rites which were customary
at this season, Moffat wisely determined to postpone the

question of a treaty until he could get him quietly to himself. He did, however, inform him of the report that he had entered into an alliance with the Boer Republic, and was relieved when the king told him very emphatically that there was absolutely no truth in it.

A week or two later, when the excitement of the Great Dance had subsided, he secured a further audience, and cautiously opened the more vital object of his visit. He found Lobengula at first suspicious. Other white men had freely used the name of Queen Victoria, and professed to be charged with messages of friendship. It took Moffat some time to convince him that he was a properly accredited representative of the Crown charged with a special mandate. But he exercised great patience, and constantly stressed the importance to the king of securing a shield of defence against intrusions by Boers from the Transvaal and by the Portuguese on his eastern frontiers, who were showing a disposition to dispute his sovereignty over Mashonaland. These arguments, coming from the son of the man whom Mziligazi had trusted, carried great weight. Lobengula knew the perils which were threatening him, and was genuinely anxious to have the support of a Power which could help him to stave them off. He bade Moffat write his proposals on paper, so that they could be repeated to his leading councillors without whose concurrence he was reluctant to commit himself. On February 11 a final discussion took place in the King's private quarters in the presence of Nungu and Bozungwane, the two chief witch-doctors, and Mhlaba, the 'Regent'. The text of a treaty, as set down by Moffat in writing, was read again and again, but no decision was reached until much beef and beer had been consumed and the pros and cons had been talked out in the manner so dear to African natives and so tedious to white men. Moffat bore their cross-examination with growing confidence, for he saw that his warnings about the

Boers and Portuguese were carrying weight, but he must have been profoundly relieved when, at the close of a discussion which seemed interminable, Lobengula took the pen which was offered him, and scrawled a clumsy cross at the foot of the paper.

By the terms of the treaty Lobengula promised that peace and amity should continue for ever between himself and his people and ' Her Britannic Majesty ', and gave a pledge to use his utmost endeavours to prevent any rupture. But the most pregnant clause was that by which he undertook ' to refrain from entering into any correspondence or treaty with any foreign State or Power to sell or alienate any portion of his country, or upon any other subject, without the previous knowledge and sanction of the High Commissioner '. In persuading the King to tie his hands to this extent Moffat achieved a master-stroke. His liveliest imagination could hardly have pictured the far-reaching consequences which were to flow from it, but he was entitled at least to feel that it sounded the death-knell to the aspirations of the Transvaal Boers.

Moffat's treaty had of course to be ratified by the Imperial Government, but the Little Englander party was no longer in office, and Lord Knutsford (the new Secretary of State for the Colonies) who received it on April 10, lost no time in conveying his approval by cable to Robinson, and authorising him to make it public. It appeared accordingly in a *Gazette Extraordinary* at the end of the month.

Equally prompt were the governments most directly concerned—those of Portugal and the Transvaal—in entering protests. The former objected that the new treaty interfered with their long established sovereignty over Mashonaland, based on a compact made in the sixteenth century between the Emperor of Monomotapa and the Governor of Mozambique. This, as may be imagined, received very short shrift from the Foreign Secretary (Lord Salisbury), who refused to recognise that Portugal had any rights whatever in a country where not a solitary Portuguese settlement existed, and where for fifty years no attempt had been made by her to dispute the possession of the Matabele king.

President Kruger's challenge was characteristically subtle. A few days after Moffat's agreement was published he issued a proclamation announcing that in accordance with treaties existing between the Republic and Mziligazi and Lobengula, and at the direct request of the latter, his Government had decided to appoint a representative, with the title of ' Consul ', to reside permanently at the King's capital town. For this post they had selected Mr. Pieter Daniel Cornelis Johannes Grobler. The proclamation went on to say that as Lobengula had expressed a desire to be protected against an influx of evil-doers all persons wishing to enter Matabeleland should obtain permits and register their names with the Consul.

The text of the treaty with Lobengula which was said to have prompted this move was not at first disclosed. Possibly it had not yet been manufactured, but as this suggestion requires justification it would be as well in the first place to glance at Grobler's record, which was not a particularly creditable one.

We first hear of him in 1880, when he arrived from the Transvaal at Shoshong with a waggon-load of ammunition, which, being in great demand among the ba-Mangwato, met with a ready sale. In the following year he returned with a number of horses which he guaranteed as ' salted ', the understanding being that if within a specified period any of them died of horse-sickness he would refund the purchase price—a recognised and usual arrangement in countries, such as Bechuanaland, where this scourge was prevalent. On these terms he succeeded in disposing of them in exchange for cattle. Khama himself bought four, and also bought and paid for a waggon, which he allowed Grobler to take away for certain necessary alterations. Within the next few months most of the horses sickened and died, but by that time Grobler had left the country, and was careful not to return. Neither did Khama again see his waggon, for which he had paid thirty head of cattle, valued at £6 apiece. Having thus made Bechuanaland too hot for himself Grobler turned his attention to Matabeleland, and in the course of the next few years made several trips to Bulawayo with horses and waggons for sale. Apparently his transactions in that quarter were more successful, and encouraged him to believe—or at any rate to assert on returning to the Transvaal—that he had acquired great influence with Lobengula, who, according to his account, was hankering for friendly relations with the Government of the Republic. Whether Kruger credited this statement or not it was an opportunity too good to be lost. A cleverly-worded document was drafted to give effect to Lobengula's supposed wishes and entrusted to Grobler, who once more set out for Matabeleland, accompanied this time by his brother, Frederick. According to the account given long afterwards by Kruger the mission was successful. On July 30, 1887—six months before Moffat's arrival—the King and four of his principal councillors affixed their marks to the agreement as prepared in token of approval. The document so obtained was the 'treaty' which was triumph-antly produced by Kruger in support of his protest against that which Moffat had negotiated.

On the surface the Boer story was a plausible one, but the most cursory examination of the treaty itself proves abun-dantly that it was never executed—probably never even seen—by the King, nor any of his councillors. It was, in short, a fabrication of so obvious and clumsy a nature that it seems incredible that the officials at the Cape could have given it a moment's serious consideration. The agreement was stated to have been signed at ' Omchaunien '—a place which had no existence. The only white signatories were Grobler and his brother; and the names of the *indunas* who witnessed Lobengula's mark bore not the slightest resemblance to those of any of his councillors, or indeed to Matabele names at all.[1] Even if its existence had not been explicitly denied by Lobengula in his statement to Moffat, the so-called ' treaty ', in which he was supposed to have pledged himself to eternal friendship with those who were his age-long enemies, and undertaken to give them armed assistance whenever called upon, stands revealed, by internal evidence, as a transparent fraud.

Grobler's career as ' Consul for the Republic ' came quickly to an end through an accident. Upon leaving the Transvaal to enter upon his duties he took with him a ' pont ', or ferry-boat, which he placed on the Limpopo at a point where it bordered on the Protectorate, and used it to transport his waggons over the river, being thus able to make a short cut across a portion of Khama's country. This he did without the permission of the Chief, who allowed no one to pass through his territory into Matabeleland except by way of Shoshong. Khama was enraged when he heard that not only Grobler (who had swindled him, and had good reasons for giving his town a wide berth) but a number of other Boers had stolen through by a new and unauthorised route, and to guard against a repetition of the trespass sent a detachment of ba-Mangwato to the spot. After a brief stay in Matabeleland Grobler was returning to

[1] Those familiar with the Matabele will agree that *Moluchelu, Nowcho, Postochau* and *Omownd*, the names given as those of the assenting *indunas*, have no likeness to real persons. Mr. Basil Williams, in his admirable life of Rhodes (p. 119) expresses the opinion that Grobler ' did undoubtedly obtain, in July, 1887, a document purporting to give the Transvaal wide powers of jurisdiction over their own subjects settled in Matabeleland, and to keep a Consul in residence at the King's kraal '. The evidence is, however, all to the contrary.

the Transvaal to fetch his family, and with him travelled several other Boers, including two women and some children. When they approached the river their waggons were stopped by Khama's men. A fracas ensued, and Grobler received a bullet wound from the effects of which he died a fortnight later.[1]

Grobler's death, occurring at a critical moment, was a serious blow to Kruger, who had no one ready to replace him. He realised that his opening gambit had failed, and, having prepared no alternative move, was obliged for the time being to confine himself to attacks on paper. He bombarded the High Commissioner with despatches containing a good deal of special pleading and many unwarranted assertions—there was even a suggestion that the attack on Grobler had been instigated by Moffat !—but the rush of events which followed Moffat's treaty was too rapid for the slow-moving Boers, who found it impossible to stay their course.

[1] Sir Sidney Shippard, who held a searching enquiry into this affray, came to the conclusion that Grobler was accidentally shot by one of his own party. (*Blue Book*, C. 5918, pp. 131, 132.)

CHAPTER XIII

THE MATABELE CONCESSION

I. BIRDS OF PREY

THE Moffat treaty, which dashed the hopes of the Boers and Portuguese, had the opposite effect on the ever-widening circle of speculators interested in South African mining ventures, who hastily assumed that it meant an ' Open Sesame ' to the northern goldfields. Signs of this feeling were not long in appearing at Bulawayo. Even before Moffat's arrival Lobengula had met with a certain amount of annoyance from white men seeking permission to prospect for gold, and as soon as it was known that British subjects were free to enter his dominions—for that was how the treaty was interpreted—their numbers swelled and their importunities grew more pressing. The discoveries at the Rand had shown that gold formations might be found in the most unexpected places in South Africa. Although Tati had proved a disappointment there were reasonable grounds for thinking that the Mashonaland reefs, depicted in such glowing language by Mauch twenty years earlier, might be as rich as those of the Transvaal—if not richer. Men reminded one another of the legends of Monomotapa and the Land of Ophir, which had persistently clung for centuries to this sealed and secret land, and a new life was unquestionably given to these old stories by the publication, just about that time, of Rider Haggard's half fantastic, half serious romance *King Solomon's Mines,* which hinted at vast hoards of gold and diamonds hidden somewhere in the mysterious precincts of ancient Zimbabwe, and of further incalculable treasure still unrevealed and awaiting the miner.

The disbandment of Warren's force had released a number of enterprising young Englishmen and British Colonials, a few of whom, in search of further adventures and with the vision of rapid wealth at the back of their minds, made their way to Bulawayo. But they found that the mere mention of prospecting put Lobengula on his guard. He knew what had happened in the Transvaal, and felt that if he once yielded and allowed digging in his own country it would speedily be overrun by hundreds of miners, and he would no longer be able to call it his own. His people also were nervous at the appearance of so many new-comers, and it was only by keeping his soldiers constantly engaged in marauding expeditions at a distance that he could guard against an outbreak of violence. This was the one thing he dreaded, for, with the lesson of Cetewayo fresh in his memory, he foresaw that an attack on white men—above all on Englishmen—would be the signal for an armed invasion from the south, and would eventually lead to the dissolution of his kingdom. But it was no easy matter to keep the peace, and more than once he was embarrassed by the indiscretion of white men who, having obtained leave to shoot game, were found to be scratching about with pick and shovel in the hope of lighting on a payable reef. It is probable indeed that his consent to the treaty was partly inspired by the thought that he could count on the assistance of the 'Great White Queen' in restraining the movements of her subjects, who were causing him nearly as much anxiety as the Boers. But to his disgust the treaty gave him no such relief. As soon as it was made public—that is about the middle of 1888—there set in a regular race to secure rights to mine for gold. The traders already in the country put themselves in communication with speculators at the Cape and elsewhere, pointing out the advantageous position they enjoyed for making terms with the King, and they were soon joined by others who had received the promise of financial backing from the City of London, or even in some cases from New York or Berlin. Rhodes was one of the first to join in the scramble. As soon as Moffat had cleared the ground he sent up a private agent—one of the de Beers staff, by name Fry, who had a long experience with natives, and being a competent Zulu linguist would, he thought, be just the man to tackle Lobengula on the subject of a concession.

This game of 'concession-hunting' was no new thing in South Africa. For many years white men had played on the avarice or ignorance of native rulers to induce them to grant exclusive rights—not only for mining, but for trading and other purposes. Swaziland was a glaring example of the resulting evils. There the king, Umbandine, who had asked in vain for British protection, had been victimised by dozens of adventurers—mainly Boers and British—who bribed him with firearms, drink or blankets into granting them monopolies for every conceivable object. The country was entangled in a network of conflicting concessions for banking, postal and telegraph services, customs, not to mention land and mineral rights, all acquired with a view to exploitation if the Transvaal or British government assumed control. Swaziland was in consequence overrun by ne'er-do-well white men and was in a state bordering on anarchy. Other native territories in the south were afflicted in a lesser degree, though Matabeleland had so far escaped. Morally, of course, it was all scandalous and wrong. The concession-hunters had no thought of extending or advancing civilisation, but were one and all actuated by self-interest, and the hope of turning their 'rights' into cash.

The question will naturally be asked ' How came it that

Rhodes, who was already a man of immense wealth, and whose aims were professedly lofty and altruistic, lent himself to this rather sordid business of angling for grants of mineral rights, first from Lobengula and later from other savage chiefs ? ' The answer is that if he was to succeed in his cherished design of obtaining an opening for British influence he had no alternative. He knew that it was useless to try to convince the authorities at home that it was their duty, in the interests of humanity, to put an end to the barbarous despotisms of the dark interior by the straightforward course of forcible occupation. Ten years earlier Sir Bartle Frere—the most Imperial-minded High Commissioner, except Milner, that South Africa has known—had vainly endeavoured to impress upon the Government that there could be no security, either for the European colonists or for their black neighbours, until autocracies of the Zulu type were uprooted and replaced by British institutions. His advice was flouted, and when the Zulu War came he was made a scapegoat. The Matabele régime was one of the Zulu type. Every thinking man in South Africa, including the missionaries, realised that its existence, cheek by jowl with civilisation, was a dangerous anachronism, and must be brought to an end.

But invasion and occupation of independent native states, however desirable in the interests of themselves or those around them, were acts which the conscience of a large number of Englishmen in the late nineteenth century would strongly reprobate. The spirit of Clive was dead ; the finger of Kitchener had not yet pointed the way. Native rights were sacrosanct, and any encroachment on them would be regarded in certain quarters with pious horror. And in these quarters were people with votes, and votes counted more with the politicians in office than the demands of the distant dependencies whose fortunes they controlled.

On the other hand there were continental Powers—Germany and Belgium in particular—whose public consciences were not so squeamish. Even the Portuguese—the most decrepit nation in Europe—would not have waited for provocation from Lobengula—would not have hesitated to snatch his country—had they felt themselves strong enough to attack him. For the moment the Moffat treaty had checked such aspirations, but any faltering on the part of Britain in following it up would infallibly have played into foreign hands.

Rhodes knew that his plans must be devised in such a way as to give no offence to cranks and hypersensitive philanthropists at home. Any advance into the interior must be—ostensibly, at all events—based on the consent of the native kings and chiefs. It must have the semblance of peaceful penetration, and be completely divested of any outward show of force. That is why, determined as he was to bring into the British sphere of influence the magnificent stretch of rich and fertile country in which the Matabele had hitherto run riot, he resorted, in default of better means, to the well-worn expedient of a concession on which he could found a right of entry.

II. MANOEUVRES

The selection of Mr. Fry to open the campaign was unfortunate. He had in him—though he had no suspicion of it—the germs of cancer. The long and arduous waggon journey to Bulawayo brought the disease to a head, and he was obliged to return to a death-bed without having accomplished anything. Much valuable time was thereby lost, and other financial groups were already bestirring themselves. It was essential for Rhodes's project that a new move should be made without delay, and as soon as he heard of Fry's illness he decided to bring his heavy guns into action. His plan was to despatch a deputation of a much more weighty character, entrusted with full discretion as to the terms to be offered to Lobengula, and he conceived that it might be possible to secure for it, indirectly, some measure of official support.

As is well known he selected Mr. C. D. Rudd, a cool-headed business man who had been his partner in several mining transactions in Kimberley and Johannesburg; Rochfort Maguire, an Oxford friend of brilliant attainments, though without any previous experience of up-country conditions, and F. R. Thompson, a South African colonial, who had spent his life in handling natives and spoke Zulu as easily as his mother tongue. This curiously assorted trio reached Bulawayo in September, 1888—not a moment too soon, for besides a number of independent adventurers whom they found encamped round Lobengula's kraal, and trying by persuasive means to ingratiate themselves with him, there arrived, almost simultaneously, an expedition equipped and financed by a wealthy German speculator, and another supported by a strong syndicate of London financiers—both on the same errand as themselves. Surrounded by so many rival parties and individuals Lobengula hardly knew which way to turn. The crisis he had so long anticipated was now imminent, and he had to play practically a lone hand. All the suitors for concessions—even those who represented the German capitalist—were British, and he had committed himself to befriend the subjects of the Queen, but he had a difficult task to protect them from molestation at the hands of his people, especially the young soldiers, who were becoming more and more restless at the sight of so many newcomers, all intent on something which was neither hunting nor trading, and therefore clearly having some sinister purpose. They utterly failed to grasp the danger of interfering with them. A few of the older councillors realised, as Lobengula did, the risk of violence, and urged the King to make terms with the party which seemed the most to be trusted, on condition that all others should be sent about their business. The missionaries gave the same advice, but even if he had been disposed to follow this course, the question was which of the various candidates it would be safe to trust, and how much he could concede without jeopardising his own freedom of action. He was outwardly civil to all ; accepted their presents, and allowed them to attend him at his kraal, where he regaled them with quantities of cooked meat and *tshwala* (native beer) ; but he was desperately careful to avoid committing himself to any definite promises. Meanwhile the position was growing more precarious, and was aggravated by the intrigues which were going on among the white men themselves, each trying to steal a march on his rivals by cajoling the King, who ended by suspecting them all. Rudd's party was at first in no better favour than the others, and made no progress.

At this juncture it was brought to Lobengula's knowledge that Sir Sidney Shippard, the Commissioner of the Protectorate and the nearest representative of the ' Great White Queen ' (for Moffat had not yet been accredited as British Resident in Matabeleland), was travelling north to visit him. In the ordinary way he would have welcomed the opportunity of laying before a high British official his uneasiness at the plague of rapacious white men who infested his country, but some of the hangers-on at the kraal, who had good reason to fear that the Commissioner might expose their pretensions, began to circulate mischievous reports as to the purpose of his visit, and the credulous Matabele at once took alarm. It became known that Shippard was accompanied by mounted soldiers—in reality an escort of an officer and sixteen other ranks of the Bechuanaland Police—and these were magnified, and said to be the vanguard of an army of invasion. Other reports credited

Shippard with being a magician of deadly powers, whose real intention was to bewitch the King and seize the country.[1]

Shippard was one of the ablest men in South Africa. After a distinguished career at the bar he had been raised, at an unusually early age, to the bench of the Supreme Court, but his strong Imperial leanings tempted him to abandon the monotonous security of a judicial post for the more creative and active life of a pioneer administrator. He was really too big a man for such a job, but no doubt he was fascinated by the prospect of the developments which were on foot, and hoped to have a share in them ; for he was in thorough sympathy with Rhodes's ambitious ideas of northern expansion, and was to a great extent in his confidence. The primary object of his present expedition was to hold an official enquiry into the death of Grobler, which the Boers alleged had been deliberately instigated by Khama. On the completion of this he was instructed to try to find a solution of the long-standing difference between Khama and Lobengula as to the ownership of the ' disputed territory ' north of the Macloutsie river, and for this purpose to visit both. He found Khama willing to come to terms with Lobengula and learnt that the latter had made a significant gesture by sending a peaceful deputation of *indunas* to Shoshong, evidently with a view to a settlement, but the situation was still complicated by the disturbing

---

[1] The late Brigadier-General W. Bodle, C.M.G., who was at that time Regimental Sergeant-Major of the Bechuanaland Border Police, and was one of Shippard's escort, informed the writer that the latter idea originated with a Matabele who had been engaged on the road to help with the waggons. This man, who was possibly a spy, peeped one evening under the skirt of Sir Sidney's tent while he was having a hot bath, and took the whole proceeding to be a mystic rite, and the soap with which he lathered his naked body to be a magic and potent ' medicine '.

The fact that Shippard's party travelled by night ' like wolves and ghosts ' gave additional ground for suspicion.

presence of several irresponsible white men, striving to get concessions in the disputed area from both chiefs, and playing one against the other.

Towards the end of September Shippard, with his escort, which was commanded by Major Goold-Adams,[1] and accompanied for the first part of his journey by a few of Khama's men to act as guides, set out on the road to Bulawayo to carry out the more delicate part of his errand. On reaching the first of Lobengula's military kraals his progress was stopped by a number of young Matabele soldiers, and when he protested to the local *induna* he was informed of the reports which had reached the King of his evil designs, and told that his further advance would not be permitted unless he consented to reduce his escort to four men only. Shippard of course refused to comply, but this unexpected hindrance only whetted his determination to carry through his plans, and after a good deal of parleying he obtained leave to send a letter to Lobengula requesting him to give orders that the whole party should be allowed to resume their march without being subjected to vexatious opposition from his underlings. While waiting for a reply to this he was exposed to the most humiliating annoyance. Fresh detachments of *matjaha* arrived daily, and their attitude became increasingly threatening. Although they refrained from actual attack they indulged in war-dances, rushing up to the *scherm* of bushes which the police escort had built round the Commissioner's camp, shouting out insults and trying to provoke the troopers to some retaliation which would justify them in massacring the whole party on the plea of self-defence. Shippard's men, however, preserved an admirable restraint, and when some of the most truculent of the savages brandished assegais within a few feet of them showed not the slightest sign of flinching—refrained even from displaying their carbines.

[1] Afterwards Sir Hamilton Goold-Adams, Governor of Queensland.

Their dangerous predicament was partially relieved a few days later when a letter was received from Bulawayo authorising them to proceed, but the Matabele soldiers were resolved not to let them out of sight and marched on either side of the party for the rest of the way. From the inhabitants of the villages passed on the road they suffered every sort of irritating treatment, short of actual violence, until they were within a day's journey of the capital, and Shippard began to have grave doubts as to the reception he might receive from the King himself.

There is no reason for thinking that Lobengula was a party to these demonstrations, though he had undoubtedly been upset by the absurd reports which had reached him as to Shippard's intentions. Whether he believed them or not he had thought it proper to take precautions, and had been busy with his witch-doctors concocting ' medicine ', and painting his body with powerful antidotes to counteract spells. It was the ' soldiers ' accompanying the mission that caused him uneasiness, and it required all Moffat's efforts to reassure him by explaining that such an escort indicated the high rank of the ' Queen's Induna ', and should be interpreted as a compliment to himself.

Shippard learnt that Lobengula had betaken himself to one of his ' country seats ' at the Umgusa river, and at once made his way there. After the rough treatment he had encountered on the road he was agreeably surprised to find that his reception was almost overpoweringly cordial. In accordance with native etiquette a couple of days were allowed to pass to permit the exchange of presents—a fat ox from the King, and a roll of cloth from the Commissioner —and to give the distinguished visitor time to rest. On the third day Shippard was conducted by two of the principal generals—Lotje and Sekombo—into the King's quarters for a formal preliminary interview. He had with him Goold-Adams as A.D.C. and Moffat, together with the Rev.

Charles Helm, the head of the London Mission, as official
interpreter, and Dr. Knight-Bruce, Bishop of Bloemfontein,
who had come up to ask leave to open an Anglican church
mission in Mashonaland. Beyond a polite interchange of
courtesies no business was transacted, but the two principals
made a favourable impression on each other—Lobengula by
his towering bulk, his kingly presence and natural suavity,
and Shippard by his dignified official demeanour, his
immaculate attire of frock coat, gloves and imposing topee,
and the glittering star of St. Michael and St. George, which
was pinned to his breast. The proceedings were of the
friendliest character, and appointments were made for further meetings at which matters of state should be discussed.

These later interviews took place at Bulawayo, under the
shade of the famous ' Indaba Tree ' (still preserved on the
site of the former kraal), and what passed between the king
and Sir Sidney was not revealed by the latter in his general
report. The conversations formed the subject of a separate
and confidential despatch, which was not allowed to see the
light of day through the medium of a Blue Book, but
remained hidden in the archives of the Colonial Office. For
reasons which will afterwards appear we may feel certain,
however, that the king appealed to Shippard for advice on
the subject which was most exercising him—how to deal
with the numerous parties who were badgering him for
concessions. In fact in a memorandum which Shippard
furnished some months afterwards to the High Commissioner he disclosed that he had impressed on Lobengula that
the Government was not concerned with mining schemes or
trading ventures, and added, with somewhat exaggerated
emphasis, that no Government officer had anything to do
with the concession obtained by Rudd and his colleagues
a week after these very interviews.[1] In his anxiety to
dissociate himself and his subordinate Moffat from any

[1] *Blue Book*, C. 5918, p. 153.

overt connection with such a transaction he had ordered the latter to leave Matabeleland for a time, without giving any reasons to Lobengula, who was surprised at the decision.[1]

It was manifestly undesirable that the outside world should have grounds for suggesting that representatives of the Crown had used their position to support a particular individual in his efforts to drive a commercial bargain with a native chief, but it is nevertheless difficult to believe that Shippard gave no hint to the King that he would be safe in coming to terms with men of the standing of Rhodes's three delegates. It can hardly be a pure coincidence that within a few days of their confidential talk Lobengula, who up to that moment had been keeping all concession-hunters at arm's length, should so suddenly and completely have changed his mind in Rudd's favour. It is well to be frank about this matter. Rhodes wanted an official aegis for his negotiations, and Shippard was only one of several Imperial officials who, knowing Rhodes's ultimate purpose, felt justified in helping him.

In conversations with Moffat and the old hunter Sam Edwards—the two men best qualified to judge—Shippard found that they took a most gloomy view of the immediate outlook in Matabeleland. Both were of opinion that a massacre of whites was imminent, and would probably be provoked by some attempt by filibusters from the Transvaal to push their way into the country. Both were doubtful of Lobengula's capacity to keep in hand his young soldiers, whose loyalty was wavering, and who were daily becoming more impatient at the presence of so many white immigrants. From the ease with which they bullied and butchered the miserable Mashonas they had come to think themselves invincible, and to regard the killing of a handful of white men as a bagatelle. They were quite incapable of

[1] *Blue Book*, C. 5918, p. 127.

discerning the possibility of such an outrage recoiling on themselves.[1]

III. LOBENGULA YIELDS

From what has already been said it will be gathered that, as soon as Shippard started on his return journey, Rudd's party set to work with renewed confidence on their negotiations with the King, and, within a week, they had the satisfaction of concluding an agreement for an exclusive mineral concession over the whole of the territory of which he claimed the sovereignty.

The terms of this agreement were drafted by Rudd and Maguire and set out on paper by the former in his own handwriting, while Thompson was mainly responsible for the difficult task of bargaining with the King as to the conditions, and inducing him and his leading councillors to view them favourably. In this he found a staunch supporter in the old *induna* Lotje, whom he had succeeded in convincing of the advantages of an alliance with the Rhodes group and the rejection of all others. At a prolonged and final *indaba* on October 30 the agreement was ' fully interpreted and explained to Lobengula and his full Council of *Indunas* ' by the Rev. Mr. Helm, who appended a certificate to that effect, adding that ' all the constitutional usages of the Matabele nation had been complied

---

[1] Apart from the two missionaries, Helm and Carnegie, who lived at Hopefountain, close to Bulawayo, with their families, the most prominent white men in Matabeleland at this time were Mr. E. A. Maund, formerly one of Warren's officers, who represented an influential syndicate of London financiers (the Exploring Company) ; Mr. W. Renny-Tailyour, who was there on behalf of Herr Lippert, a wealthy German speculator ; Messrs. A. Boggie, J. Cooper-Chadwick and B. Wilson, who were at first acting independently, but afterwards threw in their lot with the Rhodes party ; Messrs. James Dawson, James Fairbairn and a few other resident traders, and of course Messrs. Rudd, Maguire and Thompson, with their transport manager, Dreyer.

with prior to its execution'. The King made a cross on the paper in token of acceptance, and Helm wrote ' *Lobengula, his mark* ' round it. Everything in connection with the agreement was above board and in order.

Judged by the ordinary civilised standards the conditions are perfectly clear. In return for an undertaking to pay to Lobengula, his heirs and successors, £100 in cash on the first day of every lunar month ; [1] to deliver 1,000 Martini-Henry rifles and 100,000 rounds of ammunition at the royal kraal, and to place on the Zambesi—for what purpose was not stated—a steamer armed with guns, the King granted to Rudd, Maguire and Thompson, ' their heirs, representatives and assigns, jointly and severally ' the ' complete and exclusive charge of all metals and minerals situated and contained in his kingdoms, principalities and dominions '. These were the main provisions ; there were others which will be referred to later.

This concession, which was to form the foundation stone of the Chartered Company, and is still recognised as constituting its original title to the minerals of Southern Rhodesia, has often been discussed and criticised from the point of view of the grantees. For the purpose of the present narrative it is more pertinent to try to discover what was in Lobengula's mind when he agreed to it—how far, in fact, he really understood the full import of its legal phraseology as ' interpreted and explained ' to him.

Did he or his councillors, for instance, comprehend what was meant by the word ' assigns ' ? It is possible—indeed probable—that Shippard had informed the King that behind Rudd and his partners, whom he could see for himself, was a group of trustworthy and honourable Englishmen, headed by one Rhodes—a group possessed of large resources, and

[1] *i.e.* at each new moon. Calendar months were of course meaningless to natives, who measured time by the moon. But it was an inconvenient arrangement, and was afterwards modified.

ready to spend money freely in his country. But could Lobengula have foreseen that the intentions of this group were to introduce many hundreds of other white men to dig the gold, and that every one of them would be an 'assign'? Could he have contemplated that the words 'to do all things they may deem necessary to win and procure the minerals' would be held to include the formation of permanent townships; the employment on the mines and otherwise of large numbers of his slaves; the erection of telegraph lines; the construction of waggon roads in all directions and the thousand and one other innovations— necessary and inherent to the business of mining, but utterly inconsistent with the retention of his own control, and utterly subversive of the privacy he and his subjects had hitherto enjoyed?

To carry the enquiry a step further: could Mr. Helm himself—a simple, straightforward clergyman, familiar no doubt with the 'constitutional usages' of the Matabele, but with little knowledge of the vast programme of colonisation in the minds of Rhodes and his partners—have envisaged the revolutionary effects of the contract? And if he did have some notion of its real implications could he— proficient though he was in the Matabele tongue—have unfolded them in such language as to make them comprehensible to the intelligence of natives, whose sequence of thought runs on entirely different lines from that of educated Europeans? It is of course probable that Helm had gathered from conversations with Rudd or Maguire some general idea that a great effort was on foot to open up Mashonaland, and that in the interests of the Matabele he did his best to explain this to Lobengula; but it is hardly credible that he should have warned him that by signing the concession he would be parting with a vital part of his sovereignty, and would be giving the freedom of his country, not merely to the three men he knew, but to as many others as they might choose to bring in for their mining operations.

Lobengula was no fool. In fact he was one of the most astute natives that white men have ever had to deal with. He needed no hint from Helm to tell him that he had arrived at the parting of the ways. If he could have had his wish he would have made a clean sweep of all the whites in Matabeleland, but he knew that it was too late for that. Either he must make terms with some of them—and these three were, he was assured, the most to be trusted—or he and his tribe would have to move on, as they had moved before in his father's time, and find a new country. The conditions of the Rudd concession show that he was impelled not so much by motives of personal aggrandisement, as by a genuine belief that it offered the only means of preventing his people from being eaten up. To that end he would have to make sacrifices. The income of £1,300 a year was no doubt an attractive bait, but it was all he got out of the concession for himself. The rifles and the gunboat show the real trend of his thoughts. They were for protection against the Boers and Portuguese. But most important of all was the clause which empowered the grantees to keep at a distance all the other sharks. ' Whereas I have been much molested of late by divers persons seeking and desiring to obtain grants and concessions of land and mining rights in my territories, I do hereby authorise the said grantees . . . to take all necessary and lawful steps to exclude . . . all persons seeking land, metals, minerals, or mining rights therein, and I do hereby undertake to render them all such needful assistance as they may from time to time require . . .' There was nothing to indicate that Rudd and his friends would bring in their train a still more persistent and dangerous following ; nobody to warn him, as Joubert had once warned him, that the English never let go. He probably thought of Tati—the only mining right that had so far been given—where the few diggers gave him no trouble. Another grant on the same lines would be a small price to pay for getting rid of all the disturbing elements which harassed him and upset his people.

This is the only reasonable explanation of Lobengula's readiness to sell his mining rights for a consideration which was equivalent merely to a few thousand pounds. It is impossible to think that with full understanding he put his signature to a deed which was virtually a surrender of the whole of Mashonaland to a commercial company.

The Rudd concession is as remarkable for its omissions as for its comprehensions. On Lobengula's part it contains no specific reservations—except one in favour of the Tati Company—but on the other hand it confers on the grantees no power of making laws or regulations for the maintenance of order, and no land rights. As regards the latter it is true that Lobengula undertook to make no concessions of land to other parties, but this negative provision could hardly be construed as giving the parties represented by Rudd the right to mark out town sites, mining areas or farms for themselves. At a later date, when Lobengula took alarm at the influx of pioneers, he tried, in a spirit of pique, to go back on this guarantee by granting to the German, Herr Lippert, the sole right of dealing with land in Matabeleland and Mashonaland, but he completely defeated his purpose, for Rhodes bought the right for the Chartered Company, and thereby entrenched himself in a stronger position than ever.

Rhodes knew that the concession would have to be approved by the Imperial Government, and on Rudd's arrival in Capetown a copy was at once sent to Sir Hercules Robinson for transmission to the proper quarter. In the meantime a general knowledge of its terms had leaked out in the City of London, and had even reached the Secretary of State (Lord Knutsford), who displayed some qualms as to the propriety of sanctioning the delivery of rifles and ammunition to Lobengula as part of the consideration. Of course Lobengula's object in obtaining them was obvious. He saw that by continuing to depend on their stabbing assegais his regiments were at a grave disadvantage when engaged against an enemy using firearms. This had been proved not only in their former collisions with the Boers, but more recently when their attacks on native tribes at Lake Ngami and elsewhere had failed owing to their inability to rush in to close quarters in the face of well-directed gunfire.

The General Act of the Brussels Conference, which condemned the traffic in firearms with natives, was not passed until a year later, but most of the European Powers, including Britain, had already expressed agreement with the principle, and Lord Knutsford was nervous of the responsibility of departing from it. He therefore telegraphed to the High Commissioner asking whether this clause might not lead to complications, and his enquiry gave rise to some illuminating official by-play. Sir Hercules consulted the accommodating Shippard, who at once reassured him by pointing out that a Matabele armed with a rifle would be far less formidable than when ' assegai in hand, he stalks his victims as at present ' ; that the butchery in raiding expeditions would be greatly reduced if Lobengula's *impis* took to fighting at long range, and that their abandonment of the assegai in favour of the rifle would thus be ' a distinct gain to the cause of humanity '. He pointed out that if Lobengula were prevented from getting the guns in question he would undoubtedly secure all he wanted through the Transvaal, which would lead to more troublesome complications. Shippard made another amazing statement. On his way south he had discussed the condition as to firearms with Khama, who was apprehensive that it might imply hostile intentions on Lobengula's part against the ba-Mangwato, but as Rudd was prepared to give arms and ammunition to Khama also for defensive purposes ' the relative positions of the Chiefs would remain unchanged ' ! [1]

These rather specious and transparent arguments were successful in allaying official doubts, and the Colonial Secretary offered no further objection to the concession.

The condition as to the gunboat on the Zambesi was prompted by Lobengula's anxiety to get even with the river tribes of Barotseland, who, in their dug-out canoes, were slippery customers to tackle, and possibly also with some idea of restricting the activities of the Portuguese, who were said to be using their ancient settlements at Zumbo and Tete as bases for encroachments on territory claimed by him to the south of them. No arrangement was suggested as to who should control the movements of the vessel, or how it should be manned ; in fact the condition was never treated very seriously, and was tacitly suffered to lapse on payment of £500, the alternative mentioned in the concession.

[1] *Blue Book*, C. 5918, p. 153.

CHAPTER XIV

THE ORDEAL OF LOBENGULA

I. THE ENVOYS

ANY relief of mind that Lobengula may have gained from the bargain he had struck was short-lived. Rudd, with the concession in his pocket, had not left his presence more than a week or so when Bulawayo began to buzz with new alarms. In the first place disquieting reports came to hand of threatening movements by the Portuguese, both from the Zambesi and on the eastern side of Mashonaland. Lobengula had heard already from Moffat of their pretensions to his country, but as long as these were not translated into active aggression he paid very little attention to them. Now, however, it was stated that armed bodies of *askaris* led by white officers were visiting Mashona chiefs who had for years paid tribute to him and his father before him ; persuading them to acknowledge the sovereignty of the King of Portugal, and in some cases to hoist the Portuguese flag in token of submission. The reports were too circumstantial to be disregarded, and Lobengula began to cogitate on the advisability of appealing to the British sovereign, whose friendship had been guaranteed by the Moffat treaty.

Before he had made up his mind a further complication arose. Shortly after the death of Pieter Grobler his brother Frederick had arrived in Bulawayo, and tried hard to inveigle the King into an admission that he had entered into an agreement with the deceased 'Consul' which took precedence of that with Moffat. In this he failed utterly, and Lobengula, on being shown by Moffat a copy of the alleged agreement, made a written declaration under his hand and seal that his conversations with Pieter Grobler merely related to some 'old treaty of general friendship' made by his father Mziligazi with the Boer leader Potgieter. But the ingenuity of the Boer intriguers was by no means exhausted, and Shippard's official visit and the appearance at Bulawayo of so many English concession-hunters stimulated them to fresh exertions. Towards the end of the year (1888) they circulated rumours that there was no such country as England ; that the 'Great White Queen' was a myth, and that Shippard and Moffat, who had professed to be her representatives, were impostors. Such wild statements carried little weight with Lobengula himself, but they spread quickly among his credulous subjects, and created such a hubbub that he felt it imperative to take action.

It has been mentioned that among those who were seeking concessions was Mr. E. A. Maund, who was already well known to Lobengula, having, as one of Warren's officers, been sent officially to Matabeleland in 1885 to announce and explain the protectorate established in Khama's country. He was a man of commanding presence and engaging manners, and had made a good impression on Lobengula, who still looked on him as one of the 'Queen's Indunas ', and now, in the absence of Moffat, sought his advice. Notwithstanding the Rudd concession, of the extent of which he only had a general idea, Maund had not given up hope of being able to negotiate some advantageous arrangement for his own principals—the Exploring Company—and had in fact already intimated to them that there was a probability of securing at least a trading monopoly. But he felt that the Rudd concession was a serious obstacle to his plans, and that some means must at once be devised to attack it.

TSHOVU, ONE OF LOBENGULA'S WIVES

Taking advantage of Lobengula's anxiety he cleverly suggested that he should proceed to England as his emissary carrying with him a confidential letter to H.M.'s Government in regard to the Portuguese encroachments, the details of which he would personally explain. He also offered to take with him a deputation of Matabele natives to clear up the doubts as to the reality of the Queen, and to ask for advice as to the best way of dealing with the plague of white men seeking concessions to dig for gold. Lobengula was greatly attracted by both proposals and took immediate steps to give them effect. Two headmen were selected to form the deputation, one of them, Mshete, being a relative of the King but otherwise of no particular standing in the nation, while the other, Babyaan, was a man of some weight and intelligence, and Mr. Johann Colenbrander, a Natal Colonial and a fluent Zulu linguist, who had arrived in Bulawayo as a member of Herr Lippert's expedition, was attached to the party as interpreter. With Maund's assistance Lobengula prepared a letter addressed to the Queen in person, asking her to defend him against the Portuguese, and he agreed to defray the expenses of his headmen during their absence.

The party started off without loss of time and reached Capetown at the end of January, 1889. There they were interrogated by Sir Hercules Robinson, who after reading the letter which Lobengula had intrusted to Maund, and satisfying himself that the two natives had no other purpose than to obtain proof—ocular if possible—that the Queen actually existed and was not a creature of imagination, gave them leave to proceed. He does not seem to have suspected that the mission had any connection with the Rudd concession to which he had already given his blessing, and it may be taken for granted that Maund did not volunteer information on that point.

During their stay of some weeks in this country the two

headmen witnessed artillery practice with heavy guns at Shoeburyness, and a field day at Aldershot. They were shown over the bullion vaults of the Bank of England, and were given opportunities of seeing portions of the fleet, dockyards, manufacturing towns and other spectacles, all a tremendous revelation to raw savages of the wealth and military strength of the land of the Great Queen. Finally they were allowed to gratify their hearts' desire by beholding Her Majesty in person. The Queen gave them an audience, and ordered them to be presented with a large portrait of herself and other gifts for conveyance to Lobengula. The stage management of the whole tour was admirable, and its results might have been equally satisfactory had the Colonial Office handled the occasion with common sense, and had no outsiders been permitted to create false impressions in the minds of the two central figures.

The vacillations of successive Colonial Secretaries in regard to South African affairs had become proverbial, but rarely was this habit more deplorably exhibited than in Lord Knutsford's manner of dealing with the various proposals for opening up Matabeleland, and especially with the opportunity now offered by Lobengula's obvious desire to invoke the aid of the British Government in restoring tranquillity to his country. To appreciate this it is necessary to retrace the erratic course of his policy.

Some months before Rudd brought off his coup the Colonial Office had been approached by the Exploring Company through its Chairman, Mr. George Cawston, a City financier, who announced that it was intended to send an expedition to Matabeleland to try to obtain a concession. He was informed in reply that the Government could not countenance any concession or agreement unless it was concluded with the knowledge and approval of the High Commissioner, but in spite of this discouragement the

Exploring Company went on with its plans and Maund, as we know, became its agent for carrying them out. In the case of Rhodes and Rudd there is nothing in the published correspondence to show that they made any such preliminary advances to the Government, and Lord Knutsford's first knowledge of their concession was apparently derived from rumours which reached him towards the end of 1888.[1] On December 17 he telegraphed to Robinson to ascertain the facts, and received confirmation of the concession by cable on the following day. Public interest in the matter was by this time aroused, and on the 20th the Government was asked in the House of Commons what steps it was proposed to take in regard to it. To this the Under Colonial Secretary replied that as Great Britain had no protectorate in Matabeleland the Government had no right to interfere in any grant or concession which Lobengula might choose to make. A week later a copy of the actual agreement, together with Rudd's explanation of the circumstances in which it was executed, and of his future intentions for giving it effect, were in Lord Knutsford's hands, Robinson having sent them forward in a despatch in which he expressed the hope that ' the effect of this concession to a gentleman of character and financial standing would be to check the inroad of adventurers as well as to secure the cautious development of the country with a proper consideration for the feelings and prejudices of the natives '.

Whether Lord Knutsford shared this pious hope or not does not appear from the official correspondence, but as the right of the Government to interfere had already been openly disclaimed it may be presumed that he did not intend—in spite of the fact that so far as he knew the High Commissioner had not been consulted during the negotiations—in spite, too, of his anxiety about the rifles referred to

[1] *Blue Book*, C. 5918, p. 129.

in the last chapter—to put any obstacles in Rudd's way.
On the other hand he took a very definite stand a fortnight
later in regard to a proposal in which the Exploring Company was again interested. This was contained in a letter
from Lord Gifford, of the Bechuanaland Exploration
Company, who stated that it was intended to amalgamate
interests already acquired in Khama's country, and expected to be acquired in Lobengula's, by the two companies,
and asking whether the Government would give its blessing
to such a scheme in the shape of a charter. Lord Knutsford
replied once more that the suggestion could not be entertained without the recommendation of the High Commissioner.

Faced with these inconsistencies one cannot resist the
inference that the Secretary of State was anxious to dis-
courage all proposals for developing the resources of Lobengula's territory except the one behind which, as he must
surely have known, stood Rhodes and the powerful group
of financiers—among others the house of Rothschild—
associated with him. And in this, apart from the maladroit
manner in which he carried out his policy, he was no doubt
guided by motives of expediency. The Government
wanted Matabeleland, but were loth to spend any money
in obtaining it. If they could get the country opened up
to British enterprise by a commercial syndicate, and be
relieved of responsibility or cost, they were quite prepared to acquiesce, and this object was more likely to be
attained by the Rhodes group than by any other body of
speculators.

When, however, he was confronted by the two Matabele
headmen, escorted by Maund, who, as agent of the Exploring Company, had every reason to get the Rudd concession set aside—Lord Knutsford seems to have been
disposed to hedge and to seek refuge in ambiguities.
What action he took in regard to the Portuguese difficulty

was not at the time disclosed, but the message brought by the two headmen (or *indunas*, as they called themselves), and the reply he gave to it, were made public. The message was as follows :

Lobengula desires to know that there is a Queen. Some of the people who come into his land tell him there is a Queen, some of them tell him there is not.

Lobengula can only find out the truth by sending eyes to see whether there is a Queen.

The *Indunas* are his eyes.

Lobengula desires, if there is a Queen, to ask her to advise and help him, as he is much troubled by white men who come into his country and ask to dig gold.

There is no one with him upon whom he can trust, and he asks that the Queen will send someone from herself.[1]

With full knowledge of the concession held by Rhodes and his supporters, to which he had—tacitly, at all events— extended his approval, Lord Knutsford delivered to the envoys for conveyance to their king a long, and in some respects irrelevant reply containing, among other pieces of advice, this dangerous sentence, which bears obvious marks of Maund's influence :

They [the headmen] say that Lobengula is much troubled by white men who come into his country and ask to dig gold, and that he begs for advice and help. . . . The Queen advises Lobengula not to grant hastily concessions of land, or leave to dig, but to consider all applications very carefully. It is not wise to put too much power into the hands of the men who come first, and to exclude other deserving men. A king gives a stranger an ox, not his whole herd of cattle, otherwise what would other strangers arriving have to eat ?

What could have been more disconcerting to Lobengula ? It flung him back into the hands of the concession-hunters, all of whom would want their share of plunder, and it would

---

[1] *Blue Book*, C. 5918, p. 162. For the letter see Appendix III.

make him feel that he had already made a terrible blunder
by granting a monopoly for digging gold—' giving his whole
herd '—to use Lord Knutsford's precious, and doubtless
inspired, metaphor—' to strangers '. And what could have
been more short-sighted from the Government point of
view ? So far from easing their responsibilities it was calculated to throw Matabeleland into the same toils as those
in which Swaziland was already entangled, and from which
Bechuanaland had narrowly escaped.

This crude attempt to restore Lobengula's peace of mind
was made still more mischievous by the intrusion into the
affair of the Aborigines Protection Society, a body of well-
meaning but ill-informed philanthropists who, for some
obscure reason, chose to regard the Matabele as the down-
trodden victims of white oppression, and were seized with a
yearning to take them under their wing. They quite lost
sight of the wretched Mashona and other suffering tribes
who for half a century had groaned under the hideous persecutions of their new protégés.

The Society entertained the headmen at a breakfast
party in the Westminster Palace Hotel and a number of
politicians and prominent business men were asked to meet
them. The invitation card stated that Babyaan and
Mshete had visited England ' to ask the " Great White
Queen " to protect Matabeleland from being eaten up by
intruders ', and this supplied the keynote of most of the
speeches. During the proceedings a letter from the Society
to Lobengula was read and subsequently handed to the
Matabele guests for delivery to him. In it he was informed
that the aim of the Society was ' to help the weak to live '.
' We have ', it said, ' to oppose the actions of our fellow-
countrymen when they do wrong, although those they are
wronging may be strangers to us and men of another race '.
Lobengula was warned—as if he needed any warning !—to
be on his guard against white men seeking permission to dig

for gold, and the letter wound up by exhorting him ' to be
wary and firm in resisting proposals that would not bring
good to him and his people '.

A few days later the headmen, puffed up with self-
importance, took their departure, still in charge of Maund,
who, on arrival at the Cape learnt by cable, to his extreme
chagrin, that his company had effected a fusion of interests
with Rhodes, and that he was thenceforward to throw his
weight on to the side of the Rudd concession. It was with
very mixed feelings that he set out for Bulawayo to try to
undo the mischievous effects of his own machinations.

II. DISCORD AT BULAWAYO

The concession itself gave Lobengula at first no qualms.
He accepted the monthly payment of a hundred sovereigns,
and fully understood that as the rifles and ammunition had
to come from England some time must elapse before they
could reach him.   One provision in his agreement—that
whereby he had promised to co-operate with the concession-
aires in keeping out newcomers seeking to obtain gold-
rights—was at once put to a practical test.   A fortnight
after Rudd had left, the King received an application for
permission to enter the country from two Englishmen—
Mr. Alfred Haggard (a brother of the novelist) and the
Hon. John Wallop—who were in charge of an expedition
sent out by a new London company.   He at once authorised
Maguire to turn them back, and detailed an *induna* with an
armed force to support him.   On December 3 they met
the party with their waggons at Tati, and in spite of indignant expostulations insisted on their leaving the same day.
The humour of being expelled by an army of naked savages
led by a former Fellow of All Souls was quite lost on
Haggard, who protested bitterly to the High Commissioner
at this outrageous treatment of British subjects.   But Sir

Hercules Robinson declined to interfere, and when some weeks later the aggrieved members of the expedition returned to England Lord Knutsford refused even to see them.[1]

This was the only incident which relieved the tedium of Maguire's sojourn at Bulawayo, where he was thoroughly out of his element. He had nothing in common with the other white men who frequented the kraal, and although the object of his remaining was to prevent the king from being disturbed by outside influences he disliked the idea of paying court, as the others did, to a corpulent black man whose habits and surroundings were equally offensive. In truth, for all except those engaged in business, the daily life at Bulawayo was a purgatory. The proximity of a large Matabele kraal is at no time agreeable. The filth, the stench of native bodies and decaying garbage, and above all the innumerable flies and other insect pests make life a burden unless it is relieved by sport, trading or some regular occupation. Maguire had no resources of this kind, and he held himself aloof from both white men and natives. He was conscious of espionage on the part of the latter, several of whom had once stealthily watched him bathing in the Umguza, and when they saw him completing his toilet by using blood-red tooth paste had crept away to spread the news that he was bewitching the stream with some terrible ' medicine '. Thompson was more used to natives and more callous to the unpleasant conditions. On him fell the main responsibility of keeping the king's mind at rest, but though assiduous in his attentions and glib in the Zulu tongue he lacked the urbanity and impressive condescension by which such a man as Maund commanded respect, and never managed to establish himself in Lobengula's good graces.

[1] *Blue Book*, C. 5918, p. 155.   Letter from A. Haggard to *Pall Mall Gazette*, March, 1889.

III. FLIGHT OF THOMPSON

With Rudd and Maund, their two most formidable competitors, out of the way, the hopes of the remaining concession-hunters began to revive. None of them had any precise knowledge of the rights granted to Rudd, but the fact that they were extensive and exclusive soon leaked out through correspondence received from Cape Colony, where the press had plenty to say on the subject, and all sorts of extravagant reports and rumours were flying about. The schemers at Bulawayo, however, were by no means inclined to give up the contest at the first round, and began to cast about for some means of effecting a counter-stroke. For the time being most of them made common cause and also enlisted the sympathy of some of the traders, who were easily persuaded that the privileges they enjoyed would rapidly be curtailed once a footing was gained in the country by a rich commercial syndicate.

The campaign opened immediately after Maund left on his diplomatic errand to England. It was freely stated to some of the *indunas* that Rudd had obtained from the King a paper which gave away the rights over the whole country. So far as mineral rights were concerned this was strictly true, but it was noised about that the country itself had been sold, and the *indunas* were filled with the utmost alarm. They repeated the story to the King, who stoutly denied its truth. ' Those were not my words ', he said, ' and the paper which was read to me only gave them the right to dig holes for gold ', but the suggestion made him uncomfortable nevertheless, and he resolved to interrogate Helm. It was the season for the garnering of the early crops, and the King was busily engaged in the usual preparations for the ' Big Dance ', but he undertook that as soon as the ceremonies were over he would hold an enquiry, to which Helm, Maguire, and Thompson should be summoned to meet the other white men and the principal *indunas*, so that the matter might be cleared up.

Towards the end of January, 1889, an announcement appeared in a Mafeking newspaper over what purported to be Lobengula's signature to the effect that as a misunderstanding had arisen about what he had granted all action under the concession was suspended pending an investigation which was to be held. As one of the leading Capetown journals [1] observed, ' Anyone can put an advertisement in a newspaper and sign it "LOBENGULA ", and it would be of interest to have some witnesses' names appended to the document '; but, genuine or not,[2] its appearance, following so soon after the despatch of Maund's mission, told Rhodes that all was not going well in the North, and that it would be wise for him, or someone in his confidence, to proceed there without delay. Rhodes himself was on the point of starting for England, where he was anxious to open negotiations for obtaining a Royal Charter, and he persuaded Dr. Jameson, his most intimate friend, to undertake the journey on his behalf.

Jameson, though it sadly interfered with his lucrative practice at Kimberley, left at once, and reached Bulawayo on April 2, having made the last stages of his journey in

[1] *Cape Argus*, Feb. 26, 1889.

[2] The original notice from which this was copied remained in the custody of the late James Dawson, who was the leading trader at the time in Bulawayo, and many years afterwards was given by him (together with other interesting documents bearing on the Rudd concession) to the present writer. It is not of course signed by the King, for he could not write, nor does it bear his mark, but it is stamped with the impression of the ' Elephant Seal ', the use of which he sometimes—not always—authorised on letters and other documents. The notice also bears the signatures of G. A. Phillips, James Reilly, W. F. Usher and W. Tainton, the first three having signed as witnesses and the last as ' Interpreter '. It is undated, but its identity is established by a mistake in the spelling of Maguire's name which is repeated in the published version. Facsimiles of both the printed notice and the written original appear in the writer's *Making of Rhodesia*, on page 107.

company with the waggons carrying the first consignment
of the rifles for Lobengula. Shortly before his arrival the
promised enquiry had taken place in the presence of most of
the white men then in the kraal, and for two days there had
been a wrangle between Thompson and the King's councillors as to the exact terms of the concession. A copy produced by Helm showed clearly that Lobengula had parted
with the entire mineral rights of his country, but many of
the *indunas* who had been present during the negotiations
vehemently declared that his expressed intention had been
only to allow Rudd and his partners ' a hole to dig in '.
They flouted Thompson, who appears to have been cowed
and intimidated by their angry demeanour, and rated
Helm for false interpretation, telling him he was no longer
fit to be a teacher. The King was not present at the meeting,
but from time to time what passed was reported to him by
his *indunas*. At the close of the second day's discussion
he appeared, and pointing to Helm's copy of the agreement
said : ' White men, that thing is all lies ! Men of the
Amandebele, that thing is all lies ! ' He demanded that the
original should be sent for, and stated that if it also contained lies he would repudiate it.[1] By this he demonstrated
pretty clearly that he wanted to gain time.

As might be expected after this agitating dispute Jameson found the King in a morose and fretful mood, his nervous
condition being aggravated by an attack of gout combined
with ophthalmia, for which ' The Doctor ' was able to give
him relief, winning thereby his gratitude and paving the
way for cordial relations. He then proceeded to ease his
mental disquietude, employing his well-known gifts of
persuasion, coupled with a little discreet banter, which
proved as effective with the harassed old savage as with

[1] This summary of the proceedings is based on minutes taken down
at the time by James Dawson, and afterwards given by him to the
author.

all others who came under the spell of his genius. He talked to him about Rhodes, and explained the advantages of an alliance with so powerful a force—how it would enable him to snap his fingers at Boers and Portuguese, and would bring peace of mind to him and education, commerce and steady occupation to his unruly subjects. Lobengula's fears were dissipated, and the two men parted with an excellent mutual understanding.

Jameson also interviewed many of the white men, and assured them that they had nothing to lose and all to gain by identifying themselves with the forward movement, of which the concession was the first stepping-stone, and Rhodes—already, as he knew, a name to conjure with—the guiding spirit ; that those who lent their aid to him in the initial stages of the great venture would not be forgotten in the general settlement of claims, and that, as the men on the spot, they would have exceptional opportunities of benefiting by the good time coming. He did succeed in winning over the majority, but when he started on his return journey he left behind a small clique of irreconcilables who were as determined as ever to play their own hand, which meant the dangerous game of working on Lobengula's doubts and inducing him to repudiate his bargain.

Maguire went off with Jameson, thus leaving Thompson as the only direct representative in Bulawayo of Rhodes's interests. Though supported now by most of the established residents of Bulawayo, he was not strong enough to cope with the tactics of the opposition group. Shortly after Jameson's visit a letter was sent in Lobengula's name to the Queen stating that his *indunas* would not recognise the concession, and repeating his demand that the original document should be sent back for inspection, but carefully avoiding a personal repudiation. Although it bore the elephant seal the authenticity of this letter is doubtful, but in any case it reached England too late to disturb the progress of Rhodes's proposals for a Royal Charter, the draft of which had already been prepared. It is clear that at this stage the King was torn between his reluctance to throw overboard the advantages to be gained from the concession and his desire to soothe the agitation of his *indunas*. He was waiting for the return of his envoys, confident that they would have some reassuring message which would help him out of his dilemma.[1]

When these at last arrived—early in August—he was disgusted to find that they brought with them no relief. The letters from Lord Knutsford and the Aborigines Protection Society only aggravated his perplexity. That advice about not parting with his whole herd of cattle— eagerly seized upon by the opponents of the concession— made him feel that perhaps after all he had been duped. It is impossible not to have some compassion for this bewildered man, who was so greatly superior in intelligence to the rest of his people ; who had striven according to his lights to act in their interest, and who had never known a moment's freedom from anxiety since he put his mark to the Moffat treaty, which had promised so much, and from which he had reaped so little.

Still shrinking from an open disavowal of the concession, but forced to appease his restive *indunas*, he took the course —the only one which his native diplomacy suggested—of looking for a scapegoat, and he pitched on the veteran councillor Lotje, who had been the principal advocate of the arrangement with Rudd, and had ever since been

---

[1] At a later date, after the return of the envoys, he wrote a second letter to the Queen, again complaining about the trouble caused by white men wanting to dig for gold, and asking her not to credit any story that he had given away his whole country. But there is nothing in either letter to justify the conclusion of Mr. Stanley Portal Hyatt (*The Northward Trek*, p. 154) and other writers that Lobengula then or at any time intended to cancel the concession.

Thompson's firm ally. On September 10, 1889, the luckless old man was denounced as a traitor and led off to execution, his death by strangling being followed by the barbarous massacre of his wives and his whole household. It may seem a brutal thing to say, but there can be no doubt that the responsibility for this sacrifice to public opinion among the Matabele was directly attributable to the failure of Lord Knutsford to tackle the situation firmly, and to the indecent haste of the Aborigines Society to judge a question of which they had only heard one side.

Thompson had driven out that day with a Cape cart and four horses to visit Helm at his mission station, and when returning at sundown he met, on the outskirts of Bulawayo, a native who told him the news of Lotje's dismal fate. In his youth Thompson had seen his own father barbarously done to death by kaffirs in one of the native risings, down country, and the memory of that horror still haunted him. His nerves were strained to breaking point by his long ordeal, and he pictured himself as the next victim of Lobengula's fury. Hastily making his way to the nearest store, which was Fairbairn's, he outspanned one of his cart team, borrowed a saddle and bridle, mounted, and rode for his life, hardly daring to draw rein till the horse foundered not far from Sam Edwards' camp at Tati.

IV. RHODES'S QUANDARY

From Tati Thompson, still badly shaken, went on by post-cart to Mafeking, where he wrote to Rhodes, explaining his reasons for flight, and giving an alarming account of the state of affairs in Matabeleland. In his over-wrought condition he may have painted the picture somewhat blacker than reality, but the crisis was undoubtedly a serious one and the very fact of Thompson's abrupt departure, without notifying the King—without even stopping to collect his belongings, was calculated to make it worse. For one thing it deprived Rhodes of a direct representative on the spot, and left the King more than ever at the mercy of those who were pressing him to revoke the concession. It also endangered the safety of the remaining white men, for the atmosphere was so highly charged that the slightest false step on the part of any of them might provoke an outbreak and lead to a general massacre.

Rhodes had just returned from England, where he had been successful in reconciling all conflicting interests, and in securing the Government's approval for his cherished scheme of a Royal Charter. He had also impressed the Colonial Office with the necessity of despatching a new letter definitely conveying to Lobengula the Queen's approval of the concession, and undoing as far as possible the mischief wrought by the previous one. He was daily expecting to hear by cablegram that the Charter had been signed,[1] but on receipt of Thompson's agitated report he realised that the fate of his whole project hung in the balance. The Rudd concession was its main pivot, and if that were to break there must in any case be an indefinite postponement of action, while at the worst the Charter might prove to be still-born. His first impulse was to turn to Jameson, who, six months before, had acquired so strong an influence over Lobengula, and Jameson, throwing all personal considerations to the wind, readily undertook once more to make the long journey to Bulawayo and to endeavour to restore the king's shaken confidence. He left Kimberley without a moment's delay, carrying Rhodes's full authority to take whatever steps he might think fit to retrieve the situation. Although he was prepared to act alone he took with him, at Rhodes's suggestion, two men experienced in dealing with natives—Denis Doyle, a de

---

[1] The Charter was actually sealed under Letters Patent on Oct. 29, 1889.

Beers Compound Manager, and Major Maxwell, an old
frontiersman of the Diamond Fields Horse ; he picked up
Thompson at Mafeking and induced him to return, and at
Tati he enlisted the aid of Sam Edwards, who had more
weight with Lobengula than any other white man, and
agreed to throw it into the scale in support of Rhodes. Thus
reinforced he managed by great efforts to reach Bulawayo
on October 17—barely five weeks from the date of Thompson's precipitate flight.

Rhodes was by no means certain that Jameson would
succeed, and he could not expect to hear from him for
several weeks. He was busily engaged in arranging for the
despatch of new expeditions—to Barotseland, whose king,
Lewanika, had already made tentative overtures to the
British Government ; to Katanga, Gazaland, Nyasaland,
and other native territories which he hoped to draw into his
net. But Lobengula's country was the key position, and he
had made up his mind that the eastern portion—Mashonaland, where the gold prospects were most favourable—
should be occupied in the coming dry season of 1890. If
this could be effected with Lobengula's acquiescence so
much the better. If Lobengula or his people proved ob-
structive some means would have to be devised to circum-
vent them. He was anxious that the career of the Charter
should, if possible, open peacefully, but he did not intend
to be balked by a troublesome tribe whose long and bloody
tyranny should have been brought to an end years before.
There was no one in authority near enough to consult. Sir
Hercules Robinson had retired, and his successor, Sir Henry
Loch, had not arrived. The duties of High Commissioner
were being carried on by the General Officer commanding
at the Cape, who was not to be counted on for assistance.

Just about then Rhodes happened by chance to come
across a young man who had not long returned from the
north, where he had got into trouble with the natives.

This was Mr. Frank Johnson,[1] who had served in the Warren expedition, and afterwards in the Bechuanaland Border Police, in which he rose to be a Warrant Officer. On taking his discharge he and two or three other time-expired members of the force, all of them fired with the lust of adventure, had made their way to Matabeleland, where they obtained leave from the king, against the advice of his *indunas*, to visit Mashonaland to search for gold reefs. (It was before Rudd had obtained his concession.) The *indunas* in their rage at this disregard of their counsel trumped up a number of ridiculous charges against them and forced them to return to Bulawayo, where Johnson, as the leader of the party, was tried by Lobengula, and besides being sentenced to pay a heavy fine was ordered to leave the country. He had no alternative but to comply, but the unjust treatment filled him with bitter resentment, and he made up his mind to seize the first opportunity of getting even with his accusers and his judge. Such an opportunity, he thought, had now arrived.

At Kimberley the air was full of reports as to Rhodes's intention of sending an expedition to the northern goldfields, and there was much speculation as to how it would contrive to penetrate a country overrun by so fierce and warlike a tribe as the Matabele, whose evil reputation was notorious throughout South Africa. Johnson, with the impulsiveness and confidence of youth—he was only twenty-three years old at the time—approached Rhodes with a plan for secretly organising the prospectors and traders scattered about the Protectorate, nearly all of whom had military training; supplementing them with picked men from the Colony; equipping them with horses and arms, and holding them in readiness to make a sudden swoop on Bulawayo to seize the place by surprise and capture the person of the king.

[1] Now Lieut.-Col. Johnson, D.S.O.

It is possible that at first sight this plan may have appealed to Rhodes, for with the knowledge he then possessed it must have seemed essential that the power of the Matabele should be broken before the settlement of Mashonaland could be contemplated. The general opinion of all who were familiar with the conditions—including many missionaries—was that the peaceful occupation of any part of the region between the Zambesi and Limpopo rivers was hopeless as long as it was dominated by this detestable handful of ruthless pillagers. Moreover they were a relic of the old barbarous times which it was the prime object of the newly formed Chartered Company to bring to an end, and on grounds of humanity alone Rhodes would have been justified in adopting summary means for destroying their military system, and resorting to force if no alternative presented itself. He knew of only one road to Mashonaland— that which led through Lobengula's kingdom, and it would have been sheer madness to regard that road as a possible thoroughfare while Matabele *impis* were infesting it.

But a little reflection must have shown him that Johnson's plan was open to fatal objections. For one thing it would gravely imperil the lives of the missionaries and their families, as well as the other white folk in and around Bulawayo—Jameson among them—who would probably be butchered without scruple by the natives when they found themselves attacked. Another defect was the absence of open and direct provocation to justify such an assault. However reasonable it might appear to South Africans to clear out the Matabele like rats from a barn public opinion outside had to be considered. It would never do to ruffle the feelings of sentimentalists at home, who would have been horrified at the idea of an unprovoked raid on a native tribe—even a tribe that made raiding its livelihood. Johnson assured Rhodes that a *casus belli* would not be long in appearing, either in the shape of an outrage in Matabeleland itself, or through an incursion by a raiding *impi* into the territory claimed by Khama, who would then look to the British for protection. But these forecasts might not come to anything, and an armed force could not be kept waiting indefinitely.

Fortunately, however, the necessity for resorting to such extreme measures never arose, for close on the heels of Johnson came the hunter Selous, who knew the country intimately, and had a far more attractive plan for entering Mashonaland by a route which should skirt round the comparatively small area inhabited by the Matabele proper. Almost simultaneously Rhodes had word from Jameson that Lobengula's excitement was evaporating, that he had shown no disposition to break faith, and that there was every hope that, properly handled, he would, before long, consent to the entry of a body of miners and prospectors who would provide the thin end of the wedge for occupation on an extensive scale. Johnson's proposal consequently fell flat. Nevertheless Rhodes was considerably impressed by its boldness, and by the apparent capacity and confidence of its author, and marked him down as a person to be utilised when a suitable occasion arose. And before long it did arise, as we shall see.

CHAPTER XV

THE NORTHWARD ADVANCE

I. HORSEGUARDS AT BULAWAYO

WHEN Jameson left Kimberley he took with him the original of the concession, and at his first interview with the King he adopted the bold course of producing it. Lobengula recognised his mark at the foot of the paper, and when it was read aloud and translated by Moffat he agreed that its words were the same as those contained in Helm's copy, but maintained that it went far beyond his own intentions, which were to give Rudd and his friends ' one hole to dig in '. He said that the whole matter must again be discussed with his councillors, but to Jameson's great relief he did not, as might have been expected, tear the document up, or even expressly repudiate it. He handed it to Moffat for safe custody until it should again be wanted.

Both Lobengula and Jameson were playing for time. The former clung to the ' one hole ' idea in the hope that he might use it to stop the grumbling and hostility of the *indunas*, and save him from an actual disavowal of the whole transaction, which would, he knew, leave him in the air, exposed to all his old trouble with Boers and other importunate white men. He was quite aware that he had promised much more, but was loth to admit it until the people were in a better frame of mind. Jameson, on the other hand, provided he could keep the concession alive, was prepared, as a temporary step, to start with one hole, and trusted to his own powers of persuasion to induce the King by degrees to confirm his original undertaking. What he was anxious to avoid was the substitution of a new and less favourable document. Before he left Rhodes in September there had been no talk of a military expedition on a large scale to occupy Mashonaland, and neither then nor later did he think such an expedition would be necessary. Unlike the majority he had no very high respect for the fighting capacity of the Matabele *impis*, and thought their threats and truculent attitude were mainly bluster. His conversations with the King at this time were based on the assumption that the occupation would best be effected by the steady introduction into one district after another of small bodies of prospectors, who could concentrate on any sign of danger and whose numbers would gradually become sufficient to render them secure from attack. Accordingly, to make things easier for Lobengula, he told him that he wanted at first to begin digging in the direction of Tati, and if no gold were found there to try another spot in Mashonaland. To this the King raised no objection, and shortly afterwards an old prospector named Maddox was sent with a few workers to make a start in the Ramoquabane district, south of Bulawayo.

Jameson remained at Bulawayo until the middle of February—practically the whole wet season—and paid almost daily visits to the King, listening patiently to his doubts, attending now and then to his bodily ailments, and steadily gaining more and more of his confidence. During the last week in January the second 'Queen's letter' was received. It was dated November 15, when the Charter was less than three weeks old, and the changed attitude of the Government was manifested by their ready agreement to a suggestion by the Duke of Abercorn (who had been appointed President of the new company), that it should be conveyed to Bulawayo by a military escort. Two officers of the Royal Horse Guards and the senior non-commissioned officer were selected for this novel duty,[1] and to lend additional *éclat* to their mission they were provided for the road journey of 700 miles from Kimberley with a special coach, drawn by eight mules, and gorgeously painted in scarlet, with the royal cipher and imperial crown in gold on its doors.

Lobengula received them with exceptional graciousness, and at their first interview, when the only others present were Moffat, Jameson and Doyle, went to the unusual length of providing chairs for the whole party. The splendour of the guardsmen, as they marched into the royal enclosure in their blue and gold uniforms, with cuirasses and plumed helmets, filled the crowds of native onlookers with awed amazement, and appealed so strongly to the King himself that he made a special point of their attending the 'Great Dance' in the following week in full panoply By way of contrast his own costume for the audience consisted of nothing but a narrow strip of monkey-skin and a naval cap with a blue ostrich feather.[2]

The 'Queen's Letter' was read out by Moffat and translated by Doyle to Lobengula, who listened attentively and made a few comments. Before the close of the interview a number of presents brought out by the envoys—a handsome revolver and a pair of field-glasses from the Duke of Abercorn, some good hunting knives and other attractive articles—were produced, and accepted by the King with royal condescension. Such compliments he regarded as his due, and his store huts were stacked with similar gifts.

As for the letter—which, though purporting to give the Queen's own words, was of course prepared in the Colonial Office and signed by Lord Knutsford—it contained so com-

---

[1] Surgeon-Major Melladew, Captain Victor Ferguson and Corporal-Major White. Major Gascoigne of the 'Blues' was also with the party, but in an unofficial capacity.

[2] Narrative of Major Melladew, in Mathers' *Zambesia*, pp. 163-79.

plete a reversal of the policy expressed in the previous one that it is hard to believe that both emanated from the same person.   In March, with full knowledge of the concession granted to Rudd, Maguire and Thompson, Lord Knutsford had conveyed the Queen's advice to Lobengula ' not to grant hastily concessions or leave to dig, but to consider all applications very carefully', and warned him against putting too much power into the hands of those who came first to the exclusion of other deserving men.   In November Lobengula was told ' the Queen approves of the concession made to some white men who were represented in his country by Messrs. Rudd, Maguire and Thompson, . . . thinks he is acting wisely in carrying out his agreement with these persons '—he had not yet carried it out, but that is a detail—' and hopes that he will allow them to conduct their mining operations without interference or molestation from his subjects '.[1]   This *volte-face* must have puzzled him, but he was too much of a diplomat to betray surprise.

Rhodes was not mentioned in the letter, but Moffat and Jameson were both referred to by name as the persons to whom Lobengula should look for guidance—the one as being ' in the confidence of the Queen' and also as ' a true friend to himself and the Matabele people ', and the other as the principal representative of those who had acquired the concession.   By this recommendation the position of both was materially strengthened, and they were not slow to take advantage of it.   Moffat, who had of course been

---

[1] Mr. Ian Colvin (*Life of Jameson*, p. 120) says that the letter was such ' unintelligible rubbish ' that Jameson, ' who never stood upon any official punctilio, persuaded the mission to give him the letter, rewrote it in a style calculated to please a savage monarch, and had it translated.   It was then read to the King with excellent effect '. No authority is quoted for this statement, and it is difficult to believe that Moffat, to whom the envoys were instructed to hand the letter for delivery to Lobengula (*Blue Book*, C. 5918, No. 137, enclosure, p. 240), would have countenanced any tampering with an official document of such importance.

made acquainted with the terms of the Charter, was able for the first time to come into the open on the side of its promoters. Previously he had been compelled by official convention to conceal his sympathies with Rhodes's enterprise and to remain a dummy. Now he could, and did, explain to Lobengula that the Charter was an instrument by which the Queen gave authority to certain of her trusted subjects, of whom Rhodes was the head, to introduce the benefits of civilisation on British lines to Matabeleland and other native territories with the consent of their rulers ; that in so far as Matabeleland was affected he, Moffat, as the Queen's *induna*, was responsible for seeing that the conditions laid down were faithfully carried out, and that as the Charter conferred on the new company, among other powers, the right to raise troops for preserving the peace and safety of the country it had the effect of constituting a British protectorate throughout Lobengula's dominions.

When Jameson's turn came he thought the hour ripe for outlining the company's immediate intentions in regard to the concession. He had learnt by letter that a new programme was being discussed in the South, but it was not yet sufficiently developed for details to have reached him. He made no reference therefore to armed forces, but told the King that it was proposed in the approaching dry season to send into Mashonaland a strong party of gold-miners ; that it would be followed by others, and that they would take a road which would keep clear of his kraals. What Lobengula's true thoughts were it is difficult to say. He may have realised that the course of events was getting beyond his control, and that may have made him resigned to fate ; more probably he had fallen under the spell of the Doctor's frankness and easy assurance, and was lulled into a feeling of security. One begins to perceive that these Scotsmen possess some subtle wizardry, which enables them to strike a responsive chord in creatures outwardly insensitive to human appeal. As Dr. Moffat with Mziligazi, as Dr. Livingstone with Sebitoane, so now Dr. Jameson with Lobengula. At any rate the King yielded, and gave his approval. He even promised to lend some of his young men to help cut the road for the waggons of the expedition, and a few days later he ordered the rifles, which all this time had been awaiting his pleasure, to be sent out to his kraal at Mvutjwa and placed in charge of Chadwick—an action which was construed as a formal sign that he would abide by his agreement.

The King's confidence spread to his people, who, for the time being, were almost genial to the white men in their midst. The Great Dance, at which the guardsmen were present, stoically enduring the dust and sweltering heat in all their pomp of steel breast-plates and jack-boots, passed off without any display of rancour towards the white spectators beyond a certain amount of impudent horse-play. Before the Queen's envoys left Bulawayo the small British community organised a race-meeting, for which the King and some of his *indunas* entered horses. Athletic sports followed, with events and prizes for the natives, who took part in the proceedings with great gusto. The general atmosphere seemed to have cleared all round, and when Jameson ' got the road ' a day or so later he could feel that whatever the future might have in store for the Company the immediate omens were propitious.

II. SELOUS' PLAN

The march of the Chartered Company's Pioneer force into Mashonaland was a memorable and dramatic achievement, but as this chronicle does not profess to record the doings of the white settlers—except so far as they shed light on the behaviour of the natives affected—only the barest outline of the expedition can be given. The complete story has been told by several of those who actually took part in the exploit, and to their accounts the reader is referred.[1]

There is, however, one misunderstanding as to the origin of the expedition which it may be as well in a few words to remove. It has generally been taken for granted that the decision to send an elaborately equipped military force arose from Rhodes's anxiety to get the Pioneers safely past the Matabele danger zone. This is only partly true. Up to the end of 1889 there was no such intention. Had it not been that outside factors suddenly thrust themselves on his notice he would probably have adopted some such plan as that which Jameson favoured, and for which he had more or less prepared Lobengula—the gradual introduction into Mashonaland of compact bodies of prospectors, well-armed, of course, and ready for emergencies, but organised on lines which could convey no suggestion of a military invasion. By that means it was believed that the occupation would be accomplished without causing Lobengula any misgivings, and without upsetting his people, who would in time become used to the presence in their neighbourhood of a peaceful white community.

In December, while Jameson was still in Bulawayo trying to win the King's consent to this programme, news was brought down from Mashonaland by F. C. Selous which caused Rhodes some disquietude and led him to reconsider his plan of campaign. A new scheme was adopted, and as its development put a severe strain on Lobengula, and created an acute crisis at Bulawayo, the position as revealed by Selous must be glanced at.

The Mashonaland plateau was his favourite hunting ground, and he had usually entered it by what was known as the ' Hunter's Road ', leading from Bulawayo in a north-

---

[1] F. C. Selous, *Travel and Adventure in South East Africa* ; A. R. Colquhoun, *Dan to Beersheba* ; W. H. Brown, *On the South African Frontier*, etc.

easterly direction along the watershed of the rivers Zambesi
and Limpopo,[1] but when he turned up in Cape Colony in
December, 1889, he had just explored another route.
Earlier in the year he had undertaken to join and guide a
small prospecting party to the gold-belt on behalf of Frank
Johnson (who, owing to Lobengula's decree, could not go
himself), and to avoid interference from the Matabele they
had decided to go by way of the Zambesi, travelling in
canoes from its mouth as far as the ancient Portuguese town
of Tete, from which they proposed to strike southwards
with native porters across the escarpment, and so reach
the Mazoe river. Their progress, however, was greatly im-
peded by the movements of small parties of so-called Portuguese, whom they found making determined efforts to
obtain the submission of various petty Mashona chiefs—
all in the Matabele raiding area, and accustomed to pay
tribute to Lobengula. At the head of this activity was
Senhor Paiva d'Andrade, a gallant and energetic officer of
pure descent, while most of his subordinates were half-
breeds, of shady hue and still more shady antecedents, in
the service of the Portuguese Government.[2] Selous saw
enough to convince him that if Mashonaland, with its fine
climate, its perennial streams and reputed mineral wealth,
was to be rescued for British colonisation there was not a
moment to be lost.[3] In a few months the Portuguese might
be too firmly ensconced in the northern and eastern dis-

[1] Approximately the line now followed by the Bulawayo-Salisbury
railway.

[2] Though they all bore high-sounding Portuguese names many of
them were merely natives. The most notorious was Manoel Antonio
de Souza, a Goanese of great force of character, who had amassed
wealth by slave-trading and other nefarious practices, and was the
Governor of a large strip of country bordering on Mashonaland, with
the rank of General in the Portuguese army.

[3] The *Times* of January 4, 1890, contained a long letter from
Selous dealing with the Portuguese movements and the general
position in this part of Africa.

tricts to be dislodged, and there was a danger also of the southern portions being appropriated, in defiance of the Moffat treaty, by Boers from the Transvaal. He knew that Rhodes had a scheme for the occupation of the gold-belt under the Rudd concession, but he feared that while valuable time was being frittered away in negotiations with Lobengula d'Andrade and his coffee-coloured myrmidons might forestall him. In that event the ultimate struggle for Mashonaland would not be between the British and the Matabele, but between the Portuguese and the Boers.

On reaching Cape Colony Selous at once sought Rhodes, and found him quick to grasp the state of affairs and the urgent need for action. Up to then he had been mainly concerned about the Matabele, but he now realised that there was a graver problem to be tackled. It was Mashonaland he wanted in the first instance. No doubt in process of time Matabeleland would be gathered into the net, but in the meanwhile it could be left to take care of itself, for there was little likelihood of the Boers—still less the Portuguese —risking an encounter with its dreaded warriors. But Mashonaland could not wait. Lobengula's title to it was by no means unimpeachable, and, so far as white races were concerned, it was to all intents a no-man's-land, open to the first who could establish effective occupation.

Rhodes was well aware that he could count on very little support from Downing Street in resisting the claims of a Continental Power—even of one so feeble as Portugal. The Government knew, from direct representations made at the time of the Moffat Treaty, that the Crown of Portugal asserted sovereignty over Mashonaland, and had repeatedly been warned since then that insidious steps were being taken to substantiate the claim. Lobengula himself had complained in his letter to the Queen—that mysterious letter which was the real, though camouflaged, object of Maund's mission to England—of Portuguese encroachments. But beyond sending curt reminders to Lisbon as to the 'British Sphere of Influence' the Foreign Office had brought no pressure to bear, and appeared to treat the Portuguese pretensions with Olympian indifference. In regard to the Boers the Colonial Office was likely to be equally supine. Time and again it had proved a broken reed in clashes between the interests of British South Africans and the Transvaal.

Mashonaland could not wait, but there was apparently no means of access to Mashonaland except by way of Matabeleland, for the Portuguese held the coast-line and the Transvaal the southern border, and if the projected expedition was made strong enough to block both Boers and Portuguese its very strength might provoke a collision with the Matabele.

In this dilemma Selous, with his unrivalled knowledge of the country, came to the rescue.

'Why go through Matabeleland at all?' he asked. 'Why not keep to the south and east of it, and cut a road which will avoid all the Matabele outposts?'

'Can such a route be found?' said Rhodes.

'Most assuredly it can', was Selous' reply, and he proceeded to sketch it out on a map, at the same time offering his services as guide; and Rhodes went off to think it over.

Within a day or two of this conversation the new High Commissioner, Sir Henry Loch, arrived at the Cape, and Rhodes at once laid the situation before him, together with Selous' proposal, which he had already satisfied himself provided the only solution. Loch took counsel with recognised authorities—Sir Francis de Winton, then Commissioner of Swaziland, Sir Frederick Carrington, Commandant of the Bechuanaland Police, Sir Sidney Shippard and others, who were unanimous in their approval,[1] and early in the new year the ball was set rolling.

[1] Selous, *Travel and Adventure*, p. 312.

The composition of the expeditionary force was at first the subject of a good deal of discussion. Rhodes, anxious that the forward movement should have as little about it as possible to suggest warlike intentions, would have liked to send up a compact body of young colonists of the farmer and artisan class, leavened by a sprinkling of older men with some knowledge of practical mining and other trades— the initial unit of the self-supporting community which he hoped to see follow—though he was obliged of course to admit the necessity of their being trained to arms and kept at first under some sort of discipline. In this idea he was supported by Frank Johnson, who now stepped into the picture again with an offer to raise, train and equip a corps of about 250 men of the required type, who should construct a waggon-road from Khama's borders to Mount Hampden, a point on the high veld selected by Selous as the most suitable objective. Once there they could be dispersed to mark out free farms and gold claims, and Johnson undertook to get them there for £90,000. But the question of numbers was a stumbling-block. Johnson is said to have affirmed that with 250 men he would 'walk through the country '.[1] Very likely he did, and possibly he might have succeeded, but expert opinion, influenced by the general conviction that the Matabele would show fight, was strongly in favour of a much stronger and more military force being provided as an escort for the road party. In the end it was decided to limit Johnson's corps—the 'Pioneers' as they came to be called—to 200 ; to include in his contract the erection of a chain of forts, and to raise an additional force of 500 mounted police under trained British officers, who should enter the country with the road-makers, and remain to furnish garrisons for the forts and form a permanent defence for the territory.

The enrolment of the two bodies started forthwith. The

[1] Colvin, Life of Jameson, p. 122.

guidance of the expedition was entrusted to Selous, and the command of the combined column to Lieut.-Colonel E. G. Pennefather of the 6th Dragoons. During April the first contingents began to assemble in camps on the southern border of the 'Disputed Territory', and detachments of the Bechuanaland Police were under orders to move to the north of Khama's country, as a reserve to be thrown forward if the column were attacked.

III. THE 'PIONEERS'

When Jameson returned to Cape Colony in March he found these preparations in full swing, and though he was not the sort of man to get worried he must have known that trouble would arise when they came to the knowledge of Lobengula, who had been led by him to suppose that the company's expedition would consist merely of a strong party of miners on their way to Mashonaland to dig for the gold. And this was exactly what happened, for as soon as it became known to his people that a 'white *impi*' was marching northwards through Khama's country the old suspicions, which had for a time died down, were revived, and it needed all the King's cautious firmness to prevent the fiery *amatjaha* from rushing off to meet it. 'Wait for my word' he told them again and again, but he was by no means easy in his mind, and began to feel that he had been duped.

Maxwell—now the company's chief representative— succeeded, to some extent, in pacifying the King, but was quite incapable of coping with the bellicosity of the young soldiers, whose insolence became at last so unbearable that he began to lose his nerve. In his letters to Rhodes he expressed his belief that the King would be unable to hold them back much longer, and that they would wreak their anger on the few white men in the country. He laid par-

ticular emphasis on the critical position of the missionaries
and their families, and his reports were so disquieting that
Jameson, who had scarcely been in the Colony five weeks,
resolved to pay another flying visit to Bulawayo to adminis-
ter a few more doses of 'soothing syrup' to the King. He
arrived on April 27, and found Lobengula in a querulous
and resentful mood. When the whole programme was
boldly disclosed he became still more exasperated.

'Why should the Pioneers not come through Bulawayo
so that he could see them ? Why had Jameson called them
a "working party" when they were really soldiers ? Why,
since Rhodes was the man at the back of all these movements, did not Rhodes come up personally to consult him ? '

Jameson answered and explained, laying special stress on
the Portuguese threat, and succeeded in mollifying him in
some degree ; but the real danger lay not with Lobengula,
but with his people, and those he could not reach. Had he,
in addition to his other talents, been endowed with the
gift of tongues, he might have addressed a mass meeting of
the Matabele, and convinced them that their fears of attack
were groundless, for he possessed the rare faculty of swaying
multitudes as well as individuals. As it was he had to rely
on the King alone. Of him he felt fairly confident—if only
he could hold back his *impis*. 'I don't think there will be
any fighting', he wrote to his brother, 'but you never know.
In any case we'll be there this winter'. [1]

Five days later he was off again, and with the removal of
his cheery presence the situation of the few remaining white
people seemed to grow still more gloomy. Most of those
who could get away, including all the concession-hunters,
had already packed up and left, but two or three traders,
together with Maxwell, Colenbrander and Wilson—all
company's men—stayed on, and Chadwick stuck to his
guns (literally) at Mvutjwa. The last-named has given a

[1] Colvin, *Life of Jameson*, p. 132.

vivid description of those anxious days, some extracts from which may be quoted :

' Day after day the different *impis* came pouring in to the King demanding the white men's blood in the country, and for leave to attack the army which was coming up to eat them. Meetings of the excited warriors were held, and it became a question whether Lobengula would be able to restrain them or not. At one stormy meeting held at Bulawayo the old men, who sided with the King, stood up and said the young soldiers must fight them first before attacking the few whites, who were the King's visitors. The King's position was now an unenviable one, the whole nation rising against him, and it required his utmost tact and judgment to deal with them without losing his dignity or showing want of courage. . . . It became no longer safe even to let our horses out to graze ; they were frightened away by the people and the herd boys beaten and stoned, so we had to keep them in camp and fall back on our grain supplies to feed them, as even, for a long time, the girls were prevented and flogged if caught selling corn to the " white dogs "—which was our usual appellation. . . .

' The first definite news we heard from below was a letter to Major Maxwell from the Chartered Company, warning all whites to leave the country by 1st June or remain at their own risk, as the expedition would, on that date, cross the border. . . .[1] A rapid consultation was held, and we agreed to give the missionaries time to get out of the country first with their wives and families ; messengers were at once sent to them, and with a few hours' warning all were ready to leave the country and say good-bye to the King. Lobengula offered no objection to their going. . . . The fact of all the missionaries, who were considered permanent residents, going away, deserting their homes and leaving cattle, sheep and all their household goods behind, considerably added to the disturbances among the people, and made matters more serious for the few remaining whites. . . .

' Now that the time had come for the Pioneers to enter Mashonaland the King avoided any discussion about his agree-

---

[1] The Pioneers actually forded the Macloutsie river on the 27th June, and the Shashi, the recognised border of Matabeleland, on the 11th July.

ment, and said there was only one road to Mashonaland, and
that was through Bulawayo.   Although Lobengula probably
did not want to fight, still he was never friendly disposed towards the expedition entering by the route they did, and it was
in sheer defiance, and prepared to resist, that they cut their
road to Mount Hampden, in spite of the several threatening
messages sent to stop them . . . .'

The agitation in Bulawayo reached its highest pitch when
it was learnt that the column had arrived at the Shashi
river, and the King, realising that the time had come for
a decisive step, declared to his excited regiments that he
would allow it to advance no further.   He summoned
Colenbrander and Chadwick, and gave them a letter, telling
them to ride down to the Shashi and hand it to Jameson,
who was said to be in command of the force.   They were to
be accompanied by a party of his own *indunas* carrying a
verbal message ordering the white men back.   Several
versions of the letter have been given, but it is agreed that
its general tenor was to enquire why a white army was
attempting to enter the country without permission and by
an unauthorised route, and to deny that Jameson had ever
obtained leave to dig for gold in Mashonaland.   On arrival
at the Shashi after eleven days' travelling the party found
the Union Jack flying over a newly-built fort, garrisoned by
a detachment of police, and learnt to their surprise that the
main body was already well ahead.   The *indunas* decided to
wait at the fort while Colenbrander was sent in pursuit of
the column, which he caught up near the Lundi river,
150 miles further on.   He delivered the letter, and brought
back a written reply from Pennefather, which he handed to
the *indunas* for conveyance to the king.   'We are marching',
it said, ' under orders from the Queen, which are that we
should go on to Mashonaland '.

By the time this reached Bulawayo the column had
gained the plateau, and was safe from attack.   It was just

what Lobengula had anticipated when he despatched his own messages. By this clever device he had escaped from the necessity of breaking his word to Jameson, and had held his obstreperous soldiers on a leash until the quarry had passed out of range.

CHAPTER XVI

LOBENGULA'S DOWNFALL

I. THE INEVITABLE WAR

Out of sight, out of mind. For the first hundred miles of their march the Pioneers were closely watched by Lobengula's *impis*, which hovered on their flanks and kept them in a constant state of vigilance ; but as the column drew further eastward the agitation of the Matabele began to abate, and by the time it reached Mount Hampden its existence was nearly forgotten by all except the King and a few of his older councillors, who knew that the real burden of its presence was yet to come.

The expedition made a final halt on September 12, 1890 ; the last of the chain of forts was thrown up on the site of Salisbury, and the British flag was hoisted in formal token of occupation. The old ' Hunters' Road ' fell into disuse, and Bulawayo itself was only visited by occasional travellers bound for the Zambesi. As soon as the crisis was past the missionaries returned to their forsaken homes, and Moffat and Colenbrander to their posts as guardians of the interests of the Imperial Government and Chartered Company. But for these, and half a dozen traders, the place would have been a backwater.

The wet season which followed the occupation was the heaviest within living memory. Most of the prospecting parties, transport-riders and others making for the goldfields in ox-waggons from Kimberley and Mafeking were held up—sometimes for weeks—by floods and swollen rivers in the low country, where many fell victims to fever. The Pioneers and the few miners who succeeded in reaching Mashonaland before the rains set in were in hardly better plight, for all work came to a standstill and their food supplies were nearly exhausted. It was not until the middle of 1891 that the first loads of provisions arrived, but after that there was a steady and increasing traffic along the new road, which speedily became a thoroughfare, with stores and rest-houses at every convenient outspan. The first two hundred miles of the track lay through thick bush, crossed by a number of good-sized rivers and broken by towering, dome-like peaks of granite and piled-up clumps of boulders, among which were perched small villages of Banyai and other tribes—the survivors of the dense population of former times. Having been raided and persecuted for fifty years they were at first timid and suspicious and fled panic-stricken at the approach of white men, but when they found they were not attacked they lost their shyness and were glad to barter their poor produce for beads and cheap calico. All travellers carried firearms as a matter of course, but they were only required for shooting game for the pot, and for protection against lions, which infested many parts of the route. There were no other enemies. The Matabele, held in such dread a few months before, seemed to have disappeared altogether, and might have been non-existent for all the settlers saw of them.

It was contrary to South African experience that this tranquillity should endure, for all the elements of disturbance were present. The settlers, though by no means looking for trouble, were of an exploring and adventurous character, little inclined to confine their activities to a limited radius round the forts and mining camps. The Matabele before long began to chafe at the loss of their freedom to go where they pleased and raid whom they liked.

It was inevitable that sooner or later a clash should occur, and the surprising thing is that, with two dynamic elements in such close proximity, it was staved off for nearly three years. A large measure of the credit for this is unquestionably due to Jameson, who, without any previous experience of government, assumed, at Rhodes's request, the duties of Administrator. It was no easy post to fill. The small white community was composed almost exclusively of young men suddenly released from military discipline, and scattered over a large area ; all round them were wild savages of uncertain temper ; the nearest outpost of civilisation was Mafeking, 1000 miles away ; the necessaries of life had to be dragged all that distance in slow-moving ox-waggons, and luxuries were unobtainable ; there was no telegraph line and letters took three or four weeks to reach the rail-head. Yet by his tact, a marvellous faculty of quick decision, and a strong sense of humour, Jameson managed to keep the more daring settlers out of mischief, and the whole community more or less contented.

At the same time the part played by Lobengula in maintaining peace, under conditions even more trying, cannot be overlooked. He was called upon to recast his whole system of government to suit the whim of a crowd of aliens who had no regard for the customs and institutions which he looked on as sacred, and who claimed the right to shut him and his people out of a large part of their own territory. He had to stifle his private feelings and—more difficult still—to train his subjects to submit quietly to the new order.[1]

[1] That he accepted it himself was demonstrated in a curious way. He was induced to take out a prospecting licence, and commissioned James Dawson to peg out a block of claims in his name in the Umfuli district. A small battery was erected on the property—actually the first to start work in Mashonaland—and in due course a substantial lump of gold was solemnly handed to Lobengula as the result of a few months' crushing. Whether it came from the 'Lobengula Reef' or not it would perhaps be indiscreet to enquire.

The position was made more irksome on both sides by the anomalous constitution of the settlement, which was based on a fiction. In theory Mashonaland was a native territory under British protection ; Lobengula was still its king, and the white men were there by his permission. In practice the Chartered Company made their own laws and regulations and enforced them by their police ; instituted magisterial courts with jurisdiction over natives as well as Europeans ; parcelled out farms, and generally conducted their operations as if the country were their private estate. Lobengula and his tribe were debarred from all freedom of action over an immense area recognised as theirs in the very document on which the company's occupation was founded. The situation was an artificial—almost a Gilbertian one ; it could only be maintained by keeping flint and steel apart, and an explosion was bound to occur at the first impact. These conditions are not mentioned to support an argument that the British settlers had no right to be in Mashonaland, or that it was not in the interests of humanity at large that they should be there, but simply to illustrate the dangers ahead of them, and to supply an explanation of what happened.

After the first year of apparent calm several incidents took place which showed, either that Lobengula had not fully comprehended the extent to which he had surrendered his liberty, or else that his grip on his headstrong soldiers was weakening. The Mashona chief Lomagunda, whose district was not more than seventy or eighty miles from Salisbury, and had been thrown open to prospecting, was raided by a small Matabele *impi* on the pretext that he was a defaulter in payment of his customary tribute. He and his family were put to death with the usual barbarous accompaniments, and the young women and boys of his villages were driven off as captives. Not long afterwards similar treatment was meted out to Tshibi, a chief of the

Banyai tribe living not far from the southern section of the pioneer road, who was suspected of intrigues with Transvaal Boers. As both these raids happened within the jurisdiction assumed by the Chartered Company, Jameson sent messages to the King cautioning him that such acts would not be tolerated, to which Lobengula retorted that they were punitive measures against his own subjects, and that there was no intention of interference with the whites. Possibly Jameson's remonstrances were taken to heart, for eighteen months passed without further raids on Mashonaland chiefs, but in July, 1893, a large *impi* appeared without warning close to the mining township of Victoria and started an orgy of butchery among the unfortunate inhabitants of the neighbouring kraals. The Matabele seemed to have got completely out of control, for they came on to the town lands and murdered natives working for white men. They drove off a large number of cattle, including some belonging to farmers round the township, set fire to the villages over a wide stretch of country, and wherever they went left behind them a trail of dead bodies and blackened ruins.

The story of what followed has often been told, and nothing more than a bare outline need be given. Jameson proceeded to Victoria, sent for the leaders of the raiding *impi*, and ordered them to quit the district forthwith. As some of them were defiant and continued their outrages he despatched a patrol to drive them away, and in the brief skirmish which ensued about a dozen of the Matabele were killed.

Jameson now represented to the Imperial authorities that only by breaking down Lobengula's military power once and for all could the lives and property of the settlers—among whom by this time there was a proportion of women and children—be made safe, and, as a precautionary step, he began to organise a force of volunteers to be held in readiness to march on Bulawayo. The High Commissioner spared no effort to patch up a settlement, but the temper of white men and natives alike had been strained to breaking point. Both were itching to get at each others' throats, and before long there were outpost collisions which made it impossible to avert war. The advance of the small army of volunteers was therefore authorised, and they moved forward early in October.

Without going into details of the campaign two or three incidents may be related as throwing light on the attitude of Lobengula in the crisis which had been forced on him by the wanton acts of his troublesome warriors. He was just as anxious as the British Government to prevent what he knew must be for him a life-and-death struggle, and when he first heard from Colenbrander of the Victoria affray wrote to Jameson expressing a certain amount of contrition. He explained that his soldiers had been sent to punish a petty chief for some delinquency and had lost their heads, and he expressed the hope that all cattle stolen from white men had been returned. But a few days afterwards the *induna* who had been in chief command returned with his own version of the occurrence, which was to the effect that a number of his people had been induced to leave their arms behind and come into Victoria for a discussion, and that thirty of them had then been shot without cause.[1] Lobengula had elementary notions of honour, and he was, or professed to be, enraged at this act of treachery, aggravated by the fact that Jameson, who had posed as his friend, was a party to it. He dictated an indignant message (which Moffat sent down to the nearest telegraph office for transmission) to the High Commissioner, refusing to pay compensation for the damage done, and demanding the surrender of certain Mashonas who, in their extremity of terror, had taken refuge in the fort at Victoria. His next step was to recall an army of 6,000 men which had gone north on an expedi-

[1] *Blue Book*, C. 7171, p. 65.

tion to Barotseland, and he ordered the remainder of his regiments to muster at Bulawayo with their fighting equipment for inspection and mobilisation.

In spite of these ostentatious preparations there is ground for believing that in his heart he dreaded war, but had to 'talk big' before his people.[1]   When he heard that Jameson's force was actually on the move he determined to make a last-hour appeal to the High Commissioner for intervention in the vain hope of warding off a catastrophe the vision of which had haunted him for years.   But the fates were conspiring against him.   His letter [2] was entrusted to three *indunas*—one of them his half brother Ngubogubo— and the trader James Dawson, at the king's request, undertook to escort them safely to the Cape.   At Tati they found a strong detachment of the Bechuanaland Police, which had been moved there to be held in reserve, and the *indunas* were handed over to a guard, while Dawson, without explaining their errand, foolishly left them and went off to see some friends.   In his absence they jumped to the not unnatural conclusion that they had been led into a trap. One of them snatched a bayonet and before he could be overpowered inflicted ugly stabs on several members of the guard, while all three attempted to break away.   There was a scuffle in which two of the Matabele received fatal wounds.[3]

[1] Despatch from Sir H. Loch.   *Blue Book*, C. 7171, p. 72.

[2] It will of course be understood that Lobengula's letters were always written for him by someone else.   Until the critical period with which we are dealing this duty was invariably undertaken by a white man—often one of the missionaries—who translated the king's words into English, but from this time forward he became to a great extent dependent on two semi-educated aliens—John Jacobs, a 'Cape Boy', who was a fugitive from justice in the Colony, where he had a bad criminal record, and Mvulana, a Fingo native, who styled himself Karl Kumalo, in pretence of a relationship with the Zulu stock (Kumalo) from which Lobengula was descended.   Both were unmitigated rogues and subsequently exercised an evil influence on Matabele politics.

[3] *Blue Book*, C. 7284, deals entirely with the enquiry into this affair.

The impression made on Lobengula by this unlucky mishap may well be imagined. The Secretary of State directed Sir Henry Loch to write a letter of explanation and regret, but no regrets could disabuse the king's mind of the belief that his envoys had been the victims of a deliberate plot— another act of treachery, as he considered it—and he came to the conclusion that the white men were no longer to be trusted, an idea that was destined to have further serious results at a later date.

He was not left long, however, to brood over this griev- ance. Jameson's force, after beating off a determined attack at the Shangani river, encountered the flower of the Matabele army on November 1 at the Bembesi, a stream not more than twenty miles from the capital, and routed them with heavy loss. The return in disorder of the broken fragments of his crack regiments, with the news that his own bodyguard, the Imbezu, had been 'wiped out', and that the enemy was still pressing forward, told the dis- traught king that nothing could save Bulawayo, and that the only alternatives before him were surrender or flight. He chose the latter course, but he was resolved to leave nothing for Jameson, and gave orders that the great kraal should be burnt as soon as he was out of it.

In one of his storehouses there was a quantity of gun- powder and about 80,000 rounds of rifle ammunition, and there is evidence that he intended to have this brought away, but in the general panic his wishes were forgotten. On the morning of November 3 the town was fired in four places ; the flames spread rapidly in the dry thatched roofs, and in a few hours not a hut was left standing. The king's quarters were included in the holocaust, and the ammuni- tion blew up with a tremendous report which was plainly heard by Jameson's troopers fifteen miles away.

Even in this hour of supreme trial Lobengula's conduct lifted him above the common herd and proved that he possessed a sense of generosity and honour rare among his kind. Two white men—James Fairbairn, the keeper of the royal seal, and a trader named Usher—had steadfastly remained at Bulawayo throughout the crisis, trusting to the King to protect them from mob violence at the hands of his people. Their confidence was not betrayed. Lobengula gave strict orders that Fairbairn's house should be left untouched, and that neither he nor Usher should be molested. When, two days later, the victorious little army of settlers, with Jameson at their head, marched into the place they were found safe and unhurt—the only living creatures, except for some hundreds of wandering and ownerless dogs, in the gutted and forsaken capital.

II. LOBENGULA'S LAST TREK

The abandonment of Bulawayo was not entirely a new idea to Lobengula. Long before, when pestered by concession-hunters, he had thought of a complete evacuation of Matabeleland as a means of escape from their unwelcome presence, and if he could have found a suitable domicile in the north would have moved there with his whole nation. But flight before an armed invasion was a different matter, and had only occurred to him when he heard of the rout of his *impis* at Shangani. It was then that he began to make preparations, and one of his first steps was to safeguard his treasure.

As the nature and whereabouts of this treasure have provided a fascinating subject of speculation in Rhodesia for many years it may not be amiss to say something about it. Besides ivory in the tusk, of which he undoubtedly possessed a great store—partly inherited, and partly looted in the course of raids or received as tribute from conquered chiefs—he is generally supposed to have accumulated a quantity of uncut diamonds, exacted by him from his own men on their return from Kimberley as payment for the privilege of being allowed to go and work there. The existence of hoarded treasure of some kind was known to Jameson and one or two other members of the column who had visited the king, and immediately after the occupation of Bulawayo the gutted ruins of the royal quarters were diligently searched and raked over in the hope of discovering valuables. But nothing was brought to light beyond a number of half-burnt sporting rifles—presents given to Lobengula from time to time by hunters—a model in silver of an elephant, a gold signet ring, and a few other trifles. Had tusks of ivory been left in the storehouses they could not have been so utterly destroyed by fire as to have left no charred remains, and it was clear that the king had removed them—probably to some safe repository underground. The supposed hoard of diamonds may have been a myth, though the Cape boy, Jacobs, who was afterwards made a prisoner, was found to have in his possession a few small stones which he said had been given him by Lobengula from a large collection kept in a paraffin tin, and professed to know where this was hidden.

Lobengula must have had in his possession a considerable sum of money. For nearly five years he had been regularly drawing the monthly subsidy of £100 under the Rudd concession, which was always paid in gold, and he had frequently received cash for transactions in cattle. Apart from this there is some ground for thinking that he inherited a quantity of gold coin from his father. Some time after the occupation a visit to Bulawayo by his chief consort and several of his lesser wives was followed by the appearance in circulation of a number of sovereigns of early nineteenth century issues, which must have been hoarded for many years. Some, if not all, of his gold the king took with him on his flight, as we shall see later, but although there have been several theories as to the way in which he disposed of the remainder of his treasure—that he had it secretly conveyed to some spot beyond the Zambesi, or buried in a pit dug near the Umguza are two alternate conjectures— no definite clue has ever been found. It is improbable that any natives who knew the secret now survive, and the mystery is never likely to be cleared up unless by an accidental discovery.

As to Lobengula's ultimate intentions when he fled from his capital nothing can be said with certainty. It may be that he had some notion of crossing the Zambesi and founding a new settlement for his tribe in the Batoka country, but his movements seem rather to indicate that he was waiting on events, and looking for a chance of drawing the British force, whose small numbers were of course obvious, into an ambush, or another battle on ground less favourable for their tactics. Although some hundreds of his best fighting men had been killed, a large portion of his army had not yet come into action. Of the Imbezu bodyguard barely 200 remained after the battle of Bembesi, out of a total strength of 700, and the Mhlahlanhlela regiment had suffered nearly as severely, but the Induba and Insukamini, which had also fought at Bembesi, and the Ihlati and Siseba—all highly trained units of the first line—were more or less intact, and Lobengula had with him his most experienced general, Mjaan, the leader of the Imbezu, who was eager to avenge his defeat, and now assumed the chief command. The most important absentee was the King's son-in-law, Gambo, who commanded the district west of Bulawayo, and had not been able to join him, if indeed he ever wanted to, which is doubtful. But there were other leading *indunas* among those who stuck to him, including Bozungwane, the chief witch-doctor, and Magwegwe, the *induna* of Bulawayo, both eager for another trial of strength.

Either deliberately or from stress of circumstances the

King at first moved slowly. He was hampered by the presence of a number of his wives and of a crowd of other women with their children, and by the herds of cattle and a few horses, which had to be grazed and carefully guarded. Towards the middle of November the rains began and the track became heavy and in parts water-logged. The King had started with five waggons for the conveyance of his household and necessary stores, but contrary to his usual practice he travelled himself in a bath-chair, drawn by relays of slaves. With non-combatants, cattle and transport, his train was a cumbrous one, and at the end of the first week he had only advanced as far as Shiloh, an abandoned station of the London Missionary Society, about thirty miles north of Bulawayo. To cover his retreat the fighting force was spread over a line of about twelve miles in rear, with its outer flank resting on the old mission station of Inyati, which the *ama-tjaha* proceeded to loot.

While halted at Shiloh Lobengula received a letter from Jameson brought out by three mounted colonial natives, who had gallantly volunteered for the dangerous duty. The Doctor urged him to come at once to Bulawayo to discuss terms of peace with a view to stopping further useless slaughter. He reminded Lobengula of their former friendship, and guaranteed his personal safety and kind treatment. The messengers were detained for two days and then sent back with the King's reply (written by Jacobs) to the effect that he would come. But he qualified this by asking what had become of the messengers he had sent to the Cape, mentioning by name the three sent down with Dawson, two of whom, as he was well aware, had been killed in the affray at Tati, while the third, his brother Ngubogubo, was hurrying to join him ; when these returned, the letter said, he would come into Bulawayo, though as all his houses had been burnt he did not know where he could live.[1] The

[1] This letter, written in indelible pencil, is in the author's possession.

letter is not consistent with his other actions, which indicate no intention of surrender. It would appear to have been written with the object of gaining time, or it may even have been a fabrication by his amanuensis Jacobs, who immediately afterwards deserted and gave himself up to the military authorities at Bulawayo. Whichever explanation is the correct one Lobengula, so far from returning, once more began to move in the direction of the Zambesi.

After waiting a few days Jameson, concluding that the letter was a blind, despatched a strong patrol under Major Forbes to reconnoitre in the direction of Inyati, and a week was wasted in hunting for the *impi* reported to be in that vicinity. When it became known through spies that the King was continuing his northward movement Forbes was ordered to march across country to Shiloh, where he arrived on November 25, and at once took up the spoor of the waggons. By this time the King had increased the distance between himself and Bulawayo to seventy-five miles, and was making his way as fast as he could towards the Shangani river thirty or forty miles further on. But the difficulties of his flight were growing. Owing to continuous rain the country had become a quagmire ; many of the trek oxen had died of poverty, and though an attempt was made to haul the waggons by man-power three of them, together with the bath-chair, had perforce to be abandoned ; smallpox made its appearance, and every day people sickened and had to be left behind to take their chance. When Forbes left Inyati the force under Mjaan's command rejoined the King, but was reduced by desertions to about 3,000 men, many of whom had lost their fighting spirit. The King himself fell ill ; the unaccustomed hardships of the march in wet weather brought on a severe attack of gout, and he was unable to leave his waggon. From the reports of his scouting parties he knew that the white troops were hot on his scent, and must soon catch him up. His con-

dition bordered on despair, and as a last resort he determined to try to secure a respite by offering his pursuers a
bribe.

When near the Shangani he sent back three messengers,
Patshane, Sihuluhulu and another, to intercept the patrol.
He handed them a large sum in gold done up in bags—
perhaps £1,000, perhaps more ; the amount was never
known—and ordered them to seek out the white men's
induna and speak in his name these words : ' White men,
I am conquered. Take this money. Stop your *impi*, and
let us meet and talk '.

But Lobengula's persistent ill-luck still dogged him. His
messengers instead of hitting the head of the column fell in
with a couple of orderlies—one of them an off-coloured
man—who were leading baggage mules, and lagging in
rear. These caught sight of the bags of gold and their
cupidity was aroused. They paid little attention to the
message, the full import of which they doubtless failed to
grasp—if indeed they understood it at all. The column had
moved on and they were unobserved ; the natives were
unarmed, scared and anxious to discharge their errand and
creep away. Without much hesitation they parted with
the bags to the troopers, and were told to go back and say
' it was all right '. Needless to remark neither the gold nor
the message ever reached their commanding officer and
Lobengula's last overtures, like his previous ones, came to
nought.

On the morning of December 3 the fugitives, now only
seven or eight miles ahead of the column, arrived at the
Shangani, a wide river, but still shallow enough to be
fordable, and with some difficulty managed to get the two
remaining waggons with their worn-out teams across. In
one of them sat the unhappy King, who in spite of his
enfeebled condition braced himself for a final effort, and on
reaching the north bank was helped on to a horse so that

he might make a few miles more. Bozungwane and Mag-wegwe rode by his side, while Mjaan was left with his soldiers to delay the pursuit as best he could. The tough old veteran thereupon divided the force into two portions, keeping one on the north bank to defend the King, and sending the other back across the river to harass the column in the thick bush through which it was advancing.

It was at this stage that Forbes despatched Major Allan Wilson with twenty men to reconnoitre the position in front and get what information he could as to the whereabouts of the King and the disposition of the forces with him, for the smoke still rising from the fires at their last camp showed that they were only just ahead. The party appears to have actually reached the waggons, in which they assumed Lobengula was concealed, but Wilson, finding the camp strongly guarded, and not wishing to risk his small force, withdrew to a position in the bush, and sent back several of his men with a request for reinforcements. By the time these got back to the column it was nearly dark and rain was falling heavily, but a further patrol of twenty men under Captain Borrow was hastily detailed to join Wilson and inform him that the main body would follow at daybreak.

Early next morning (December 4) the column was attacked on both flanks in the bush by Mjaan's southern *impi*, and had barely shaken it off and resumed the march when the river came down, as African rivers do, in sudden flood, putting all hopes of crossing out of the question. During the fighting the sound of firing from the opposite side showed that Wilson was also engaged, but it died away, and almost simultaneously three more of his party who had been sent back, and had managed to swim the river, arrived with the report that the two patrols were together, but were defending themselves against a greatly superior force of Matabele and were in imminent danger of being surrounded. But the news came too late. The Shangani was now a raging torrent, and Forbes could do nothing. After waiting some time in vain for the water to subside he was obliged to order a retirement.

The last stand of the patrols ranks, with the defence of Rorke's Drift, as one of the classic episodes of colonial warfare, and this is not the place to attempt to do it justice. Wilson's men might perhaps have extricated themselves but for the arrival of Mjaan's southern *impi*, which was just able to cross the river before it became unfordable, and hurried forward at once to join in the attack. The patrols were then caught in the jaws of a vice. They formed their horses in a ring, and as they dropped under the fire from the Matabele encircling them in the bush, used their bodies as cover. For several hours, in spite of thinning numbers, they kept the enemy at bay, and dealt out death to those who showed themselves. At last their ammunition gave out. The few still alive stood up, shook hands, and calmly awaited the final rush. They died shoulder to shoulder, and there was no survivor.

The accident of the flooded river saved Lobengula from what he most dreaded—capture and confinement. The despot who had never bent his knee or bowed his head to another, before whom all men had grovelled in abject veneration, could not brook the thought of humbling himself to aliens, and it was as well for all concerned that he was spared that bitterness.

Lobengula's cup of misery, however, was not yet full. Delivered from one peril he ran into others. With three of his sons, some of his wives and a few faithful *indunas*, he struggled on as far as the Mlindi river, which he struck at a point not more than forty miles from the Zambesi. There the fugitives found themselves in a belt of tsetse fly, which meant death to their cattle. A few of the loose oxen which had lagged behind escaped, but their trek animals perished and they were left stranded. This misfortune, coming on the top of the long-drawn anxiety of the preceding weeks, broke Lobengula's spirit, and robbed him of the desire to live. His limbs were swollen with gout ; his massive frame was racked with pain, and he was even denied the solace of his favourite *u-tshwala*. Death was the best thing that could befall him, and his release came towards the end of January. Mjaan and Bozungwane stood by him to the end, and as far as possible paid him the tribute due to his kingly rank. But his interment was shorn of the pomp and ceremony which Zulu tradition prescribed for departed chiefs. There could be no sacrifice of cattle, for the herds brought up from below had been all but annihilated by the tsetse poison. Out of the miserable remnant that survived two black oxen were killed, and in their freshly-flayed hides the great body of the dead King was sewn up and buried where it lay.[1]

It was a far cry to the Matopo Hills, where the grim figure of Mziligazi peered out in constant vigil from his tomb in the granite,[2] and the two *indunas* may have wondered whether the spirit of Lobengula would ever find its way back to play a part in the future destinies of the Matabele.

[1] Such particulars as are known of Lobengula's last days were obtained by James Dawson, who, in company with a trader named Patrick Riley and one *induna*, volunteered to proceed to the Shangani as soon as the rains abated. It was not until February 23 that they were able to cross the river, on the north side of which they met Mjaan and other *indunas*, whom they induced to return with them to Bulawayo and surrender. Dawson also found and buried the bodies of all but one of Wilson's party, which had been collected by the natives at one spot, and though stripped had not been subjected to the usual mutilation. Copies of Mr. Dawson's letters giving an account of this mission are in the possession of the writer.

[2] See chap. viii, p. 124 footnote.

CHAPTER XVII

KHAMA THE REFORMER

I. SIDELIGHTS ON HIS CHARACTER

It is time to return to Khama, who, when we last took note of him, was engrossed in the domestic reforms upon which he had embarked at his accession, but keeping an ever-watchful eye on the Matabele and the Boers on his borders. As to the Protectorate which had held out such glowing prospects he was moderately enthusiastic, but it was not long before he began to find fault with some of its conditions. On Sir Charles Warren's recommendation the northern boundary had at first been fixed at the 22nd degree of south latitude, and while welcoming the general scheme, and accepting the right of the Queen's government to exercise a benevolent supervision over blacks as well as whites, Khama vigorously protested against this arbitrary and imaginary line, which, as far as he could understand it, seemed to cut his country in two. According to his showing the Mangwato dominion extended at least 250 miles north of the 22nd degree, and embraced an immense tract of country reaching up to the Zambesi. His pretensions, however, were hardly substantiated by the actual conditions.

The people of his own tribe—the ba-Mangwato proper—occupied a ridiculously small area in the immediate vicinity of Shoshong, which lay in the south-east corner of the vast territory claimed by him, and the bulk of them were contained within the town itself, which about 1890 had a population variously estimated at from 15,000 to 30,000 souls. The country outside this limited radius was inhabited by tribes over which Khama exercised a somewhat precarious authority, chiefly kept alive by the maintenance of a number of cattle-posts—sometimes, but not always, in charge of a Mangwato headman—and by frequent trading and hunting expeditions, organised by the king himself, for the purpose of obtaining skins—the manufacture of *karosses*, or rugs made of dressed hides being one of the staple industries of all the Bechuana tribes. These expeditions were carried as far as the Botletle river and Lake Ngami, whose shores were occupied by the ba-Tauwana, and northward towards the Chobe and Mababe, affluents of the Zambesi, where there were only a few wandering Masarwa, a low type of nomads akin to the Bushmen of South Africa who tilled no land but eked out a wretched existence by hunting. In the lake and the rivers entering it were large numbers of hippopotamus; giraffe, zebra and other big game were abundant wherever there were water pools, and even in the drier parts on the west, where the country gradually became merged in the Kalahari desert; but these were inaccessible to any but Bushmen on account of their aridity, and no ba-Mangwato ever visited them.

On the east, between Shoshong and the Victoria Falls, Khama's rights were restricted by the proximity of the Matabele, who at one time conducted regular raids in all that region, though after the rough handling they received from the ba-Tauwana in 1885 [1] they gave it a wide berth. But Khama had not ventured to assert any claim beyond the trade route to the Zambesi, and his most eastern cattle-post was more than twenty miles from Tati.

The comparatively small strip between the Macloutsie and Shashi rivers was still a bone of contention when the

[1] See chap. xi.

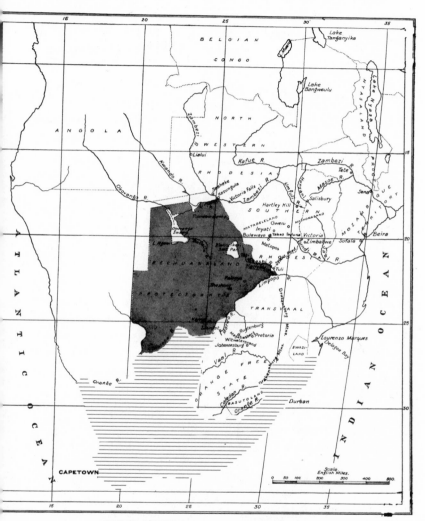

SOUTH AFRICA AT **CLOSE OF 19th CENTURY.**

Pioneers entered Mashonaland, and its ownership was never actually settled during Lobengula's lifetime.

It will be seen that Khama's sovereignty over the nor-thern Protectorate was extremely nebulous.[1]

The first practical proof of the reality of the Protectorate was the official visit of Sir Sidney Shippard in connection with the death of Grobler. Although the enquiry disclosed that some of the ba-Mangwato had been guilty of deceit and treachery Khama himself was expressly acquitted from blame, while the Transvaal Boers were required to give pledges to respect his frontier. Khama began now to feel that the British were in earnest ; anxious to stand by him, and guard him not only from the Boers but from the Mata-bele, and he was emboldened to take a step which he had long been contemplating—that of moving his capital town to a more suitable spot nearer the Matabele border. Sho-shong had so far been retained because of its strong defen-sive position among the hills, but in every other respect it was a most undesirable site for a large native town. The cultivable land around it was limited and worked out ; the water supply was scanty at all times and hopelessly in-adequate in seasons of drought ; owing to this, and to the unclean habits of the native population, the sanitary con-dition of the huge overcrowded kraal was deplorable, and there were constant outbreaks of fever and other diseases due to filth. A new site was chosen at Palapye, sixty miles to the north-east, and only seventy from the Matabele border, on the edge of a plain thickly wooded with acacia and other trees, and drained at all seasons by several streams of good water which found their way through kloofs to the Lotsani river just below.

[1] The extent of the whole area claimed by Khama was roughly 110,000 square miles—considerably larger than Great Britain. Much of it, however, was comprised in the ' Thirst-land ', as the Kalahari Desert is called by South Africans.

All stages of the move were personally supervised by Khama, who selected the site and planned the lay-out of the new town, clearing a central space for his *kothla* and allotting to the various sections of the tribe the positions they were to occupy round it. In the dry season of 1889 the whole population migrated in a body from Shoshong, taking with them their simple possessions, and driving before them their cattle and small stock. On arrival at the new site each family was ordered to cut the necessary poles and thatch and puddle the clay required for its own tenement, and in an incredibly short space of time the community settled down in comfort. Excellent as was the site the approaches were so bad as to baffle description. From the south the only means of access was through a belt of some miles of distressing sand, over which bullock-waggons had to crawl at a snail's pace, while the ' road ' on the opposite side resembled a staircase of rock, liberally strewn with loose boulders, the smallest of which were as big as footballs. It did not seem to occur to Khama to improve these abominable tracks, though they were a serious impediment to trade.

As soon as the move was satisfactorily accomplished Khama's energy, always directed towards the well-being of his people, became astounding. Rising every morning at dawn he spent a large part of each day in the saddle—he was an excellent horseman—visiting the workers in the fields, advising them as to their crops, arranging for the sale of their produce or for the purchase of ploughs and other implements. Later on he would be found sitting in his *kothla* administering justice or interviewing traders and other white men on business. He was never idle, and his tall wiry figure, always clad in European clothes, could be seen here there and everywhere till the evening, when it was his custom to hold a prayer-meeting for as many as he could induce to attend. Truth to tell his religious fervour was not

shared by the general body of the tribe, who found it
rather burdensome, though many of them made a great
parade of reading bibles and singing hymns when Khama
himself or the missionaries were about. Khama's fanatical
zeal for temperance led him to prohibit the manufacture of
' Kaffir beer ', which in some form or other is used throughout Africa as a beverage, and is in fact a wholesome and
necessary element in the native dietary. In this he defeated his own purpose, for not only was there a good deal
of secret brewing, but the natives sought opportunities of
obtaining cheap spirits from low-class traders His attempts
to repress polygamy were productive of equally bad results,
and Palapye became notorious for the profligacy of its
women.

But no failures could restrain him from his self-imposed
task of regenerating his tribe. He was fired with an ambition to erect a church worthy of his new town, and besides
subscribing £3,000 from his own purse levied a compulsory
contribution from all his people to meet the cost. Unfortunately this led to a quarrel with the resident missionary,
Mr. J. Hepburn, who had come to Shoshong twenty years
before as Mackenzie's colleague, and had proved a staunch
friend to the ba-Mangwato through many vicissitudes.
Khama would brook no opposition to his plans, and finding
Hepburn unwilling to give way ordered him out of the
country at a moment's notice, denying him even the right
to return and collect his belongings.

The opinions of Khama's character published by white
men who came in contact with him at this period vary
remarkably. Selous makes constant references to his single-
ness of purpose and the beneficial influence which he exercised in uplifting his people. Mr. H. A. Bryden, who spent
some time at Palapye in 1890, speaks highly of his generous
behaviour to white men, and particularly to himself, a total
stranger, and considers that the appointment of a British

official at his capital, with authority to perform acts of administration, provided him with a just grievance, implying that Khama was fully capable of carrying out the duties of government without such assistance.[1] The missionary writers—as is natural, seeing that Khama was the most notable exemplar of a converted black man—were unanimous in their admiration for him, in spite of his shabby treatment of Hepburn, and many others have testified to his sterling qualities. On the contrary Décle, the eminent French explorer, described him (in 1891) as spoilt by the favours heaped upon him by the British Government, and as growing daily more self-important and dictatorial in his attitude towards white men, whom at the bottom of his heart he hated and despised.[2] Mr. D. C. de Waal, an Afrikander politician who passed through Palapye in 1890 in company with Sir Henry Loch and Cecil Rhodes, gives instances of Khama's autocratic and bullying demeanour towards the Bechuanaland Exploration Company and other trading firms, which so incensed Rhodes that he avoided intercourse with him.[3]

In the face of such a conflict of opinion among reputable authorities it is difficult to form a correct estimate of Khama's true character, but it may not be out of place to give, for what they are worth, my own impressions formed during a short stay in Palapye in the same year (1891), and jotted down at the time. It appeared to me that Khama was strangely different from those around him, and quite out of place among them. The ba-Mangwato as a rule were inert, unmannerly and, while cringing to those they feared, disinclined to render the least service to white men, or even to one another, except for payment. In energy, in courtesy and in anxiety to help others Khama stood alone. He

[1] *Gun and Caméra in Southern Africa*, pp. 274-5.

[2] *Three Years in Savage Africa*, p. 36.

[3] *With Rhodes in Mashonaland*, pp. 38, 39.

could meet white men on equal terms of intelligence, and with a modest dignity which was respectful without a trace of servility. At the same time he was arbitrary and extremely tenacious of his own opinion. A later visit, on a slightly contentious matter of official business, proved that he could be obstinate to the extent of pigheadedness, and quite uncompromising where his wishes were thwarted. Most outstanding natives try to gain their ends by diplomacy. This was a quality which Khama seemed to lack, but he made up for it by a sincere conviction that he could never possibly be in the wrong.

Without doubt he was a genius—or some might say a freak, and it would be difficult to point to another native of Bantu descent so widely diverging from the normal. Like many men of genius he was given to fantastic obsessions; like most Bantu he was deficient in a sense of proportion. Had he not chanced to come under missionary influence he might have proved a dangerous factor in South African politics, for it is certain that he would never have remained quiescent.

In June, 1890, on hearing from Selous of the projected expedition to Mashonaland, Khama supplied him with a working party under one of his headmen to cut the first section of the road across the 'disputed territory' to the Shashi river, and when the force was ready to cross the Matabele border, and he learnt that a number of coloured boys attached to the column had deserted in a panic, he sent a further body of two hundred men—some of whom were mounted—to replace them. Selous warmly commends his action in thus coming to the assistance of the Pioneers, and especially points out that he placed 'his favourite brother', Raditladi, in command of the contingent, but no doubt Khama was fully alive to the advantage he would derive from the entry of a British force into the country of his long-standing enemy. As for Raditladi, so far from

being his favourite brother he was one of the most unruly
of his troublesome family, and had always been a thorn in
his side. In his earlier days he had done his best to stir up
dissensions between Khama and Macheng, and he eventually
became such a source of mischief that Khama was led to
banish him altogether. While Selous, whose partiality for
the ba-Mangwato may have been inspired by his detesta-
tion of the Matabele, writes in glowing terms of the services
rendered by Khama's men, whom he employed as scouts,
other members of the column found them an unmitigated
nuisance, and their leader Raditladi an obstreperous
braggart.[1] Long before the Pioneers reached the high veld
they were sent back, but on the first day of their homeward
march they caused a good deal of trouble by spreading a
false report that a large *impi* of Matabele was advancing to
attack the column, which was in consequence kept in a
state of extra vigilance for the whole of one night.

The unreliability of the ba-Mangwato, and the peculiar
mentality of their king were exhibited still more markedly
in 1893, when the movement of Jameson's little army from
Mashonaland was being supported by the advance of a
combined force of Bechuanaland Police and volunteers,
under Colonel Goold-Adams, from the south. Khama,
elated by the thought that Lobengula was to be hunted
down, was anxious to be in at the death. Of his own accord
he offered the services of 1,800 of his men, including a
mounted troop, and announced his intention of commanding them in person. They were accepted, and joined the
white force on November 1. On the 3rd a portion of Goold-

---

[1] An American member of the force wrote, ' They were the most
annoying people it has ever been my misfortune to meet. . . . It
was stated that they had been brought with the expedition to please
those people in England who take special interest in the ba-Mangwato
nation because they profess Christianity. They read the Bible, pray
and sing a good deal, but the men of the expedition who had been at
their town, Palapye, all agreed that their religion was not deep-
seated ' (W. H. Brown, *On the South African Frontier*, pp. 90, 91).

Adams's column was attacked by an *impi* under Gambo, Lobengula's son-in-law, while breaking laager near the Ramoquebane river (which separated the Tati Concession from Matabeleland proper) and a sharp engagement followed, in which the ba-Mangwato took part, behaving well and losing three men killed, besides other casualties. Two days later, just as the column was preparing to resume the march, Khama informed its commanding officer that he and his people must get back to their own country, as small-pox had broken out there, and the time had arrived for ploughing. He was reminded that he had pledged himself to go in with the British, and that his men were drawing pay and rations as an integral part of the force, but he adhered to his determination to retire, and marched away with his whole contingent. Not content with this desertion in face of the enemy he off-loaded and dumped on the veld a quantity of stores which had been placed in his charge, and refused to lend his waggons to Goold-Adams to carry them any further.[1]

II. KHAMA *versus* RHODES

By leaving Goold-Adams in the lurch at a critical moment Khama seriously damaged his own interests. Besides receiving a smart rap over the knuckles from the High Commissioner, who told him that it would be difficult for him to regain the confidence of Her Majesty's Government, he forfeited all claim to consideration from Rhodes and Jameson, and found himself left out in the cold in their subsequent arrangements for settling Matabeleland. He felt the official rebuke bitterly, and attributed the whole blame to the Company, whose proceedings he thenceforth watched with jealousy and mistrust. He ignored the fact that the break-up of the Matabele tyranny had freed him

[1] *Blue Book*, C. 7290, pp. 11, 42-3, 86.

from a threat which had been hanging over him and his people as long as he could remember, and chose to harbour a suspicion that the Company's next step would be to serve him as they had served Lobengula in order to appropriate his country.

More than a year elapsed before he came once more into the limelight, for he was kept fully engaged in dealing with the pressing problems confronting him at home. The occupation of Matabeleland was followed by an extraordinary rush of white men from other parts of South Africa and from Great Britain, anxious to profit by the opening up of a new field for enterprise, and Palapye, as a half-way house between Mafeking, where the railway ended, and Bulawayo, where a great township was rapidly springing up, was flooded by a constantly swelling stream of traffic. Traders, prospectors, professional men, transport-riders, and adventurers of all sorts passed through in every kind of vehicle, generally halting for a few days to replenish their stores or rest their cattle. No outspan regulations could save the veld round Palapye from being eaten bare, and there were frequent grass-fires due to the carelessness of travellers. The kraal natives were unsettled by the coming and going of so many strangers, whose oxen broke down their fences and damaged their crops, and whose coloured waggon-boys hung about the outskirts of the town and pestered their women. Khama's old-time privacy was rudely broken into, and instead of being free to attend to church affairs and his various schemes of reform he found his days occupied in settling disputes and keeping watch on troublesome aliens. All these worries were due, according to his way of thinking, to the Chartered Company.

His domestic concerns were also causing him anxiety. As a strict monogamist he had escaped the complications which most great African chiefs brought on themselves by indiscriminate matrimonial ventures, and his family was a small one. His first wife, generally known as Ma-Bessie,[1] lived with him contentedly for twenty-seven years, and had several daughters and one son, called, after his grandfather, Sekhome. A year after her death Khama took to wife a sister of Bathoen, Chief of the ba-Ngwaketsi (an elder branch of the ' crocodile people '). She only survived her marriage a few months, and he was now once more a widower.[2] But Sekhome, at this time a man of twenty-five, was beginning to kick over the traces and assert his independence, while the Chief's brother Raditladi, who had a substantial following, was again making himself objectionable, his grievance arising from the ukase against the brewing of kaffir beer.

While Khama was trying to manage his family and grappling with the problems created by the boom in Matabeleland, it came to his ears that plans were on foot to extend the railway from Mafeking, through Palapye, to Bulawayo. In itself this would not have caused him any serious disquietude ; in fact it would relieve him from the waggon transport, with all its attendant evils. But it soon leaked out that the railway extension was only part of a far more comprehensive programme, which seemed to him to strike at his authority as chief—even to menace the existence of his tribe, and filled him with dismay.

It had of course long been apparent to Rhodes that no real progress could be made with the development of the northern territories so long as they were dependent on oxtransport, and immediately after the settlement of Matabeleland he began to map out a huge scheme of railway construction. It was necessary for this that he should acquire the ownership of a strip of country through Bechuana-

---

[1] See chap. v, p. 72.

[2] Later on Khama took a third wife, Semane, by whom he had a daughter and another son, Tshekedi, who became Regent on the death of his brother Sekhome in 1925.

land, and he thought that his purpose would best be served
by persuading the Imperial Government to hand over the
administration of the whole Protectorate to the Chartered
Company, allowing the territory from Mafeking southwards, which since Warren's annexation had been governed
as a Crown Colony, to be absorbed by the Cape. It was no
new idea. The first clause of the Royal Charter provided
that the 'field of operations' of the Company should include
all country to the north of the Crown Colony of Bechuanaland, and it was generally and correctly assumed that the
Imperial Government would be only too glad to be relieved
of the cost and responsibility of controlling this vast and
more or less unproductive tract, and of the complicated
problems arising from the multiplicity of native tribes
scattered over it. Rhodes had acquired for the Company
by purchase a number of land and mineral concessions
granted by the various chiefs to syndicates and individuals,
and full use of these could not be made as long as the country remained in the feeble clutch of the 'dead hand of
Downing Street'. Early in 1895, therefore, he began to
press for his rights under the Charter.

Knowledge of these designs first came to Khama through
the missionaries, who read the report of a speech made by
Rhodes in the Cape Parliament, when he outlined his views
as to the future of the Protectorate. To the Chief the prospect of exchanging the *laissez-faire* supervision of the
British Government for the vigorous methods of the Company was terrifying. He saw his supremacy threatened,
and he may even have feared that he would be driven from
his country as Lobengula had been driven. His apprehen-
sions were nourished by the missionaries, who felt that their
influence would vanish if the land was overrun by young
men of the pioneer type, and urged him to lose no time in
protesting to the authorities against the change. But
Khama needed no urging; he had already decided on a

course of action, and hastily enlisted the co-operation of his brother chiefs in the Protectorate. Within a month it was decided that he, together with Sebele, who had helped him in the old turbulent days of Macheng and had now suc-ceeded Sechele as Chief of the ba-Kwena, and Bathoen, Chief of the ba-Ngwaketsi, his own brother-in-law, should form a deputation to visit the High Commissioner at Capetown, and in default of getting satisfaction from him should proceed to England to lay their case before the Queen.

In July news of their intention reached Jameson, who, as Administrator of Rhodesia, was as anxious as Rhodes for the extension of the railway and had a special reason of his own for wanting to obtain immediate control of the Pro-tectorate. He was already deep in his plan for giving military aid to the Uitlander malcontents in Johannesburg. It was essential for him to have a plausible excuse for keeping a body of troops close to the Transvaal border, and to find a *point d'appui* from which to launch the force when the expected revolution started. If the Protectorate were placed under the Chartered Company this would, he thought, be a simple matter, and it was imperative that any opposi-tion to the transfer should be nipped in the bud. He there-fore rushed off to Palapye to reason with Khama, and thought himself fortunate in catching him at a moment when Mr. Willoughby, his principal missionary adviser, happened to be out of the way.

But although Jameson did his utmost to reconcile Khama to the change of administration, going so far as to outline the regulations he was prepared to make for safeguarding the interests of his people, and promising, as a special sop, to take Raditladi and his disaffected following away and find room for them in Matabeleland, he failed to move the chief from his purpose. If anything his intervention only stiffened Khama's resolve to block the transfer, and six

weeks later he, together with Sebele, Bathoen and some
native servants, escorted by Mr. Willoughby, were at the
Cape, where they booked passages by the next mail steamer
for England.

In interviews with the High Commissioner [1] Khama was
reserved and suspicious ; it was only with the greatest
difficulty that his real object could be extracted from him.
Sebele and Bathoen were more outspoken, and Khama
eventually admitted that the main purpose of the mission
was to protest to the Queen's Ministers against being put
under the Company.[2]   Bathoen had prepared an impas-
sioned appeal in writing, some passages of which, as it
expressed the feelings of all three, may be quoted :

' We cannot believe that the Government under which we
have found rest and peace will thus desert us and put us under
another government, especially that concerning which we have
heard such deeds in Matabeleland. . . .   Shall we be given into
the hand of a company whose work is to hunt for gold and the
wealth of the land only ?   Never ! . . .   We refuse to be thus
cast away.   We wish still to remain under the protection of the
Queen of England, where we can enjoy peace and laws which
forbid the selling of English spirits, which are the destruction of
men. . . .   Hear I beseech you, the prayer of the people of the
ba-Ngwaketsi tribe, which is in reality the petition of three
Chiefs and their three tribes '. [3]

Their conviction that the Company would flood their
country with liquor was further emphasized in a later
petition written by Mr. Willoughby on the chiefs' behalf :

' We fear that the Company will fill our country with drink
shops as they have Bulawayo and some parts of Mashonaland. . .'

Coming from Khama such sentiments were undoubtedly
sincere ; in the mouths of Sebele and Bathoen they amoun-

---

[1] Sir Hercules Robinson, who, on the resignation of Sir Henry
Loch, had once more been appointed to that office.

[2] *Blue Book*, C. 7962, p. 11.   [3] *Ibid.*, C. 7962, p. 4.

ted to rank hypocrisy, as both were notorious drunkards. They were moreover groundless, for the Company's laws provided the severest penalties for supplying drink to natives, and were in fact more drastic than those of any other government in South Africa. But the missionaries who advised the chiefs knew that such a plea was certain to make a powerful appeal to certain sections of the British public.

Another argument against the Company appearing in the same petition betrays the reckless nature of the statements put into the mouths of the chiefs by people who should have known better :

' We fear the Company because we see that they are people without gratitude ; if Khama had not helped them they could not have established themselves in Mashonaland, and again in Matabeleland, and yet they try to take Khama's country secretly.'

Although Khama signed this it is impossible to think that he really believed it. One need not attribute altruistic motives to the Company, but at least one must allow that they had no reason to be grateful to Khama for any assistance in occupying Rhodesia.

The three chiefs arrived in England early in September, 1895, and at once had a preliminary interview with Mr. Joseph Chamberlain. Having only recently succeeded to the office of Secretary of State for the Colonies he was not disposed to commit himself hastily on the transfer of the Protectorate, but he informed them that while the change would certainly be carried out sooner or later every consideration would be paid to their wishes as to the exclusion of liquor and the reservation of sufficient land for tribal purposes. He advised them to go straight to the heads of the Company and get the best terms they could, and promised to give them a definite decision before their departure.

The next two months were passed by the Chiefs in a carefully organised sight-seeing tour in London and some of the principal towns in the provinces. At Birmingham Khama was presented with a mayoral address which opened with the words ' To His Majesty King Khama '. Elsewhere they attended missionary meetings, conversaziones, and other functions arranged in their honour. They were carefully shepherded by Willoughby and other officials of the London Missionary Society, who were determined that that body should get the whole credit of their presence, and that no outsiders should have a chance of interfering as the Aborigines Protection Society had in the case of the Matabele ' Envoys ' six years before. The temperance card was played for all it was worth, and, as had been astutely foreseen, proved an infallible draw. Very soon it came to be believed that Rhodes was engaged in a deep conspiracy to corrupt the Bechuana peoples with drink and to rob them of their land. The non-conformist and ' Little England ' press raved about the wrongs of the unhappy tribes that the octopus Company was entangling in its tentacles. One of the foremost in the campaign of hysterical propaganda was Sir Ellis Ashmead-Bartlett, who controlled a journal called *England and the Union*. In one fiery article headed ' Khama's Betrayal ', after describing Bechuanaland as ' Naboth's Vineyard ', he proceeded :

' In 1881 Khama protected British colonists and refugees against the wrath of the Boers. In 1887 he actively helped Sir Charles Warren's expedition. But for his invaluable support the pioneers of the Chartered Company would never have reached Mashonaland alive. In 1891 [*sic*] his active help enabled the Southern British column to overcome the resistance of the best part of Lobengula's army. He is now rewarded by the Chartered Company endeavouring to grab his dominions and destroy his independence '.

Khama, having no experience of the lengths to which certain sections of the British public are prone to go in

lionising distinguished foreigners—especially when they
happen to have black skins—was, not unnaturally, carried
away by this misdirected outburst of sympathy. He began
to think that he really was a martyr, and was more than
ever convinced of the iniquities of Rhodes and his Company.
At a reception at Grosvenor House arranged by the Duke
of Westminster and attended by the Bishop of London
(Dr. Temple) and a galaxy of temperance reformers, he
implored his audience in moving language to help him in
averting the terrible results which would follow the handing
over of his country to the wicked Company. This appeal
was received with loud and sympathetic cheers. Lord
Loch, the late High Commissioner, who assured the meeting
that the Devil was not so black as he was painted—in other
words that one of the main planks of Rhodes's policy was to
keep drink from the natives—was received coldly, and a
framed address (prepared in advance) was presented to
Khama fervently assuring him that he would have the
unanimous support of the temperance advocates at home in
his brave efforts to preserve his people from the ' demoralisation and degradation of the liquor traffic '.

Mr. Chamberlain was unmoved by all these demonstrations, and treated the mission with dispassionate and
businesslike calm. What mattered most in his eyes was the
northward extension of the Cape railway, and after further
interviews he announced that for that purpose each of the
Chiefs would have to surrender a narrow strip of country.
All would be provided with large defined areas within which
they would live as heretofore under the protection of the
Queen, but outside these areas the British South Africa
Company would be charged with the administration, towards the cost of which the inhabitants would have to con-
tribute by means of a small hut tax. He promised that
' white men's strong drink ' should not be brought into the
Protectorate for sale, and that a special Commissioner

should be appointed to watch over the native interests. The ' Disputed Territory' was definitely assigned to Khama.

Although this settlement involved the surrender by each of them of a considerable tract of land—in Khama's case about 3,000 square miles—it was accepted with satisfaction, for it gave final and inalienable rights to the native tribes, and interposed a buffer of British territory between them and the Transvaal. If Sebele and Bathoen, who had now spent several months in unwonted sobriety, felt any qualms in contemplating the total exclusion of ' white men's strong drink' from their realms they were careful to conceal them.

The visit of the chiefs was brought to a close by two functions of a very dissimilar kind. The first was the long-hoped-for audience with Queen Victoria. Arrayed in orthodox silk hats and black tail-coats, and accompanied by Mr. Chamberlain and two of the missionaries as interpreters, they travelled down to Windsor Castle, where they were received in semi-state and entertained at luncheon by the ladies and gentlemen of the household. Afterwards they were ushered into the presence of the aged Sovereign, who told them in a few kindly words how glad she was to hear that they had come to a satisfactory settlement. Each of the chiefs presented Her Majesty with a magnificent kaross of picked leopard and jackal skins, and received in return a Bible, stamped with the royal arms, and the inevitable Indian shawls for the adornment of their wives— in the case of Khama, who had no wife at the time, for his eldest daughter.

The privilege of meeting face to face one who had all their lives been regarded as an almost supernatural being, and of beholding with their own eyes the glories of her palace and surroundings made a profound impression on these men who had so recently emerged from black barbarism, and went a long way to restore them to a proper sense of their relative unimportance.

BECHUANA CHIEFS IN ENGLAND, 1895

BATHOEN, SEBELE, KHAMA

(Standing) REV. W. C. WILLOUGHBY, REV. F. LLOYL.

(face p. 280)

LEWANIKA

IN CEREMONIAL DRESS

(see p. 300)

The last public appearance of the Chiefs was at a great farewell gathering at the Queen's Hall, Langham Place, on the day before their departure. An immense crowd of enthusiasts had assembled, and when the Chiefs filed into their places on the platform they were greeted with rapturous homage. Bouquets were presented to them, and society women flocked up to shake them by the hand— some in their ecstatic fervour bestowing the same attention on their native servants who stood behind them. After the usual adulatory speeches, to which they had by this time grown accustomed, each of them delivered a short address— Sebele, as technically the senior of the three, leading off. Khama, when his turn came, preserved on the whole a dignified restraint, but he would not have been human if he had entirely concealed his gratification, and there was a distinctly exultant note in his remark that the Queen's Government had rescued him from the clutch of the Chartered Company.

At the end of November the trio left England, and reached their respective kraals, in a somewhat blasé condition, on the eve of the Jameson Raid. In the emotional thrill which followed that miserable episode they and their grievances were completely effaced from the public memory. They had, however, the satisfaction of learning that the Chartered Company would not, after what had occurred, be allowed to retain any control in the Protectorate. The Imperial Government resumed possession, and the vast territory relapsed into a state of semi-stagnation from which it has not to this day emerged.

III. KHAMA'S RETIREMENT

The story of Khama must now be brought to a conclusion. After the English visit he never came again prominently before the world, but settled down quietly to govern his people in his own way, under the shadow of civilisation, but free from direct contact with it. It speaks well for the stability of his character that the absurd fuss made about him in England did not upset him nor fill him with an undue amount of self-esteem. As the years went on he certainly became increasingly dictatorial and masterful in his own domain, but he never obtruded himself on the outside world or came into collision with his neighbours, black or white. After the Boer War, in fact, he withdrew himself entirely from the presence of white men. Finding that Palapye was uncomfortably close to the railway he moved his capital once more—and this time further into the wilds —to Serowe, once the place of his voluntary exile, forty or fifty miles westward towards the Kalahari desert.

His last twenty years were embittered by a feud between himself and his son Sekhome, who having been educated at a missionary college in Cape Colony, absorbed notions of independence and broke away from the autocratic discipline of his father. A reconciliation took place in 1922, when Sekhome, after a long period of exile, expressed penitence, and was received back into the fold. In the following year the old Chief died of a chill caught while riding in a rainstorm. He had reigned—with a brief interruption—for fifty-one years, and will go down to posterity as a unique example among natives of a man with a consistent ideal. Singularly pure and simple in his personal life he devoted his whole career to the task of elevating the standards of those around him by Christian endeavour. Few men have had such unpromising material to work on, and it is not surprising that he only partially succeeded. It is too soon to say that his efforts have left a permanent impress, or even to point to the ba-Mangwato as having any marked superiority over tribes which did not have the advantage of the same wise handling.

CHAPTER XVIII

BAROTSELAND

I. THE RISE OF LEWANIKA

FAR away in the north, on the reeking, fever-stricken banks of the upper Zambesi, Robosi, the usurper, had, after many years of uphill struggles and changing fortunes, succeeded in establishing himself in a firm position as king of the ba-Rotse. Up to 1886 he was too busily engaged in consolidating his power to be able to bestow much thought of what was taking place in neighbouring kingdoms, but he now had some leisure to look beyond his immediate surroundings, and he began to watch with inquisitive and growing interest the doings of the white men in Bechuanaland and Matabeleland.

Though Sesheke still continued to be the chief port of entry to the country north of the Zambesi, Robosi had relegated it to the charge of one of his lieutenants, and had taken up his residence at the ancient capital of Lialui, which was situated in the marshy and malarious valley formed by the junction with the Zambesi of large tributaries from east and west. Much of this low-lying ground was inundated every year during the rainy season, when the inhabitants were compelled to betake themselves to the sand-belts which skirted it, or to islands left standing above the floods. When the waters receded, and the great river resumed its normal channel, the soil of the ba-Rotse valley, fertilised by deposits of rich silt, produced heavy crops of manioc and native cereals, and the lush grass gave pasturage to immense herds of cattle. Within the valley, which was about seventy-five miles long and from ten to thirty in width, the bulk of the pure-bred ba-Rotse were concentrated, and before the series of upheavals which started with the death of Marambwa and the ma-Kololo invasion, they lived in great ease and prosperity, relying on slave labour, drawn from their numerous subject tribes, for the care of their fields and stock, the construction of canoes and weapons, and other arduous services, and spending their own time in hunting and in certain gentlemanly arts, such as wood and ivory carving, in which they excelled.

During the thirty years before Robosi's accession the tribe had become disorganised through political feuds, and many of its institutions had lapsed into desuetude. Robosi had done something towards restoring its ancient unity, and had regained control over most of the subject peoples, whose allegiance had become loosened in the absence of a strong master-hand. Among the ba-Rotse proper, however, his authority was precarious. He reigned in an atmosphere of perpetual plots and intrigue, kept alive by the factions of other claimants to the kingship, and it was only by resorting to a policy of terrorism, and by constant executions for treason that he could keep them in some sort of restraint.

Towards the end of 1884 the spirit of unrest came to a head, and a riotous mob suddenly made a rush on the King's *kothla*, bent on assassinating him. Faced with this emergency Robosi behaved with great presence of mind. Seizing a loaded rifle he ran into the courtyard, shot one of the leaders dead and ordered the remainder to stand back. From force of habit they hesitated a moment, which gave him the chance to slip through the palisade and make his

escape, followed by one of his sons, Litia, a lad of fourteen.[1]
His boldness and promptitude saved him and he made his
way across the swamps, until, after some weeks of wandering,
he found a refuge on an island in the Okavango river. The
rebels, on recovering from their surprise, wreaked their fury
on the King's unfortunate wives and the rest of his children,
whom they murdered in cold blood, afterwards looting and
burning the royal residences. They then proceeded to elect
as their king a cousin of Robosi, known as Tatira, or Akafuna, a youth of feeble capacity, who was a mere puppet in
the hands of the revolutionary party. Robosi's supporters
were too cowed to make any show of resistance, and those
who were not put to death fled to the Kwando river many
miles to the south, where they were rallied and held together
by his eldest sister, the *Mokwae* (Princess) of Nalolo, a woman
of remarkable talents and strength of character.

But Robosi was not a man to accept defeat tamely, and
lost no time in preparing for a counter-stroke. The opportunity came before he had been nine months in exile, when
he learnt that further insurrections had broken out in
Lialui, and a new conspiracy hatched against Tatira, whose
mother was said to be a slave woman. The deposed king
straightway joined his sister, and taking command of the
loyalist refugees marched towards the Zambesi, which he
crossed near the falls of Gonye, some hundred miles south-
east of the capital. Here he met a strong opposing force and
after several hours of fighting, and heavy slaughter on both
sides, was forced to retire, but recrossing the river he worked
his way round towards Lialui, where a second desperate
battle took place a few days later. In this Robosi is said to
have exhibited great gallantry, leading the attack on horse-

---

[1] Litia, who has adopted the name of Yeta, is the present king of
the ba-Rotse. His father informed the British Resident long afterwards that he could not have fired a second shot, as the rifle he carried
was a Martini, and the belt of cartridges he hastily snatched up
belonged to a weapon of different calibre.

back, and killing many of the enemy with his own hands, but his army was outnumbered, and the day would once more have gone against him had it not been for the intervention of a body of well-armed Mambari—half-caste merchants from the Portuguese country—who had just arrived in the valley on a trading expedition, and by their timely aid turned the scale in his favour.[1] By nightfall Robosi had with their help completely routed the rebels and driven them back to Lialui, where he followed up his victory by an orgy of carnage in which none were spared.   The people of Sesheke and other ba-Rotse towns at a distance held aloof from the struggle and played a waiting game, but when they saw that Robosi had the upper hand at once flocked to his side with every profession of loyalty.

By this bold stroke Robosi, who now assumed the name of Lewanika, established himself more firmly than before, and he made his position doubly sure by mercilessly hunting down every person who had been in the slightest way connected with the revolution or had not given convincing proofs of loyalty.   The witch-doctors were kept busy ferreting out evidence or manufacturing it, and although Tatira himself was spirited away many of the principal headmen were put to death on mere suspicion of having supported him.

The King now set to work in earnest to restore the constitutional usages which were traditional among the ancient a-Luyi, and distinguished them from all other people of Bantu origin.   One peculiar feature of their system was that the sisters and female blood relations of the reigning monarch were accorded special rank, and in some cases a definite share in the duties of government.   They were treated as if they were men, were addressed by male titles and enjoyed

[1] Major St. Hill Gibbons (*Africa from North to South*, p. 154) says that Robosi was also helped by a Scottish trader named McDonald, who happened to be on the spot.   The Mambari received special trading privileges as a reward for their assistance.

AT NALOLO, BAROTSELAND, 1903

(Left to Right) MOKWAE'S TENTH HUSBAND, THE 'GREAT MOKWAE,
THE AUTHOR, MR. F. WORTHINGTON

exemption from the ordinary rules of marriage, being allowed the privilege of choosing their own consorts and
changing them at pleasure. (Only one husband was permitted them at a time and he was debarred from having
other wives.) The senior lady in the land was the King's
eldest sister—the 'Mokwae' of Nalolo, who, besides
governing her own province, where she maintained a dignity second only to that of her brother, played an active
part in the affairs of the nation at large, and was consulted
by the King on all weighty matters of state. There were
several other Mokwaes, who were local chiefs, and possessed
similar, but relatively less important privileges. The
'Great Mokwae' took full advantage of her matrimonial
freedom ; in fact she was a sort of human spider, and
Coillard the missionary relates that at the time of his arrival
she had already had nine husbands, all of whom she had
discarded and murdered in turn as soon as she had tired of
them.[1]

The King was also assisted by a council composed of a
Prime Minister—styled Ngambela—whose office was permanent—in so far as anything could be regarded permanent
in that land of intrigue and sudden death—and a number of
representative headmen, who had among themselves a
strictly defined order of precedence. The members of the
royal family did not sit upon this council, but constituted a
separate circle of advisers, with real though undefined
powers.

The provincial administration was equally elaborate, and
differed essentially from that of other Bantu hegemonies.
We have seen, for instance, that the vassal tribes of the
Matabele only came into contact with their conquerors

[1] When the writer visited her in 1903 she was still living with her
tenth husband, who although an insignificant and under-sized man,
appeared to have gained some hold on the affections of his wife,
herself a woman of enormous bulk.

through raids, and were kept in submission by cruel persecutions; while Khama's subjects, other than the ba-Mangwato, consisted of scattered groups of Makalanga, whose allegiance was slender and based on the need for protection, and of nomad families of Bushmen, who had no tribal unity at all. Lewanika on the other hand, when once he had regained supremacy over the outlying portions of the kingdom exercised a control which was neither spasmodic nor desultory. His dominion embraced some twenty tribes, differing in customs, characteristics and sometimes in language, who were kept in constant touch with the central authority through the medium of provincial ' governors '— selected headmen of ba-Rotse birth, who represented the King, and saw to it that tribute was regularly paid to him. By this means Lewanika maintained communication with every section of the heterogeneous population; their affairs were his direct concern, and he was their sovereign in a real sense. He and Lobengula might be compared to two Scottish land-owners, one of whom owns an estate with tenants, and has bailiffs to collect rents and attend to its well-being, while the other has a deer-forest in the Highlands, maintained and visited solely for the purpose of sport.

The great annual event in the ba-Rotse valley was the migration at the time of the rains, when the King was conducted in pomp in a huge state barge—newly built for each pilgrimage—to a temporary residence among the sand-hills, escorted by the inhabitants of Lialui in a fleet of ordinary canoes. There were peculiar and mysterious ceremonies connected with this proceeding, and great competition among the ba-Rotse aristocrats for a place among the paddlers of the royal craft. The Mokwae of Nalolo had her own barge and made a similar voyage.

The pure-bred ba-Rotse were the only people in the country accounted free; all others were deemed serfs, and though not harshly treated on the whole could own no property. The tribute paid by the subordinate tribes took various forms according to their locality or resources. The ma-Totela, whose country was rich in iron deposits, were skilful blacksmiths, and paid in hoes, spears and axes ; the ba-Toka, who were shepherds and hunters, in hides ; some of the river tribes supplied canoes and fishing nets, while the distant ba-Lunda, only a portion of whom acknowledged Lewanika as overlord, paid in elephant tusks. Each tribe had in addition to furnish its quota of slaves for the service of the King and the ba-Rotse patricians. The ma-Mbunda alone were exempt from tribute and menial services, but having acquired a reputation for skill in healing and magic spells they provided all the physicians and diviners of the nation. The subject tribes had no part in the public affairs of the ba-Rotse oligarchy, and in that respect were fortunate, as they escaped the constant espionage and suspicion which surrounded the well-born.

Although the ba-Rotse had reached a higher stage of political development than the peoples to the south of them they were, if possible, more deeply in the grip of black superstition and witchcraft. Trials by the ordeal of boiling water or loathsome emetics ; ceremonial observances to ensure good crops, to avert the evil eye, or to bring success in battle and hunting ; symbolical dances of a grossly obscene character, and many other practices founded on a belief in occult agencies filled their daily life and absorbed their thoughts. All the horrid accompaniments of the cult of sorcery were rife among them, and suspects were continually burnt alive, flung to the crocodiles, tortured and mutilated on no evidence beyond the word of informers or private enemies. The King himself was a firm believer in the influence of ancestral spirits on mundane affairs, and was punctilious in paying homage at the tombs of his departed predecessors. He maintained a state band, whose instruments consisted of a variety of tom-toms and *marimba* (primitive xylophones), and whose principal function was to create a hideous din all night outside his quarters to scare away demons which otherwise might molest him in his sleep.

Yet with all this undercurrent of superstition and brutality befouling their daily lives the ba-Rotse were, on the surface, the most polished of folk, and were bound by an elaborate code of etiquette and conventional courtesy. There were, for instance, many kinds of formal greeting, ranging from the *shualela*, or profound obeisance with which the King and his sister were hailed—a series of salutes commencing with a loud repetition of the words *Yo-Zho*, gradually increasing in fervour, and ending with a prostration of the body with head to ground—down to a complicated mutual handclasp and embrace between equals on meeting after a separation. No one—not even his sons or wives—was allowed to stand in the King's presence, and when he took food it was passed from hand to hand along a lengthy chain of kneeling servitors.

The King lived in a fine house solidly built of timber shaped with the adze, with partitions and passages, and a high-pitched roof of thatch. Its appointments inside and out were scrupulously neat and clean. Round it were grouped the houses of his wives (of whom there were generally fifteen to twenty), each surrounded by its own courtyard and fence. Many of the King's relatives and the higher sub-chiefs were housed with a proportionate degree of comfort, for the ba-Rotse were the most skilful builders of all the Bantu peoples.

Except on the south, where the Zambesi formed a natural boundary, the outer limits of Lewanika's realm were not strictly defined. Roughly his influence extended to the present Congolese border on the north, and from the Portuguese territory of Angola on the west to the country of the wild Mashukulumbwe beyond the Kafue river—in all about 200,000 square miles, or an area nearly as large as France. By the time the British appeared on the scene in Bechuanaland he had assumed an active control over the greater part of this enormous region, and at the close of the nineteenth century was undoubtedly the most powerful native sovereign south of the equator.

II. LEWANIKA AND COILLARD

In March, 1886, François Coillard, of the Paris Evangelical Mission in Basutoland, who had made previous abortive efforts to obtain an entry into Barotseland, arrived at Lialui, and was received with moderate kindness by the King, who granted him a site for a mission station a few miles from the town, where in the following year he was joined by his wife—a Scotswoman. It was an epoch in the history of the country, for the almost Christ-like patience and fortitude exhibited by the heroic couple, under the most depressing and often perilous conditions, gradually won them the respect and confidence of the King, and it was Coillard's influence that finally induced him to seek the protection of the British Crown.

Up to this time Lewanika's acquaintance with white men had been very slight. George Westbeech, the ivory trader, who had made several trips to Lialui, happened to be there when Coillard arrived, and was mainly responsible in securing a favourable reception for him, for the King was not particularly anxious to have resident missionaries in his country, and had already sent away two Jesuit priests, the survivors of four who had started from Panda-ma-Tenka in 1882. Another, Frederick Stanley Arnot of the L.M.S., had reached the ba-Rotse valley in the same year, during the critical period before the insurrection which led to Lewanika's flight, but after a few months' struggle, in which his health broke down under repeated attacks of malaria, he gave up all hope of doing good work among a people so hopelessly involved in tribal feuds, and left the country.[1] Apart from these and one or two traders from Angola Lewanika had only been visited by Silva Porto (1870-82), a Portuguese trader; Emil Holub (1875), an Austrian scientist, and Major Serpa Pinto (1879) the explorer, whose records all prove that, in spite of their superior intelligence, the ba-Rotse were the most treacherous and degraded of all he tribes of the upper Zambesi.[2]

Coillard was fortunate in reaching Lialui after Lewanika's restoration, when conditions were becoming more settled, and the king in a more tranquil state of mind. He gladly accepted the site offered him for a mission station, although it was in a most unhealthy situation, and with short intervals of leave remained in the country until his death from black-water fever eighteen years later. His brave wife, who had shared his hardships and anxieties, died in 1891.

When Lewanika first heard of Khama's acceptance of the British Protectorate he was still in exile, but as soon as he regained power he began to reflect on the subject, and to wonder whether he too could be taken under the same supporting arm. After Coillard's arrival he had many discussions with him as to how to set to work, and in 1889 induced the missionary to write both to Khama and to Sir Sidney Shippard to ask their counsel. Khama was chary of giving advice, but wrote back assuring Lewanika that so far as he was concerned the Queen's protection was a real blessing, and had relieved him of all uneasiness regarding the Boers and Matabele, and that he was now

[1] Arnot afterwards spent some years in mission work in Garenganze, or as we now call it Katanga.

[2] MacQueen, *Journeys of Silva Porto*; R.G.S. *Journal*, vol. xxx; Holub, *Seven Years in South Africa*; Serpa Pinto, *How I Crossed Africa*. Cf. also Arnot, *Garenganze*.

living in peace. The mention of the Matabele made a strong appeal to the King, for only two years before one of their *impis* had crossed the Zambesi and raided the ba-Toka country, and it was rumoured that they were now preparing a still bolder campaign—no less than an expedition into the ba-Rotse valley. He was not troubled by Boers, but had many qualms as to the designs of his western neighbours the Portuguese, who were showing unmistakable intentions of pushing their influence in his direction. He was also just beginning to be embarrassed by the attentions of the inevitable concession-hunters, and before he realised what it might lead to had been beguiled, by the offer of a heavy subsidy, into giving one of them—a Mr. Harry Ware of Kimberley—the exclusive right of mining in the ba-Toka country.

Lewanika's letter to Shippard was referred to the Colonial Secretary (Lord Knutsford), who sent a non-committal reply, but it was also shown to Rhodes, who was at that moment daily expecting the grant of his Royal Charter, and seized on the tentative enquiry as a heaven-sent opportunity for drawing Barotseland—of the extent of which his knowledge was extremely vague—into the sphere of his operations. With Rhodes to think was to act, and early in November, 1889—less than a fortnight after the sealing of the Charter—he despatched a small expedition consisting of Mr. Frank Elliot Lochner, an ex-officer of the Bechuanaland Police, and three English companions to open negotiations with the King for exclusive land and mineral rights over his entire territory. In the meanwhile he succeeded in acquiring, for a substantial consideration in cash and shares, the concession obtained by Harry Ware.

Lochner's party made the arduous journey of 900 miles by ox-waggon and 300 by native canoes during the worst of the wet season, and all suffered severely from malarial fever. One of them had to turn back, but the others reached Lialui in a worn-out condition in March, 1890, and were welcomed by the Coillards who patiently nursed them back to health. It was not, however, until May that Lochner, who was more ill than the others, was fit to broach the subject of his mission, and he at once found that he had to face a determined opposition from some of the King's councillors, who had been warned by interested traders against him, and told that the grant of a concession would be followed by an invasion of white men. Lochner made every effort to win these objectors over to his side. On Queen Victoria's birthday (May 24) he organised a grand fête, with sports, a feast of beef, fireworks and other entertainments, which went some way to establish him in popular favour, and shortly afterwards he was relieved to hear that the King had convened a national *pitso*, or assembly of his representatives in the outlying parts of the country, who were to meet the council and discuss the proposed concession.

The meeting, at which Coillard acted as interpreter, was a trying ordeal, and Lochner had to face a cross-examination as to the intentions of the Company, and what it had to do with the Queen, whose support was Lewanika's sole object. But after hours of wearisome talk and wrangling the scale was suddenly turned in Lochner's favour by the arrival, in the nick of time, of a special envoy despatched, at Shippard's instance, by Khama. This man craved permission to address the *pitso*, and held forth eloquently on the blessings of the British connection. He assured the councillors that the Company had a direct mandate from the Queen, and that an agreement with it would be tantamount to accepting her protection—a statement which Lochner discreetly allowed to carry full weight. In face of this argument the opposition died away, and after some haggling as to money terms, the King, his son and heir Litia, his Prime

Minister and all the councillors and provincial representatives, to the number of about forty, affixed their marks to a document giving the Company the sole mineral and commercial rights over the whole of the ba-Rotse dominions. The King bound himself to enter into no similar covenant with any other individual, company or state. In recognising the Protectorate of Queen Victoria he expressly reserved his constitutional authority as ruler of the nation, and stipulated for the freedom of his people and their towns, lands and cattle from interference. In return Lochner on his part pledged the Company to shield the nation from outside attack ; to promote the education and civilisation of the native tribes, and to secure the appointment of a British Resident. Certain defined areas were excluded from mining operations, and it was understood that the country would not be thrown open to general immigration without the consent of the King. In return for the benefits of the concession the Company was committed to the payment of an annual subsidy of £2,000. When all was satisfactorily settled the King, with due solemnity, presented Lochner with a pair of enormous elephant tusks,—the usual native token of submission.[1]

Had Rhodes followed up this initial success by appointing a representative to reside in Barotseland and keep adverse influences from disturbing the mind of the King, or had the Imperial Government, which soon afterwards ratified the concession, supplemented it by sending a properly accredited official to give reality to the Protectorate, a great deal of trouble would have been avoided. For some years, however, nothing of the kind was attempted. Rhodes was engaged in so many enterprises—in Gazaland, Nyasaland and other distant parts—that he allowed the matter to stand over. The Company had its hands full with the

[1] These tusks now decorate the Board Room of the Chartered Company.

settlement first of Mashonaland and then of Matabeleland, and the upshot was that Barotseland was left to take care of itself. Lewanika was disappointed at seeing no tangible results follow his solemn undertaking, and grew moody and suspicious. These feelings were aggravated by the insinuations of the white traders at Lialui, who, not having sufficient intelligence to perceive that it was to their own advantage to support Rhodes, endeavoured to instil into the King's mind the idea that he had been tricked and betrayed ; that the Company had no warrant from the Queen, and that the Protectorate would never become effective. In his disgust Lewanika attempted to repudiate the covenant, and was only partially reassured by a letter from Sir Henry Loch informing him that an Imperial Commissioner had been selected and would shortly arrive at Lialui. It had, in fact, been decided to entrust this post to Mr. (afterwards Sir Harry) Johnston, but circumstances prevented him from accepting it.

Months went by and no Commissioner appeared. Matters went from bad to worse. In the absence of other scapegoats M. Coillard, who had to some extent identified himself with Lochner's mission, and was known to have supported the concession, fell under suspicion, and his life was more than once in danger. It was the story of the Matabeleland business over again, and it was fortunate for the Company that neither Belgium (whose agents had already outmanœuvred Rhodes in Katanga) nor any other Power was sufficiently wide-awake to grasp the opportunity of stepping in. In 1895 a British Resident (Mr. Hubert Hervey) was actually appointed, but before he could start for Barotseland the Matabele rebellion broke out and the road to the north was closed. He joined the Company's forces, and was, unhappily, killed in action. And so another year slipped by, and still nothing had been accomplished.

III. LEWANIKA AND CORYNDON

At the close of the hostilities in Matabeleland a new move was made, and this time a definite one. At the instance of the Company the Government appointed Major Robert Thorne Coryndon, a member of Rhodes's personal staff, to the post of British Resident [1] and in 1897 he started for Lialui with a small party of white officials to undertake the dual task of representing the Crown and the Company, and lay the foundations of an organised administration.

During the seven years which had elapsed since Lochner's mission the King's patience and forbearance had been sorely tried, but in the face of great antagonism from the mistrustful chiefs and councillors he had never ceased to cherish an abiding faith in the idea of a Protectorate. Although all danger of an invasion by the Matabele was removed by the defeat of Lobengula, and the occupation of his country, he still had to reckon with the Portuguese, who had been roused from the torpor of centuries by the activity of the British and other Powers, and were making valiant efforts to assert historical claims to the hinterland of Angola. Portuguese officials, whose objects were perfectly clear to Lewanika, had for some time been touring the border districts with armed forces. Only the British could save him from their encroachments, and it was with intense relief that he saw the long-delayed Resident at last appear. From that moment his burden was lightened. He had not altogether grasped the position of the Company, but the Company was for the time being kept by Coryndon in the background, and as no mining or prospecting operations took place for some time there was nothing to remind the king of its existence. In his eyes Coryndon was the ' Queen's man ' and nothing else, and he made little demur

[1] The late Sir Robert Coryndon, who died in 1925, while Governor of Kenya.

at the administrative proposals for which his co-operation
was tactfully sought. If he occasionally felt that matters
were being taken out of his hands he consoled himself by
the thought that he was saved from the trouble of sending
military expeditions to enforce his authority in the outlying districts. The ba-Rotse were far from being a race of
warriors, and Lewanika himself, although his early life had
been passed in scenes of terrible violence, and he had won
his way to power by ruthless spilling of blood, was not by
nature a fighting man. Besides he was getting on in years,
and, now that his subjects were settling down peaceably,
was less inclined to be combative. As long as his tribute
was assured ; as long as he was looked on and treated as the
' All-Highest ' in his immense domain, and was not interfered with in his immediate surroundings, he was content
to fall in with the new régime. It gratified him also to see
that, so far from curtailing his territorial influence, Coryndon was eager to assert, and even to extend it. It was of
course in the Company's interest to do so, for under the
concession their mineral rights were co-extensive with his
dominion.

So successful was Coryndon in his handling of the somewhat delicate situation that in 1899 the King was persuaded
to accompany him to the Victoria Falls, where he met the
Company's chief representative in Matabeleland, the Hon.
Arthur Lawley,[1] and amplified the Lochner agreement by a
new one which conferred on the Company wider powers of
administration and jurisdiction within his country. He
also promised to use his best endeavours to co-operate with
the British officials in suppressing slavery and witchcraft.
The slave-trade he had never encouraged, as it was mainly
carried on by the Mambari, who, although they had earned
his favour by coming to his aid when he was fighting for his
kingdom, were too closely mixed up with the Portuguese in

[1] The late Lord Wenlock

Angola to be welcome in his country ; but domestic slavery
was an old and time-honoured institution among the high-
born ba-Rotse, and it is doubtful whether Lewanika realised
the full import of his undertaking in this respect, or in
regard to witchcraft, in which he was himself a profound
believer. It was not until some years later, and then only
under considerable pressure on the part of Coryndon and his
officials, that domestic slavery was finally abolished, and
even if the King had been in earnest as to the repression of
witchcraft he would have been powerless to eradicate
beliefs and cults which to his subjects, and especially to the
ba-Rotse, were the main inspiration of their daily lives.

Having satisfied his desire for a Protectorate, which was
now giving him a feeling of placid security, Lewanika was
seized with a longing to visit England and see with his own
eyes the great Queen, whose personality he, like all African
chiefs, regarded from a distance with profound reverence,
but the outbreak of the Boer War frustrated his wishes, and
before the way was clear he learnt to his bitter disappointment that the Queen was dead. He was partially reconciled
by the receipt of an intimation through the Chartered
Company that if he so desired arrangements would be made
for him to attend the coronation of King Edward in the
following year, and he gladly agreed to the suggestion.

It is difficult to realise what a tremendous undertaking
such a journey was to a man who had never, except during
his brief exile, set foot outside his own territory ; never
seen a railway, nor the sea, on which he would now have to
trust himself for several weeks, never even seen a white
man's town. He would be obliged to leave the control of his
people in the hands of a regent ; he would have to forego
the company of his sixteen wives, and, great king as he was
in his own world, he knew that he was about to enter a
sphere where he would only be an insignificant unit amid a
host of other and far greater princes. Nothing could better

demonstrate the confidence he had acquired in less than five years under the prudent handling of a small coterie of British officials, than the readiness with which he placed himself in their hands for a journey of such magnitude, and left his own country in their keeping.

He was accompanied by his Prime Minister and by two or three personal attendants, and conducted throughout the whole tour by a senior official of the Company's administration. As a series of object lessons of gradually culminating impressiveness the visit to England was an unqualified success, and left an ineffaceable effect on his mind. Had it taken place at any ordinary time it might have exposed him to unwholesome attentions and flattery on the part of the public, as had happened in the case of Khama. But although he took part in all the splendid functions which marked the occasion, and not only witnessed the coronation ceremony, but had a personal audience of King Edward ; [1] although he was accorded a welcome befitting his position as the ruler of a great native dependency, no undue fuss was allowed to be made of him either in public or private, no meetings or fulsome entertainments were organised in his honour and nothing was done which could inflate him with exaggerated views of his own status. He won good opinions by the natural dignity with which he conducted himself, and few who saw him in the quiet grey suit in which he went about England, or in the rich uniform which he donned for state functions, could have imagined that less than twenty years before he had been a naked savage fleeing for his life among the swamps of the Okavango, or presiding over strange rites and gory executions in the barbaric surroundings of a remote kraal in the heart

---

[1] On entering the audience chamber he somewhat startled His late Majesty by falling on his knees and rubbing the ground with his forehead, loudly ejaculating ' Yo-Zho ' several times, in true ba-Rotse fashion.

BAROTSE HOUSE OF BETTER TYPE
LITIA (LEWANIKA'S SON) AND FAMILY
IN 1903

of ' Darkest Africa '. The present writer had several opportunities of seeing and talking to Lewanika immediately before his pilgrimage to England, of again seeing him at reviews and other functions in London, and shortly after his return of spending over a year in his country and visiting him at his own town of Lialui, and is able to say with confidence that his English tour was productive of nothing but good. It widened his outlook, convinced him of the greatness of the Empire of which his country was a distant but integral part, and inspired him with feelings of deep loyalty, and an earnest desire to turn his experience to account by educating his people in the arts of peace and in habits of industry.

The remainder of Lewanika's life was comparatively uneventful. The dispute as to the boundaries between his country and the Portuguese colony of Angola was eventually referred to arbitration. The award was a disappointing one, and in his opinion robbed him of a large tract of country whose inhabitants had been the tributaries of himself and his forefathers from time immemorial. If the decision had been given a few years earlier he would probably have fought the Portuguese in defence of his rights, but he had learnt that the Empire was a bigger thing than Barotseland, and that the maintenance of political balance among outside Powers often entailed individual sacrifices. He accepted the contraction of his boundaries without loss of temper, knowing that fair consideration had been given to his claims.

Towards the end of his reign the railway line, which reached the Zambesi in 1906, was carried through Lewanika's country to the borders of the Belgian Congo, and mining operations began in earnest. But for some years there was no large immigration of white men, and no such huge activity as has since sprung up owing to the vast discoveries of copper in the northern part of the territory.

There was in fact nothing which could ruffle his pride, or lead him to foresee that the old ba-Rotse dynasty would shortly come to an end, and that his successor would be relegated to the position of an unimportant local chief.

We must now take leave of Lewanika. With his death, which took place in 1916, there passed from the stage the last of the South African despots—and possibly the wisest. Some of them had taken fright at the approach of that strange combination of ideas and institutions which they were told was ' civilisation ', and some had stood their ground for a while and fought hard to keep it back. Some had tamely yielded, and become nonentities. Lewanika was the only one who accepted it without loss of dignity or curtailment of territory. It is true that in following the path of least resistance he was obliged to abandon customs and methods of ruling which were hallowed in his eyes by tradition and antiquity, but he managed to get much in return—freedom from his enemies, peace and just treatment for himself and his subjects. The Chartered Company was fortunate in having such a man to deal with, and happy in being able to place on the spot officials who were able to draw out his good qualities, and use him as a colleague without humiliating him. To the Company belongs the credit of making the best use of the opportunity, redeeming a savage wild from utter barbarism, and converting it into one of the most promising colonies under the British flag.

CHAPTER XIX

THE OUTLOOK

Does the story of the last hundred years help to lift the curtain which hangs over the future ? Does the visible acceptance by the mass of the native population of new discipline, new restraints, and in some cases new standards justify the assumption that, after so short a period of close quarters with civilisation, they have radically changed their outlook ? Can we assert, without peradventure, that in spite of occasional and local lapses the natives as a whole are shaking off the habits, the beliefs and the impulses which, for centuries before the white men appeared, formed the background of their lives and dominated their actions ?

Such questions are not on a par with the trite one about the Ethiopian changing his skin ; they are not concerned merely with a matter of pigment, but go far deeper, and rest on the fundamental differences between the temperaments of two great divisions of the human race. They are, moreover, of paramount gravity, for upon the mutual relations between whites and blacks depends the whole political and commercial future of a large part of the African continent.

There are some who contend that the Bantu peoples are capable of rising to the intellectual level of Europeans ; that their backwardness is due to the handicap of their age-long environment ; that their brain capacity and general

303

intelligence are equal to ours, and only need the steady stimulus of education and association to enable them ultimately to play their part in the professions, in commerce and even in affairs of state. They point to colonies on the west coast of Africa, where such conditions seem to have been already achieved, and where negroes are no longer debarred from full citizenship by the colour of their skins.

Others shake their heads and argue that with improved hygiene and relief from tribal warfare the numerical strength of the native population is rapidly growing; that the effect of a veneer of education is to make them resent their present condition of inferiority, and that sooner or later a ghastly struggle is inevitable, in which the blacks, by sheer weight of numbers, will overcome and expel the intruding Europeans.

Lastly there are, especially in the Union of South Africa, where the Boer traditional view is to-day gaining ground, a great many intelligent people who believe that the two races are ordained by Providence for different ends, and that the destiny of the blacks is to serve the whites. Though it would require some courage to advocate the re-introduction of slavery there are probably some who would welcome it, if stripped of its more objectionable adjuncts.

There are fallacies contained in all these views, and the history of the past hundred years in South Africa to some extent exposes them. The most ardent champion of the natives would find it hard to deny that Khama, the idealist and reformer, Lobengula, the diplomatist, and Lewanika, the builder of a great kingdom, were rare and exceptional products of their times, and that from all the millions of black people the nineteenth century failed to bring forth half-a dozen such. Nor does there seem to be a prospect of similar products now that the two races have rubbed shoulders for a number of years, for no great native leader has risen of late above the general level of mediocrity.

What permanent impress after all have these men, whose distinguishing quality was in each case fixity of purpose, left upon their own kind ?   Khama, having achieved local reforms in an insignificant tribe, suffered himself to be effaced, and retired into comparative obscurity.   Can it truthfully be said that his example has resulted in any greater stability among the people whom he sought to uplift ?   Can the effect of his life-work be compared to that of, say General Booth, or Florence Nightingale ?   Lobengula's honest efforts to preserve the Zulu tradition of military supremacy were futile, and the younger generation of Matabele are now, except perhaps for some slight superiority in physique inherited from their fighting ancestors, indistinguishable from the general body of natives round them.   Lewanika, wise enough to seek the protection of the British, only made their object easier of attainment, and smoothed the way for the conversion of his hard-won autocracy into a colony of the Crown.   The once arrogant ba-Rotse owe their changed conditions, not to him but to the British, who have forbidden the practice of witchcraft, stopped them from killing one another and are teaching them to appreciate the ' dignity of labour '.   But they have fallen from their high estate, have no freedom of movement except in their own reserve, and have lost every shred of the authority they once exercised over a score of subject tribes. Their ' king ' is still saluted with a loud ' Yo-Zho ', and on high occasions struts about in the magnificent gold-laced coat and cocked hat bought by his father for Edward the Seventh's coronation.   In reality he is nothing more than a subsidised local chief.

In considering the future of South Africa it would be unsafe to count on the breaking down of racial antipathy. There is something mysterious about this.   It is not, as might appear on the surface, a sentiment exclusive to the white people, and it is significant that it is not so strongly felt by the Latin races—the Portuguese, for instance—as by those of Teutonic stock.   Outside Africa its force is not fully appreciated, but people who have lived for any length of time among Bantu races, except perhaps the missionaries, will agree that it is hopeless to expect that the feeling, which finds modern expression in the ' colour bar ', will ever entirely die out.   If colour prejudice has its foundation in physical aversion, or is in some subtle way connected with the instinctive abhorrence of miscegenation, it would appear that in Rhodesia and the territories with which this book deals it is more deeply seated—if not so vociferously proclaimed—than in the older colonies of South Africa. In proof of this one may cite the fact that the problem of the half-breed has never become acute in Rhodesia.   The few children of mixed blood that exist are relegated as a matter of course to the native parent—invariably the mother—and there is no such class as the ' off-coloured ' men and women who constitute so difficult and pathetic a problem in the Cape peninsula.

But the prejudice may be due to suspicion arising from the revolts of the blacks, which have more than once disturbed the progress of civilisation in South Africa.   And on this assumption the Rhodesians have good cause for being constantly on their guard.   Apart from the first Matabele war, the causes of which were perfectly natural and have already been explained in detail, there have been two formidable rebellions in Southern Rhodesia, and although both took place more than thirty years ago their shocking episodes left memories which time cannot efface.   In each case they were ushered in with the cold-blooded massacre of large numbers of isolated and unsuspecting white men, women and children, the murder roll amounting to close on three hundred.   The rebellion of the Matabele in March, 1896, was traced to a variety of causes, and should not altogether have come as a surprise, for they were by nature a race of warriors and had only been half conquered. But the fanatical and furious outbreak of the Mashona, who were not a fighting race, was conclusively proved to have been engineered by their witch-doctors, who played on their credulity and worked them up to a pitch of frenzy.

The mention of witch-doctors is a reminder that the native belief in magic is a powerful obstacle to any complete understanding between the two races. It is difficult for those who have not studied the subject at close quarters to comprehend the tremendous part which witchcraft, and its concomitant evils of terrorism, blackmail and orgiastic excitement, still play in the life of the Bantu. The natives are now fully conscious that certain practices which they invest with sanctity are repugnant to white men and have been made illegal, but evidence is constantly forthcoming that these practices are by no means dead, but are carried on in dark corners. A belief in magic is inherent in the Bantu mind. The sorcerers are not necessarily charlatans, but in most cases are the victims of auto-suggestion, and, like the Indian Yogis, have implicit confidence in their own powers. It is to be feared that the infatuation of the blacks in regard to occult forces is natural and ineradicable. Missionaries may claim to have stamped it out in certain instances, and to have replaced it by Christian doctrines, but they are apt to be misled by the specious professions of supposed converts, who outwardly call themselves Christians from motives of vanity or self-interest. This is not of course always the case, for genuine conversions are well-authenticated, but except in rare instances—such as Khama —the natives are incapable of shaking off their innate belief in spirits and all the allied and consequential superstitions which we regard with contempt. Witchcraft, though carried on in secret, is nearly as potent a force to-day as it was a hundred years ago, and so long as it endures will form an insuperable barrier between the whites and the blacks.[1]

The Rhodesian authorities have wisely recognised the vitality and invincibility of the colour prejudice, and have modelled their native policy accordingly. Without adopting any rigid form of segregation they have set aside huge areas in which the natives may lead their own tribal and communal lives, secure from white intrusion, and liable only to the ordinary hut-tax. Further areas have been earmarked wherein the progressive native may become a landowner. If, however, he desires to earn money by entering the service of a white employer in a town, mine or farm, he must adapt his ways to white conventions, comply with special regulations and realise that he belongs to a class apart. In practice the bait of good wages, quarters and food is a sufficient inducement to make the youths and adults seek work for at least a portion of the year, and many remain in service more or less permanently, only visiting the reserves for family or holiday reasons.

The danger of a widespread revolt of South African natives against white men cannot be entirely excluded, but the gradual break-up of tribal life resulting from the increased tendency of the natives to seek remunerative work at a distance from their own kraals seems to render any organised or combined movement on a large scale unlikely. Still one can never predict from experience what African natives will do in any given circumstances. Their ways and

---

[1] Since these words were written a case has been tried in the High Court at Bulawayo in which a grandson of Lobengula, born and educated in the Union of South Africa, has been convicted of extorting cattle from local Matabele natives under threats of causing them to be bewitched. The accused man, who is known as ' Rhodes Lobengula ' had as accomplice a coloured woman, who claimed to be the daughter of a female ' Kumalo ' (*i.e.* a member of Mziligazi's family) by an old-time white trader, and not the least remarkable feature of their conduct was that for the purpose of their blackmailing expeditions they toured the district in a motor-car.

motives are not ours, and they are more liable to mass hysteria which may be induced—as in the case of the Mashona rebellion—by panic, or superstition or some imaginary grievance. Quasi-religious movements, stirred up by self-proclaimed 'prophets', who are only witch-doctors in another guise, have from time to time caused anxiety, but their demonstrations have been short-lived and confined to localities, and it would seem that the Bantu people have not the necessary cohesion to maintain any prolonged agitation or to make it general.

Meanwhile, having appropriated the country of the Bantu for our own ends, we are bound, in common honesty, to regard their welfare as a trust. We shall discharge that trust with less strain if we disencumber ourselves of the ideal of raising them within a measurable distance of time to the European level, and we shall discharge it with more benefit to them if we frankly admit that the white man and the black man belong to essentially different species, which may exist side by side in harmony, but can never be welded.

APPENDIX I

THE SPELLING OF NATIVE NAMES

THE study of South African history has been made unnecessarily difficult by the queer variations adopted by different writers in the spelling of native names of persons and places. These vagaries arise mainly from the fact that as the natives in their aboriginal state had no knowledge of writing, Europeans have been obliged to fall back upon their own alphabets to express sounds which they do not always provide for, and in this respect everybody has been a law unto himself.

The ' clicks ' in the Zulu group of languages and the nasal tones in the Suto group cannot be expressed in English letters, and there are also certain vowel sounds for which we have no equivalent. Artificial expedients have been devised to get over this difficulty, but all are unsatisfactory. Sir Harry Johnston, in his erudite and monumental work on the Bantu tongues,[1] supplemented the English vowels by Greek ones to which he gave a special value, and invented half a dozen symbols to denote the clicks and other peculiar consonants, but ordinary men have had to make the best job they could with the medium at their disposal—the letters in the English alphabet. In regard to words which present no phonetic difficulty the simplest course is to accept the form of spelling which has become stereotyped by custom and familiarity—inaccurate though it may often be. It is sheer pedantry to write the name of the Matabele King ULOPENGULE, as the missionary Thomas persists in doing, when the rest of the world calls him, and spells him, LOBENGULA, and the same applies to many other well-known Bantu names.

[1] *A Comparative Study of the Bantu and Semi-Bantu Languages.*

One or two points which have led to confusion may be noted :

(*a*) The Boers tried to vocalise a certain guttural sound by using their letter G, which in Dutch is pronounced something like the CH in the Gaelic word *clachan*. This has been followed by some English writers, and has led to such lock-jaw eccentricities as KGAMA, where the second consonant indicates an effort to express an aspirated K.

(*b*) There is a sound in several of the languages of Southern Rhodesia which resembles the rolled French R (as in *roi*) so seldom acquired by Englishmen. To some ears this appears to be a Q, to others RW, or WH. It is really none of these, but the difficulty of rendering it phonetically accounts for the erratic spelling of a large number of words. Thus the name of a river in Mashonaland, which one person writes QUEQUE is given by others in the forms RWERWE, or WHOIWHOI.

(*c*) An immense number of words in the Zulu group are prefaced by a sort of soft grunt—the relic of a pronominal prefix. As illustrations may be mentioned the common words MLIMO (God or spirit) and NKOSI (chief), alternative spellings of which are MOLIMO, UMLIMO, M'LIMO, 'MLIMO ; and INKOSI, ENKOSI, N'KOSI, 'NKOSI, etc. A Scottish journalist, possibly with a laudable desire to make things easier for his fellow-countrymen, calls the river in the north of Bechuanaland McLOUTSIE, on the analogy of McKENZIE !

(*d*) There is also a semi-mute vowel sound at the end of many words—variously expressed by English writers as A, E or I, so that we get KHAMA, KHAME and KHAMI.

Throughout this book the forms of spelling sanctioned by general use have been adopted, phonetically incorrect as they often are, but for the benefit of those who refer to other works on the same subject a list of a few alternative spellings is appended.

Ordinary Spelling.	*Variants.*
ba-Kwena (tribe) -	- Bakone (Moffat) ; Baquains (Livingstone).
Bechuana - - -	- Boochooana ; Bechwana (Lloyd).
Botletle (river) - -	- Beauclekky (Baldwin).
Bulawayo - - -	- Gubuluwayo ; Bulowaigo (Baines).
Dingaan (Zulu king) -	- Umtigana (Lloyd).

Ordinary Spelling.	Variants.
Gaseitsive (chief) -	- Hasiitsiwe (Mackenzie) ; Gatzizibe (Blue Book).
Khama - - -	- Kgama ; Khame ; Khâme (Lloyd) ; Khami.
Khari (Mangwato chief)	- Kgadi (Shippard).
Kalahari (desert) -	- Khalahari (Lloyd).
Lobengula - - -	- Ulopengule (Thomas) ; Lumpengula (Mohr) ; Lopenguela, Lopingula, Lopenula (Blue Books).
Makalanga (tribe) -	- Makalaka ; Mokaranga.
Makorikori (salt lake)	- Maralerale (Posselt) ; Makhadikhadi, Makgadikgadi (Lloyd).
Matabele - - -	- Amandebele ; ma-Tebele (Bryant) ; Mantabele (Blue Book).
Matopo (hills) - -	- Amadobo (Thomas).
Matshayangombi (Mashona chief) - - -	- Umatji-yankompi (Thomas).
Mjaan (Matabele general)	- Mtyana.
Mziligazi - - -	- Mzilikazi (Posselt) ; Moselekatse (Moffat) ; Morelekatse (Blue Book) ; Masulakatse (Cloete).
Ngami (lake) - -	- Nghabe (Mackenzie) ; Ngate (Blue Book).
Ningi (Lobengula's sister) -	Mncencengni,; Ningengnee (Selous); Nini (Cumming).
Notwani (river) - -	- Ngotwane (Lloyd).
Palapye (Mangwato town) -	Palapswe ; Phalapi ; Palachwe ; Palapshe, etc.
Sekhome (Mangwato chief)	Sicomy (Cumming) ; Sekome (Livingstone).
Tshukuru (Khama's father-in-law) - - - -	- Chukudu.

APPENDIX II

MISDEEDS OF CERTAIN BRITISH SUBJECTS IN BECHUANALAND

The following particulars are extracted from the report by Sir Sidney Shippard of an official enquiry held by him, as Deputy Commissioner of the Bechuanaland Protectorate, at Shoshong in September, 1888. (The full report is printed in *Blue Book*, C. 5918.)

ONE of the oldest firms in Shoshong was that of Messrs. Francis and Clarke, who started business there as general merchants soon after Khama's accession. They appear to have consistently defied his embargo on the importation of liquor for sale to the natives, and in 1878 were mixed up in a drunken brawl, which so disgusted the chief that he ordered them to leave his country and remove their goods. The sentence was afterwards reduced to a fine, and the two men were allowed to remain on giving assurances of future good behaviour.

After the establishment of the Protectorate in 1885 they were again detected in offences against the drink regulations, and were once more ordered to quit. This time they appealed to Shippard, who persuaded Khama to allow them eighteen months to wind up the affairs of their partnership. He went so far as to pay certain debts owing to them by some of his people so as to facilitate the arrangement, but notwithstanding this generous treatment the two men, in conjunction with another Shoshong trader named Chapman, endeavoured to engineer a filibustering raid against him by Transvaal Boers, visiting Pretoria for the purpose.

On the failure of this attempt they returned to Shoshong accompanied by a Mr. Wood (an ex-member of the Cape Legislative Assembly) with the object of obtaining permission to prospect on the Shashi river, and to pass through the Mangwato country to Matabeleland, where they hoped to get a mineral concession from Lobengula. They informed Khama that if they were unsuccessful in this they would bring up an army to fight the Matabele, and urged him to promise his assistance, but he indignantly rejected the proposal, and refused to allow them to prospect in his country, though offering no objection to their passing through it on their way to Bulawayo.

A little later they returned with the announcement that Lobengula had granted them the very rights which Khama had refused in the shape of a concession over the district between the Macloutsie and Shashi. This greatly incensed the chief, who declared that Lobengula had no jurisdiction over that part, as they well knew, and accused them of deliberately trying to provoke war. He peremptorily ordered Chapman, Francis, Wood and Clarke to clear out of the place, and told them he never wanted to see them again. They had no alternative but to obey, but before leaving the first three sent letters to Lobengula urging him to despatch an *impi* to raid the district in question.

During the next few months they organised a fresh expedition in the Transvaal, and succeeded in entering Khama's territory by making use of the pontoon placed on the Limpopo by Grobler (see page 188). Khama at once sent an armed party to seize their waggons, one of which was found to be loaded with arms and ammunition. Francis and Chapman then obtained the assistance of upwards of twenty of Grobler's Boer friends, who opened fire on the ba-Mangwato, forcing them to abandon the waggons and to fly to the bush, but further aggressions were checked by the fracas which resulted in Grobler's death, and roused both British and Transvaal authorities to action.

These occurrences took place within territory nominally under British protection, and Shippard concludes his scathing comments on the scandalous behaviour of those concerned by remarking :

' Though British subjects, these men, Chapman and Francis, do not hesitate to wage war against a Chief and people enjoying Her Majesty's protection, and they would not hesitate a moment to set all South Africa in a blaze, if, by means of the conflagration, they could make money for themselves '.